Multimedia Projects in Education
Designing, Producing, and Assessing

Third Edition

Karen S. Ivers

Ann E. Barron

LIBRARIES UNLIMITED

U N L I M I T E D

A Member of the Greenwood Publishing Group

Westport, Connecticut • London

Library of Congress Cataloging-in-Publication Data

Ivers, Karen S.
   Multimedia projects in education : designing, producing, and assessing / by Karen S. Ivers and Ann E. Barron.—3rd ed.
      p. cm.
   Includes bibliographical references and index.
   ISBN 1-59158-249-0 (pbk. : alk. paper)
   1. Media programs (Education) 2. Interactive multimedia. 3. Instructional systems—Design. I. Barron, Ann E. II. Title.
LB1028.4.I95 2006
371.33'5—dc22   2005030806

British Library Cataloguing in Publication Data is available.

Library of Congress Catalog Card Number: 2005030806
ISBN: 1-59158-249-0

First published in 2006

Libraries Unlimited, 88 Post Road West, Westport, CT 06881
A Member of the Greenwood Publishing Group, Inc.
www.lu.com

Printed in the United States of America

The paper used in this book complies with the Permanent Paper Standard issued by the National Information Standards Organization (Z39.48–1984).

10   9   8   7   6   5

Contents

Preface

There is nothing more rewarding for an educator to experience than the enthusiasm and joy created by students actively engaged in a learning activity. Students *willingly* seek knowledge, spend extra time on their projects, and take pride in their work. Both the teacher and the students enjoy coming to school!

Although there are no magic potions to guarantee positive student outcomes, teachers can use a variety of strategies to ensure that learning is an active, personally relevant, meaningful process. These strategies include cooperative learning, constructivism, identifying each individual student's needs and talents, and using a variety of alternative assessment techniques. *Multimedia Projects in Education: Designing, Producing, and Assessing* (3d ed.) takes advantage of the many benefits associated with the development of multimedia and video projects and provides educators with strategies and ideas for incorporating multimedia projects into the curriculum. It provides management and assessment techniques for integrating multimedia projects in the classroom, emphasizing the importance of identifying instructional goals and relative standards and addressing situations where there may be a limited number of computers in the classroom.

Multimedia Projects in Education: Designing, Producing, and Assessing (3d ed.) begins by describing research in the areas of cooperative learning, multiple intelligences, and constructivism. It provides practical ideas as to how these theories can be applied to the development of multimedia projects. Chapter 2 introduces a model (DECIDE, DESIGN, DEVELOP, and EVALUATE) that is used to guide the reader through the rest of the book. Chapter 3 (DECIDE) discusses classroom management issues, grouping alternatives, computer-scheduling options, and other issues related to planning a project. Chapter 4 (DESIGN) introduces the reader to the design stages of multimedia development, including flowcharts, storyboards, and basic design issues. DEVELOP is divided into two chapters. Chapter 5 (DEVELOP: Media Components) addresses and defines the various media components that are available for multimedia projects and includes background information about desktop video production. Chapter 6 (DEVELOP: Multimedia Development Tools) provides an overview of development tools. Chapter 7 (EVALUATE) discusses alternative assessment techniques and assessment strategies. It also includes information on rubric design and provides examples of multiple rubrics.

Following the chapters on DECIDE, DESIGN, DEVELOP, and EVALUATE, four activity chapters provide the reader with multimedia project ideas. The activities focus on various development tools in several content areas, and they address a variety of grade levels and standards.

Throughout the book, the emphasis is on student-learning outcomes and on managing the development of multimedia projects. Each chapter begins with a scenario illustrating the implementation of multimedia projects in an educational setting. The chapters contain detailed graphics, charts, and tables. In addition, blackline masters are included that can be copied for educational purposes. Teachers, media specialists, and administrators will find this book an invaluable resource for producing, designing, and assessing multimedia projects.

This book is designed from the educator's perspective and can be used to facilitate classroom instruction as well as in-service workshops on strategies for developing multimedia projects. It is appropriate for classroom teachers and for educational technology courses at both the undergraduate and graduate levels.

Impact of Multimedia on Student Learning

A SCENARIO

Ms. Burke always used a variety of instructional approaches. Her favorite was the use of multimedia presentations, allowing students to work in groups to collect, analyze, plan, and present information. It was a multistage process that provided students with an opportunity to construct their own learning. This semester's multimedia assignment was to investigate a genetic disease. Ms. Burke's divided her high school biology students into groups of four, provided them with the assignment's objectives, the various stages of the assignment, and discussed how the assignment would be assessed (allowing student input and ideas). Nancy, Teresa, Michelle, and Deedra were eager to start, having already decided on a topic—polycystic kidney disease (PKD). Deedra's mother was recently diagnosed with this disease, so her teammates volunteered to help Deedra learn more about it. The team devised a plan, assigning members to research the Internet, contact and interview local nephrologists, search the library, and attend a PKD conference sponsored by the local PKD Foundation chapter—a chapter started by Deedra's aunt several years ago. After gathering, analyzing, and evaluating their research, the team would develop storyboards to organize and lay out their information. Once the storyboards were finished and approved by Ms. Burke, the team would work together to develop the project on the computer. Each person would be assigned a role—graphics, text, navigation, and audio—as they worked through the project. They were anxious to start—the assignment allowed them to investigate a topic of interest, draw upon and examine multiple resources of information, and share what they have learned through multimodalities. "This was learning at its best," thought Ms. Burke. "Students are engaged and want to learn."

OVERVIEW

Multimedia projects allow students to exhibit their understanding of a topic in a variety of ways, and they provide students with the opportunity to explain their work and ideas to others. Bennett (1996, 16) notes that students "know that they have learned something when they can explain their work and ideas to others or when they can successfully teach others difficult concepts or content." Multimedia provides students with a powerful communication medium and offers them new insights into organizing, synthesizing, and evaluating information. Multimedia has the potential to change the roles of teacher and learner and the interaction between them by allowing students to create their own interpretations of information.

In addition to content knowledge and skill development, developing multimedia projects offers students the opportunity to work collaboratively, engage in multiple modalities of learning and reflective thinking, and use a constructivist approach to learning. This chapter defines multimedia and examines research addressing the benefits of developing multimedia projects. Topics include the following:

- Definition of multimedia

- Why use multimedia?

- Research on multimedia and student learning

- Howard Gardner's Theory of Multiple Intelligences

- Cooperative learning

- Constructivism

DEFINITION OF MULTIMEDIA

In general terms, *multimedia* is the use of several media to present information. Combinations may include text, graphics, animation, pictures, video, and sound. Educators have been using multimedia for years. For example, it is not uncommon for teachers to support a unit on Spain with videotapes or DVDs, audio CDs, pictures, text, and artifacts. Today's technologies, however, allow educators and students to integrate, combine, and interact with media far beyond what was previously possible.

"Hyper" environments, such as hypertext and hypermedia, have added to the complexity and sophistication of multimedia's definition by providing electronic, nonlinear approaches to moving through a body of information. Hypertext facilitates interaction between readers and texts by organizing and linking information through text chunks. This can create associations, definitions, examples, and other relationships between the text passages (Maccini, Gagnon, and Hughes 2002; Rouet, Levon, Dillion, and Spiro 1996). Hypermedia adds video clips, graphics, or audio files to hypertext. Combining these elements results in greater comprehension, recall, and inference (Bagui 1998; Jones 2003; Mayer and Moreno 2002; Panagiotakopoulos and Ioannidis 2002). These multimodal approaches to education effectively accommodate students with diverse learning and cognitive styles (Ellis 2001; Lachs 1998; Maccini, Gagnon, and Hughes 2002; Morse 2003; Rasmussen and Davidson-Shivers 1998). In addition, hypermedia applications are better suited to transmitting knowledge that is not easily conveyed through print or verbal explanations (Ercetin 2003; Liao 1998; Son 2003).

Both hypertext and hypermedia can be considered subsets of multimedia. Combining the traditional elements of multimedia with hyper environments, Gayeski (1993, 4) defines *computer-based* multimedia as "a class of computer-driven interactive communications systems which create, store, transmit, and retrieve textual, graphical and auditory networks of information." In other words, computer-based multimedia involves the computer presentation of multiple media formats (e.g., text, pictures, sounds, and video) to convey information in a linear or nonlinear format. This book is based on this definition and focuses on multimedia projects created via authoring, presentation, video, and Web tools. It touches on multimedia creations possible through word processing programs and other application programs. Multimedia is driving today's technology; it is unusual for today's products not to be multimedia based! The purpose of this book is to help teachers and students design, produce, and assess multimedia projects using various multimedia development tools. Guidelines are provided for projects taking a couple of days or weeks to complete.

WHY USE MULTIMEDIA?

Multimedia projects encourage students to work in groups, express their knowledge in multiple ways, solve problems, revise their own work, and construct knowledge. Students have the opportunity to learn and apply real-world skills. They learn the value of teamwork; the impact and importance of different media, including design issues, media appropriateness and validity, and copyright laws; the challenges of communicating to different audiences; the importance of research, planning, and organization skills; the significance of presentation and speaking skills; and how to accept and provide constructive feedback. Creating multimedia projects helps to reinforce students' technology skills and to prepare them for the demands of future careers. To use technology effectively in the classroom, Yelland (1999, 44) notes that five goals must be met:

1. Integrating technology and curricula

2. Promoting active learning, inquiry, and problem-solving environments that engage the children in individual and collaborative work using higher order thinking skills

3. Using technology to present and represent ideas

4. Developing new definitions of play and new conceptions of what constitutes a manipulative

5. Developing media literacy skills that involve critically analyzing the use of the technologies and the information derived from them

The act of creating multimedia projects addresses each of these criteria. Liu (2003) notes that the development of multimedia projects can address the 21 core cognitive skills as defined by Vockell and Van Deusen (1989).These skills can be grouped into the following categories: focusing, information gathering, remembering, organizing, analyzing, generating, integrating, and evaluating.

The process of creating multimedia projects addresses the technology foundation standards for students, also, as described by the International Society for Technology in Education (ISTE). With the creation of the National Educational Technology Standards (NETS) for students, ISTE defines six broad categories designed to measure students' computer literacy. These categories include a variety of descriptors, including the following: to use a computer proficiently; to use the computer for collaboration, personal pursuits, and productivity; to promote creativity and produce creative works; to communicate information and ideas effectively to multiple audiences; to locate, evaluate, and collect information from a variety of sources; and to support problem solving (ISTE 2004).

Multimedia projects allow students to focus on course content; promote active and cooperative learning; engage students in higher-order thinking skills; and present and represent ideas through a variety of media. They also allow students to manipulate various technology tools, onscreen objects, and information models; locate and determine the best tools and resources for gathering and producing information; and critically analyze, evaluate, and organize information.

RESEARCH ON MULTIMEDIA AND STUDENT LEARNING

Over the last decade, advancements in technology have made it possible for teachers and students to develop elaborate multimedia programs in the classroom. Using Macintosh- and PC-based computers, students are able to express themselves through a variety of media—text, audio, video, graphics, animation, and sound—in linear and nonlinear formats. Although limited, research in the area of multimedia is promising, demonstrating that using multimedia can be effective for teaching and learning (Cooper 1998; Liao 1999; Mayer and Moreno 2002; Nikolova 2002; Sivin-Kachala and Bialo 2000) with all levels of students, including those with special needs (Daley 1999; Holzberg 1998; Irish 2002; Morse 2003; Pratt 1999; Xin 1999). Multimedia learning environments can support higher-order thinking and problem-solving skills (Herrington and Oliver 1999; Liu and Hsiau 2002; Oughton and Reed 1998), increase students' achievement (Chen and McGrath 2003; Liao 1999; Liu 2003; Sherry, Billig, Jesse, and Watson-Acosta 2001; Sivin-Kachala and Bialo 2000), and increase student motivation (Kasahara 2001; Marr 2000; Okolo and Ferretti 1998). In addition, creating multimedia projects reflects research on how the brain learns—helping students construct knowledge and making topics more meaningful and motivating to learn (Wolfe 2001). Bagui (1998) suggests that "multimedia may make it easier for people to learn because of the parallels between multimedia and the 'natural' way people learn" (4).

Viewing the learner as an active participant in the process of acquiring and using knowledge, educators are reexamining ways to activate appropriate learning strategies during the instructional process. These include a renewed interest in cooperative learning (Antil, Jenkins, and Wayne 1998; Johnson and Johnson 2000; Slavin 1994), a shift from behavioral to cognitive learning theories (Jonassen, Peck, and Wilson 1999), and an investigation into the theory of multiple intelligences (Armstrong 2000; Gardner, 1999). This section examines these theories and their relationship to the design and development of multimedia projects.

Howard Gardner's Theory of Multiple Intelligences

Several researchers have developed theories on various ways of knowing, suggesting that students possess several different intelligences (Gardner 1983, 1999; Samples 1992; Sternberg 1994). Perhaps the most recognized theory of multiple intelligence is Howard Gardner's Theory of Multiple Intelligences (Gardner 1983, 1999). In his book *Intelligence Reframed: Multiple Intelligences for the 21st Century,* Gardner reviews the seven intelligences he introduced in his first book, *Frames of the Mind: The Theory of Multiple Intelligences,* and adds another—the naturalist intelligence. Gardner defines *intelligence* as "a biopsychological potential to process information that can be activated in a cultural setting to solve problems or create products that are of value in a culture" (Gardner 1999, 33–34). He suggests that intelligences are neural conditions that will or will not be activated by opportunities, personal decisions, or values. He also states that everyone possesses these intelligences, noting that people acquire and represent knowledge in different ways. Gardner's proposed eight areas of intelligence include the following:

1. Linguistic Intelligence: the ability to use words effectively, whether orally or in writing

2. Logical-Mathematical Intelligence: the capacity to use numbers effectively and to reason well

3. Spatial Intelligence: the ability to perceive the visual-spatial world accurately and to perform transformations on those perceptions

4. Bodily-Kinesthetic Intelligence: expertise in using one's body to express ideas and feelings and facility in using one's hands to produce or transform things

5. Musical Intelligence: the ability to perceive, discriminate, transform, and express musical forms

6. Interpersonal Intelligence: the ability to perceive and make distinctions in the moods, intentions, motivations, and feelings of other people

7. Intrapersonal Intelligence: self-knowledge and the ability to act on the basis of that knowledge

8. Naturalist Intelligence: expertise in recognizing and classifying living and nonliving forms within one's environment. Gardner (1999, 49) notes, "The young child who can readily discriminate among plants or birds or dinosaurs is drawing on the same skills (or intelligence) when she classifies sneakers, cars, sound systems, or marbles."

Gardner identified these intelligences based on a series of tests that included eight criteria. Additional intelligences have been proposed—including spirituality, moral sensibility, sexuality, humor, intuition, and creativity—but it remains to be seen whether these proposed intelligences meet the required criteria (Armstrong 2000; Gardner 1999).

There are several important elements to remember about Gardner's Theory of Multiple Intelligences. In his book *Multiple Intelligences in the Classroom*, Armstrong (2000) states the following:

- Each person possesses all eight intelligences.

- Most people can develop each intelligence to an adequate level of competency.

- Intelligences usually work together in complex ways.

- There are many ways to be intelligent within each category.

Many educators have successfully implemented Gardner's Theory of Multiple Intelligences into their classrooms and have found these statements to be true (Cost and Turley 2000; Goodnough 2001; Lach, Little, and Nazzaro 2003; Loria 1999; Mjagkij and Cantu 1999; Willis and Johnson 2001). Applying Gardner's Theory of Multiple Intelligences can benefit all learners, including learning-disabled students, gifted students, and students from diverse cultural backgrounds (Green 1998; Vialle 1999).

Commercial multimedia applications and the development of multimedia projects encourage a multimodal approach to learning. Well-designed multimedia applications present content in several media formats and allow students to use their own individual learning styles. Although multimedia applications can effectively teach content, student-based multimedia projects allow students to gain skills beyond content-area knowledge. These skills include finding and interpreting information, articulating and communicating knowledge, and using the computer as a cognitive tool (Liu 2003; Liu and Hsiao 2002; Jonassen 2000; Jonassen, Peck, and Wilson 1999).

Applying the Theory of Multiple Intelligences to Multimedia Projects

One of the many benefits of developing multimedia projects is that it allows students to construct and communicate knowledge in various ways. Multimedia projects also encourage group work and social interaction, but they do not require a uniform experience for all students. According to Levin (1994), group work and social interaction are necessary for a multiple intelligences approach, but a uniform experience for all children is not.

When assigning multimedia design teams, students should be placed in groups that provide them with the opportunity to take advantage of their strengths, as well as nurture their weaknesses. For example, students who are identified as spatially intelligent might be responsible for the graphic content and layout of a multimedia project. Students who are identified as logical-mathematically intelligent might be responsible for designing the structure/flowchart of the project and the scripting or programming requirements. Table 1.1 correlates each intelligence with the observed student behaviors and recommended roles when developing a multimedia project.

It is important to note that all students have all intelligences, although one or more may be stronger than others. Placing students in design teams that capture the diversity of their intellectual profiles can provide them with the motivation, skills, and support necessary to learn. Armstrong (2000) comments that most students have strengths in several areas; hence, students may contribute to projects in multiple ways. For example, one student may lead the group in developing the text and music for the project, another student may lead the group in creating the graphics and flowcharts for the project, and so on.

Table 1.1.

Roles of Multiple Intelligence in the Creation of Multimedia Projects

Intelligence	Observed Student Behaviors	Leadership Roles in Multimedia Projects
Linguistic	Loves to read books, write, and tell stories; good memory for names, dates, and trivia; communicates well	Gather and develop text for project; provide narration; keep journal of group progress
Logical-Mathematical	Excels in math; has strong problem-solving skills; enjoys playing strategy games and working on logic puzzles	Design flowchart; write scripting and programming code; develop navigation routes
Spatial	Needs a mental or physical picture to best understand things; draws figures that are advanced for age; doodles a lot	Create graphics, animation, and other visual media for project; design layout
Bodily-Kinesthetic	Excels in one or more sports; good fine-motor skills; tendency to move around, touch things, gesture	Keyboard information; manipulate objects with mouse; operate multimedia equipment

Musical	Remembers melodies; recognizes when music is off-key; has a good singing voice; plays an instrument; hums a lot	Identify works for content integration; create musical score for project; input audio/sound effects
Interpersonal	Enjoys socializing with peers; has leader- ship skills; has good sense of empathy and concern for others	Coordinate group efforts; help set group goals; help solve group disputes
Intrapersonal	Has strong sense of self; is confident; prefers working alone; has high self-esteem; displays independence	Conduct independent research to share with teammates; pilot test multimedia projects; lead multimedia presentations
Naturalist	Enjoys the outdoors, plants, and animals; easily recognizes and classifies things within his/her environment	Collect or videotape outside elements for incorporation into projects; organize project work

Intellectual profiles can change over time as intelligences develop in strength. Gray and Viens (1994, 24) note, "the differences among individual intellectual profiles are the result of personal and local factors as well as cultural influences." Working in diverse groups allows students to nurture their weaknesses and capitalize on their strengths. Students are able to make valuable contributions to group projects as well as augment their intellectual profiles.

Cooperative Learning

Cooperative learning takes place when students work together to accomplish shared goals. Most cooperative conditions use small groups "so that students work together to maximize their own and each other's learning" (Johnson and Johnson 1999a, 5). Johnson and Johnson (1999b) suggest that a cooperative learning group has five defining characteristics:

1. Positive Interdependence. There is a group goal to maximize all members' learning beyond their individual abilities; members succeed only if the other members in their group succeed.

2. Individual Accountability. Group members hold themselves and each other accountable for high-quality work; students are held accountable for their share of the work.

3. Face-to-Face Promotive Interaction. Group members produce joint products, providing both academic and personal support; students promote each other's learning.

4. Social Skills. Group members are taught social skills and are expected to use them to coordinate their efforts; teamwork and task work are emphasized.

5. Group Processing. Groups analyze how well they are achieving their goals, working together, and learning.

The researchers note that a cooperative group is more than the sum of its parts and state that students often perform better academically than they would if they worked by themselves (Johnson and Johnson 1999b).

There are a variety of cooperative group techniques, including Student Teams Achievement Divisions, Teams Games Tournament, Team Assisted Individualization, Jigsaw, Group Investigation, and Learning Together (Slavin 1994, 1999, 2003; Vermette 1998).

Student Teams Achievement Divisions (STAD)—students learn something as a team, contribute to the team by improving their own past performance, and earn team rewards based on their improvements. Students are usually heterogeneously mixed by ability and take individual weekly quizzes. For example, student teams may study about the Westward Movement and take weekly quizzes on the content. Teams earn points based on each student's improvement from previous quizzes. If a student scores 5 out of 10 points on the first quiz and 8 out of 10 on the second quiz, he may earn 8 points for his team, plus 2 bonus points for improving. If a student scores 7 out of 10 points on the first quiz and 5 out of 10 on the second quiz, he may earn 5 points for his team, but no bonus points. If a student scores 10 points on both quizzes, she may earn a total of 12 points (10 points for the second quiz plus 2 bonus points for the perfect score) for her team.

Teams Games Tournament (TGT)—similar to STAD except that weekly tournaments replace weekly quizzes. Homogeneous, three-member teams are formed from the existing heterogeneous groups and compete against similar ability groups to earn points for their regular, heterogeneous group. As with STAD, high-performing teams earn group rewards. For example, existing heterogeneous groups may contain one each low-, average-, and high-ability student. During weekly tournaments (e.g., a game of Jeopardy), low-ability students form groups of three, average-ability students form groups of three, and high-ability students form groups of three. Low-ability groups compete against each other, average-ability groups compete against each other, and high-ability groups compete against each other. The winning homogeneous groups earn points for their heterogeneous teams.

Team Assisted Individualization (TAI)—combines cooperative learning with individualized instruction. Students are placed into groups but work at their own pace and level. Team members check each other's work and help one another with problems. Teams earn points based on the individual performance of each member in the group. Team members encourage and support one another because they want their teams to succeed (Slavin 1994). For example, students at different spelling levels may be placed into heterogeneous groups. The group may consist of one low speller, two average spellers, and one advanced speller. Students are responsible for learning their assigned spelling words, but they have their team members to assist and encourage them. Groups earn points based on their team members' performance on weekly spelling tests. Members take responsibility for each other's learning as well as their own.

Jigsaw—a cooperative group learning method that assigns each of its members a particular learning task. For example, learning about the Civil War may include famous men and women, battles, economic factors, and issues of slavery. Each member chooses a topic and is responsible for teaching his or her team members "all that there is to know" about that topic. Team members meet with members of other groups to form "expert groups" to discuss and research their topic. For example, the team members of the cooperative groups who chose famous women would meet together in a separate cooperative group focused on learning only about famous women of the Civil War. Following research and discussion, the students return to their own teams and take turns teaching their teammates about their topic. Afterward, students take individual quizzes and earn a team score.

Group Investigation—similar to the Jigsaw method except students do not form expert groups. Students work in small groups toward an overall class project. Each group is assigned a different task or activity. Within each group, members decide what information to gather and how to organize and present their findings.

Learning Together—incorporates heterogeneous student groups that work on a single assignment and receive rewards based on their group product. For example, student groups may be assigned to draw and label the human skeletal system. Each student would receive the same final grade for the group product.

Cooperative learning groups differ from traditional learning groups in that most support positive interdependence, individual accountability, group processing, peer responsibility, and heterogeneous membership (Johnson and Johnson 1999a). General findings conclude the following:

- Cooperative groups are appropriate for any instructional task.

- Cooperative groups do just as well or better on achievement than competitive and individualistic learning conditions.

- Cooperative conditions appear to work best when students are heterogeneously grouped, although high-ability students do just as well or better in homogeneous groups.

- Group discussion promotes higher achievement.

- Cooperative learning is more likely to have an effect on student outcomes when cooperation is well defined.

- Stereotypes are likely to be reduced when using cooperative groups.

- Using cooperative groups promotes equality among perceived ability and leadership roles among males and females.

- Cooperative learning can reduce anxiety and create more interesting learning.

- Cooperative groups can be more cost-effective than individualistic learning conditions.

- Cooperative learning appears to be effective at all primary and secondary grade levels and with groups of two to five.

- Cooperative conditions can benefit all ability levels.

- Cooperative groups support achievement-oriented behavior and healthy social development.

- Cooperative grouping can increase student self-esteem and foster higher-order thinking skills.

Although researchers report many positive outcomes using cooperative learning (Calderon, Hertz-Lazarowitz, and Slavin 1998; Johnson and Johnson 1999a; Lord 2001; Marr 2000; Rothenberg, McDermott, and Martin 1998; Siciliano 2001; Slavin 1994, 1999), others note that there are pitfalls (Johnson and Johnson 1999a; Slavin 1994; Vermette 1998). Pitfalls include the "free-rider effect" (members let the more capable members do all the work) and the "sucker effect" (more able members have the less able members do all the work). Individual accountability and grades based on the team's average individual scores can help avoid these pitfalls (Johnson and Johnson 1999a; Slavin 1994). Vermette (1998) suggests teacher monitoring, randomly calling on group members to summarize their group's progress, or requiring each student to write a concluding summary or a description of his or her group's activity, including a retelling of each individual's role and contribution. Others recommend placing students in smaller groups so that it is harder to hide or "free-ride," defining individual expectations of group members, and assigning roles that focus on the strengths of the students (Baloche 1998; Marr 2000). In the case of chronic absenteeism, Baloche (1998) recommends the following:

- Group members phone or e-mail peers with what they have missed.

- Chronically absent students be placed in larger groups so other group members are not as dependent on them.

- Group members have access to the other members' project information and material.

- Assessment is structured so that group members are not penalized for work missed by the absent student.

High expectations must be the norm for all students, where everyone is viewed as a valuable member of the team.

Applying the Theory of Cooperative Learning to Multimedia Projects

Using cooperative groups in multimedia design and development has many benefits. These include peer-teaching, increased use of metacognitive and elaboration strategies, accommodation of individual differences, self-reflection, increased motivation and positive attitudes toward learning, and increased performance (Chen and McGrath 2003; Marr 2000). The teacher's role is to guide and facilitate the cooperative groups' efforts. Table 1.2 provides examples of students' roles and responsibilities in different cooperative group settings. Cooperative group methods that require individual accountability and assign grades based on the average of the team's individual scores are recommended (see Chapter 7).

Table 1.2.

Cooperative Group Settings and Responsibilities in Multimedia Projects

Cooperative Group Method	Multimedia Project Example and Evaluation	Student Roles and Responsibilities in Multimedia Projects
Student Teams Achievement Divisions (STAD)	Groups are provided with specific questions for research and content information on the Westward Movement. They display their knowledge through group multimedia projects. Announced weekly quizzes check individual content learning. A rubric can be used to evaluate final projects for a group grade.	Students learn about the Westward Movement as a team, helping each other understand the content. Groups may alternate project responsibilities to ensure everyone has a chance to explore the content in different ways.
Teams Games Tournament (TGT)	Similar to STAD, except weekly tournaments replace weekly quizzes, and students complete against similar-ability groups to earn points for their heterogeneous group. Responsibilities remain the same.	
Team Assisted Individualization (TAI)	Groups create projects on a select genre, such as mystery stories. Groups display information about several books. The project is evaluated based on each student's book report.	Each student is responsible for reading a select book (at the appropriate level) and reporting on it through multimedia. The team project introduces and links each report.

Jigsaw	Groups create projects on the Civil War. Students are evaluated on their group's final project and their individual knowledge of all the content areas researched for the Civil War.	Each member is assigned a particular content area of the Civil War, such as famous men and women, battles, economic factors, issues of slavery, and so on. Members meet with other groups' members assigned to the same content area. For example, members researching famous battles meet together and help each other become an "expert" on the topic. Members return to their groups and share what they have learned. Students design their portion of the group's multimedia project. (This approach may also be used to learn about different skills, such as creating animation, desktop videos, and so on.)
Group Investigation	Similar to the Jigsaw method except students do not form expert groups. Students work in small groups toward an overall class project. Each has a specific task or assignment.	
Learning Together	Groups decide on a multimedia project of interest (e.g., a project about volcanoes) and present their final project to the class. Each student receives the same final grade for the group product.	After deciding on the project, students determine each other's role and responsibilities based on their interests. Responsibilities and roles may change during the project. (Individual accountability may be weak.)

Cooperative group multimedia projects support small group interactions, positive socialization, peer teaching and learning, and the development of original projects that reflect the groups' collaboration (Marr 2000; Okolo and Ferretti 1998). In addition, cooperative groups can reduce the complexity and time commitment of creating multimedia projects by assigning students to specific design roles and responsibilities. Each student contributes to the project as a whole and has the opportunity to share his or her expertise with, as well as learn from, others. Techniques for establishing, monitoring, and assessing group projects are included in Chapters 3 and 7.

Constructivism

Cognitive psychologists believe in the process of learning through the construction of knowledge. They assert that "people learn by actively constructing knowledge, weighing new information against their previous understanding, thinking about and working through discrepancies (on their own and with others), and coming to a new understanding" (Association for Supervision and Curriculum Development 1992, 2). These ideas, combined with social learning, are not new. Kilpatrick (1918) expressed the need to base education on purposeful acts and social activity, which he designed into his project method of instruction. Dewey (1929) stated that "social tools" (reading, spelling, and writing) are best acquired in a social context. Piaget believed that people try to make sense of the world and actively create their own knowledge through direct experience with objects, people, and ideas (Woolfolk 1987). Vygotsky (1978, 88) argued, "human learning presupposes a specific social nature and a process by which children grow into the intellectual life of those around them."

Professional organizations, such as the National Council for Teachers of Mathematics (NTCM), the American Association for the Advancement of Science (AAAS), and the National Council for the Social Studies (NCSS) continue to emphasize the need to engage students in constructivist thinking—decision making, problem solving, and critical thinking. Researchers (Gagnon and Collay 2001; Marlowe and Page 1998; Shapiro 2003) define *constructivist teachers* as those who

- Encourage and accept student autonomy and initiative

- Use raw data and primary sources, along with manipulative, interactive, and physical materials

- Use cognitive terminology such as classify, analyze, predict, and create

- Allow student responses to drive lessons, shift instructional strategies, and alter content

- Inquire about students' understanding of concepts before sharing their own understandings of those concepts

- Encourage students to engage in conversations with the teacher and with one another

- Encourage student inquiry by asking thoughtful, open-ended questions and encouraging students to ask questions of each other

- Seek elaboration of students' initial responses

- Engage students in experiences that might create contradictions to their initial hypotheses and then encourage discussion

- Allow wait time after posing questions

- Provide time for students to construct relationships and create metaphors

- Nurture students' natural curiosity through frequent use of the learning cycle model (discovery, concept introduction, and concept application)

These teacher practices can help guide students in their own understanding and intellectual and reflective growth. Developing multimedia projects provides an ideal forum for a constructivist approach.

Applying the Theory of Constructivism to Multimedia Projects

Research has demonstrated that developing multimedia projects can help students learn how to develop concepts and ideas, design plans, apply what they learn, refine questions, make predictions, collect and analyze research, communicate findings, and solve problems (Funk, 2003; Schacter and Fagnano 1999). Researchers (Cooper and Brna 2001; Riddle 1995) report that students are more likely to show greater descriptive detail, unique perspectives, and diverse interests and skills when using multimedia software to create and add graphics, audio, and animation to their textual communications. Other researchers suggest that developing multimedia projects allows learning to occur in more meaningful contexts (Basden 2001; Katz 2002; Rice and Wilson 1999). Designing multimedia projects can provide a concrete and meaningful context for developing higher-order thinking skills, engaging students in the learning process, and inviting them to use technology as a cognitive tool (Liu 2003; Liu and Hsiao 2002; Liu and Pedersen 1998). While developing multimedia projects, students begin to see themselves as authors of knowledge, experts within their design teams, and active participants in the learning process (Katz 2002; Liu 2003; Liu and Pedersen 1998; Schacter and Fagnano 1999).

According to Simons (1993), constructivist learning includes at least five components: active, cumulative, integrative, reflective, and goal-directed. Their definitions and relationship to the construction of multimedia projects are presented in Table 1.3. Gagnon and Collay (2001) describe similar elements, but include a sixth—grouping—noting that "small groups are necessary for students to move from personal meaning to shared meaning in the social construction of knowledge" (36). Design teams allow students to work in small groups.

Table 1.3.

Constructivist Components and Their Relationships to Creating Multimedia Projects

Constructivist Learning Component	Definition	Relationship to Creating Multimedia Projects
Active	Students process information meaningfully.	Multimedia projects allow students to be active learners by defining the content and creating the media components.
Cumulative	Learning builds on prior knowledge.	Multimedia projects allow students to connect current knowledge to new ideas through a variety of formats.
Integrative	Learners elaborate on new knowledge.	Multimedia projects offer environments in which students can create increasingly complex programs, as well as present current and new knowledge in new ways.
Reflective	Students assess what they know and need to learn.	Multimedia projects incorporate multiple levels of assessment at various phases throughout the design and development process.
Goal-directed	Learners engage in purposeful learning activities.	When assigning multimedia projects, the teacher and students work together to define specific learning outcomes.

Herman, Aschbacher, and Winters (1992) also discuss the implications of aligning instruction and assessment with constructivist learning. Table 1.4 presents cognitive learning theories and their implications for instruction, assessment, and multimedia projects.

Table 1.4.

Cognitive Learning Theories' Relationships to Multimedia Project Creation

Cognitive Learning Theory	Implications for Instruction/Assessment	Relationship to Creating Multimedia Projects
Learning is a process of creating personal meaning from new information and prior knowledge.	Encourage discussion, divergent thinking, multiple links and solutions, varied modes of expression, critical thinking skills; relate new information to personal experience; apply information to new situations.	Projects encourage knowledge construction and group efforts, stimulating discussion, and divergent thinking. Media elements provide various modes of expression.
Learning is not necessarily a linear progression of discrete skills.	Engage students in problem solving and critical thinking.	Developing flowcharts and storyboards requires problem-solving and critical thinking skills to "chunk" and organize information into linear and nonlinear formats. Students see how data relate to each other.
There are a variety of learning styles, attention spans, developmental paces, and intelligences.	Provide choices in task, varied means of showing mastery and competence, time to think about and do assignments, opportunities for self-evaluation and peer review.	Design teams offer task options, allowing students to demonstrate their skills in many ways. The process of developing projects requires students to revise and rethink, and provides students with hands-on, concrete learning experiences.
Students perform better when they know the goal, see models, and know how their performance compares to the standard.	Discuss goals and let students help define them (personal and class); provide and discuss examples of student work and allow them to have input into expectations; give students opportunities for self-evaluation and peer review.	Rubrics, goals, and expectations for projects can be decided as a whole class without sacrificing the teacher's basic objectives. Sample projects can help clarify project expectations. The process of developing projects encourages self-evaluation and peer review.
It is important to know when to use knowledge, how to adapt it, and how to manage one's own learning.	Provide real-world opportunities (or simulations) to apply or adapt new knowledge; provide opportunities for students to think about how they learn and why they like certain work.	Multimedia projects support real-world learning experiences, plus they have the potential to enhance students' communication and metacognitive skills.
Motivation, effort, and self-esteem affect learning and performance.	Motivate students with real-life tasks and connections to personal experiences; encourage students to see the relationship between effort and results.	Projects provide students with real-life tasks that they can connect to their personal interests and experiences. Projects serve as visual outcomes of students' efforts.
Learning has social components. Group work is valuable.	Provide group work; establish heterogeneous groups; enable students to take on a variety of roles; consider group products and group processes.	Multimedia projects encourage cooperative grouping techniques.

Multimedia projects can provide ideal learning environments for implementing a constructivist approach to learning. Creating multimedia projects encourages divergent thinking, multiple modes of expression, goal setting, critical thinking skills, teamwork, opportunities to revise and rethink, and more. Students are active participants, constructing knowledge that is meaningful, applicable, and memorable. In addition, multimedia projects provide educators with multiple ways to assess students' progress. Assessment strategies are discussed in Chapter 7.

SUMMARY

Multimedia combines several media to present information. Computer-based multimedia uses computers to present multiple media formats that convey information in a linear or nonlinear format. Creating multimedia projects reinforces students' technology skills and invites them to work cooperatively and use a variety of media to express their understanding. It is a process approach to learning, encouraging students to think differently about how they organize and present information. It supports a collaborative environment, self-reflection, authentic learning, and the use of technology as a cognitive tool. In addition, multimedia projects offer an effective alternative for assessing student learning and provide students with a real-world learning environment.

Research demonstrates that multimedia development tools provide students with opportunities to show greater descriptive detail, unique perspectives, and diverse interests and skills. It is possible that these tools may help students develop what may otherwise be paralyzed or "shut-down" intelligences. Opportunities to explore concepts and express understanding through multimedia may create positive turning points in the development of a student's intelligences. Students report a desire to learn, feel more confident, and consider themselves producers of knowledge rather than consumers when creating multimedia projects. By working cooperatively and constructing knowledge, students become empowered learners.

REFERENCES

Antil, L. R., J. R. Jenkins, and S. K. Wayne. 1998. Cooperative learning: Prevalence, conceptualization, and the relation between research and practice. *American Educational Research Journal* 35(3): 419–54.

Armstrong, T. 2000. *Multiple intelligences in the classroom.* 2d ed. Alexandria, VA: Association for Supervision and Curriculum Development.

Association for Supervision and Curriculum Development (ASCD). 1992. Wanted: Deep understanding. "Constructivism" posits new conception of learning. *ASCD Update* 34(3): 1–5.

Baloche, L. A. 1998. *The cooperative classroom: Empowering learning.* Upper Saddle River, NJ: Prentice Hall.

Bagui, S. 1998. Reasons for increased learning using multimedia. *Journal of Educational Multimedia and Hypermedia* 7(1): 3–18.

Basden, J. C. 2001. Authentic tasks as the basis for multimedia design curriculum. *T.H.E. Journal* 29(4): 16–21.

Bennett, D. T. 1996. Assessment through video. *Electronic Learning* 15(4): 16–17.

Calderon, M., R. Hertz-Lazarowitz, and R. Slavin. 1998. Effects of bilingual cooperative integrated reading and composition on students making the transition from Spanish to English reading. *Elementary School Journal* 99(2): 153–65.

Chen, P., and D. McGrath. 2003. Moments of joy: Student engagement and conceptual learning in the design of hypermedia documents. *Journal of Research on Technology in Education* 35(3): 402–22.

Cooper, B., and P. Brna. 2001. Fostering cartoon-style creativity with sensitive agent support in tomorrow's classroom. *Educational Technology & Society* 4(2): 32–40.

Cooper, S. B. 1998. Instructor-created computer tutorials for students in an elementary mathematics education course. *Journal of Computing in Childhood Education* 9(1): 93–101.

Cost, P. A., and J. M. Turley. 2000. Teaching the food guide pyramid using multiple intelligence learning centers. *Journal of Health Education* 31(2): 111–12.

Daley, 1999. Turning the tide. *Instructor*, 108(8): 23–26.

Dewey, J. 1929. *The sources of a science of education.* New York: Horace Liveright.

Ellis, T. J. 2001. Multimedia enhanced educational products as a tool to promote critical thinking in adult students. *Journal of Educational Multimedia and Hypermedia* 10(2): 107–23.

Ercetin, G. 2003. Exploring ESL learners' use of hypermedia reading glosses. *CALICO Journal* 20(2): 261–83.

Funk, C. 2003. James Otto and the pi man: A constructivist tale. *Phi Delta Kappan* 85(3): 212–14

Gagnon, G. W., and M. Collay. 2001. *Designing for learning: Six elements in constructivist classrooms.* Thousand Oaks, CA: Corwin Press.

Gardner, H. 1983. *Frames of mind: The theory of multiple intelligences.* New York: Basic Books.

Gardner, H. 1999. *Intelligence reframed: Multiple intelligences for the 21st century.* New York: Basic Books.

Gayeski, D. M. 1993. *Multimedia for learning.* Englewood Cliffs, NJ: Educational Technology Publications.

Goodnough, K. 2001. Multiple intelligences theory: A framework for personalizing science curricula. *School Science and Mathematics*, 101(4): 180–93.

Gray, J. H., and J. T. Viens. 1994. The theory of multiple intelligences: Understanding cognitive diversity in school. *National Forum: Phi Kappa Phi Journal* 74(1): 22–25.

Green, B. 1998. Multiple intelligence and the child with dyslexia. *International Schools Journal* 18(1): 34–43.

Herman, J. L., P. R. Aschbacher, and L. Winters. 1992. *A practical guide to alternative assessment.* Alexandria, VA: Association for Supervision and Curriculum Development.

Herrington, J., and R. Oliver. 1999. Using situated learning and multimedia to investigate higher-order thinking. *Journal of Educational Multimedia and Hypermedia* 8(4): 401–21.

Holzberg, C. S. 1998. Helping all learners succeed: Special ed success stories. *Technology and Learning* (18)5: 52–56.

International Society for Technology in Educational (ISTE). 2004. Technology foundation standards for all students [Online]. Available at: http://cnets.iste.org/students/s_stands.html. Retrieved on December 4, 2004.

Irish, C. 2002. Using Peg- and keyword mnemonics and computer-assisted instruction to enhance basic multiplication performance in elementary students with learning and cognitive disabilities. *Journal of Special Education Technology* 17(4): 29–40.

Johnson, D. W., and R. T. Johnson. 2000. How can we put cooperative learning into practice? *Science teacher* 67(1): 39.

————. 1999a. *Learning together and alone: Cooperative, competitive, and individualistic learning.* 5th ed. Needham Heights, MA: Allyn & Bacon.

————. 1999b. Making cooperative learning work. *Theory into Practice* 38(2): 67–73.

Jonassen, D. H. 2000. *Computers as mindtools for schools.* 2d ed. Upper Saddle River, NJ: Prentice Hall.

Jonassen, D. H., K. L. Peck, and B. G. Wilson. 1999. *Learning with technology: A constructivist perspective.* Upper Saddle River, NJ: Prentice Hall.

Jones, L. C. 2003. Supporting listening comprehension and vocabulary acquisition with multimedia annotations: The students' voice. *CALICO Journal* 21(1): 41–65.

Kasahara, A. 2001. Students making media. *The Active Learner* 6(1): 18–23.

Katz, D. 2002. Multimedia projects. *English Teachers' Journal* 54: 72–79.

Kilpatrick, W. H. 1918. The project method: The use of the purposeful act in the educative process. *Teachers College Bulletin.* Columbia, SC: Columbia University.

Lach, C., E. Little, and D. Nazzaro. 2003. From all sides now: Weaving technology and multiple intelligences into science and art. *Learning and Leading with Technology* 30(6): 32–35, 59.

Lachs, V. 1998. Making the computer dance to your tune: Primary school pupils authoring hypermedia. *Journal of Computing in Childhood Education* 9(1): 57–77.

Levin, H. M. 1994. Commentary: Multiple intelligence theory and everyday practices. *Teachers College Record* 95(4): 570–75.

———. 1998. Effects of hypermedia versus traditional instruction on students' achievement: A meta-analysis. *Journal of Research on Computing in Education* 30(4): 341–59.

Liao, Y. C. 1999. Effects of hypermedia on students' achievement: A meta-analysis. *Journal of Educational Multimedia and Hypermedia* 8(3): 255–77.

Liu, M. 2003. Enhancing learners' cognitive skills through multimedia design. *Interactive Learning Environments* 11(1): 23–39.

——— and Y. Hsiao. 2002. Middle school students as multimedia designers: A project-based learning approach. *Journal of Interactive Learning Research* 13(4): 311–37.

——— and S. Pedersen. 1998. The effect of being hypermedia designers on elementary school students' motivation and learning of design knowledge. *Journal of Interactive Learning Research* 9(2): 155–82.

Lord, T. R. 2001. 101 reasons for using cooperative learning in biology teaching. *American Biology Teacher* 63(1): 30–38.

Loria, W. 1999. Teaching to the multiple intelligences. *Inquiry* 4(1): 13–15.

Maccini, P., J. C. Gagnon, and C. A. Hughes. 2002. Technology-based practices for secondary students with learning disabilities. *Learning Disability Quarterly* 25(4): 247–61.

Marlowe, B. A., and M. L. Page. 1998. *Creating and sustaining the constructivist classroom.* Thousand Oaks, CA: Corwin Press.

Marr, P. M. 2000. Grouping students at the computer to enhance the study of British literature. *English Journal* 90(2): 120–25.

Mayer, R. E., and Moreno, R. 2002. Aids to computer-based multimedia learning. *Learning and Instruction* 12(1): 107–19.

Mjagkij, N., and D. A. Cantu. 1999. The public be damned! A thematic and multiple intelligences approach to teaching the gilded age. *OAH Magazine of History* 13(4): 56–60.

Morse, T. 2003. Enhancing special education students' multiple literacies through multimedia activities. *Journal of Reading Education* 28(2): 39–40.

Nikolova, O. R. 2002. Effects of students' participation in authoring of multimedia materials on student acquisition of vocabulary. *Language Learning and Technology* 6(1): 100–22.

Okolo, C. M., and R. P. Ferretti. 1998. Multimedia design projects in an inclusive social studies classroom: Sometimes people argue with words instead of fists. *Teaching Exceptional Children* 31(1): 50–57.

Oughton, J. M., and W. M. Reed. 1998. The effect of hypermedia development on high school students' knowledge acquisition, general problem-solving skills, and general design skills. *Journal of Educational Multimedia and Hypermedia* 7(4): 333–63.

Panagiotakopoulos, C. T., and G. S. Ioannidis. 2002. Assessing children's understanding of basic time concepts through multimedia software. *Computers & Education* 38(4): 331–49.

Pratt, B. 1999. Making it work. *Learning and Leading with Technology*, 26(8): 28–31.

Rasmussen, K. L., and G. V. Davidson-Shivers. 1998. Hypermedia and learning styles: Can performance be influenced? *Journal of Multimedia and Hypermedia* 7(4): 291–308.

Rice, M. L., and E. K. Wilson. 1999. How technology aids constructivism in the social studies classroom. *Social Studies* 90(1): 28–33.

Riddle, E. M. 1995. *Communication through multimedia in an elementary classroom* (Report no. 143). Charlottesville, VA: Curry School of Education, University of Virginia. (ERIC ED 384 346)

Rothenberg, J. J., P. McDermott, and G. Martin. 1998. Changes in pedagogy: A qualitative result of teaching heterogeneous classes. *Teaching and Teacher Education* 14(6): 633–42.

Rouet, J., J. J. Levon, A. Dillion, and R. J. Spiro. 1996. An introduction to hypertext and cognition. In *Hypertext and cognition*, edited by J. Rouet, J. J. Levon, A. Dillion, and R. J. Spiro. Mahwah, NJ: Lawrence Erlbaum Associates.

Samples, B. 1992. Using learning modalities to celebrate intelligence. *Educational Leadership* 50(2): 62–66.

Schacter, J., and C. Fagnano. 1999. Does computer technology improve student learning and achievement? How, when, and under what conditions? *Journal of Educational Computing Research* 20(4): 329–43.

Shapiro, A. 2003. The latest dope on research (about constructivism): Part II: On instruction and leadership. *International Journal of Educational Reform* 12(1): 62–77.

Sherry, L., S. Billig, D. Jesse, and D. Watson-Acosta. 2001. Assessing the impact of instructional technology on student achievement. *T.H.E. Journal* 28(7): 40–43.

Siciliano, J. I. 2001. How to incorporate cooperative learning principals in the classroom: It's more than just putting students in teams. *Journal of Management Education* 25(1): 8–20.

Simons, P. R. J. 1993. "Constructive learning: The role of the learner." In *Designing environments for constructive learning*. Edited by T. Duffy, J. Lowyck, and D. Jonassen. Heidelberg, Germany: Springer-Verlag.

Sivin-Kachala, J., and E. R. Bialo. 2000. *Report on the effectiveness of technology in schools*. 7th ed. Washington, DC: Software and Information Industry Association.

Slavin, R.E. 2003. *Educational psychology theory and practice*. 7th ed. Boston, MA: Allyn & Bacon.

———. 1999. Comprehensive approaches to cooperative learning. *Theory into Practice* 38(2): 74–79.

———. 1994. *Cooperative learning: Theory, research, and practice*. 2d ed. Needham Heights, MA: Allyn & Bacon.

Son, J. 2003. A hypertext approach to foreign language reading: Student attitudes and perceptions. *Australian Review of Applied Linguistics* (17): 91–110.

Sternberg, R. J. 1994. Diversifying instruction and assessment. *Educational Forum* 59(1): 47–52.

Vermette, P. J. 1998. *Making cooperative learning work: Student teams in K–12 classrooms*. Upper Saddle River, NJ: Prentice Hall.

Vialle, W. 1999. Identification of giftedness in culturally diverse groups. *Gifted Education International* 13(3): 250–57.

Vygotsky, L. S. 1978. *Mind in society: The development of higher psychological processes*. Cambridge, MA: Harvard University Press.

Willis, J. K., and A. N. Johnson. 2001. Multiply with MI: Using multiple intelligences to master multiplication. *Teaching Children Mathematics* 7(5): 260–69.

Wolfe, P. 2001. *Brain matters: Translating research into classroom practice*. Alexandria, VA: Association for Supervision and Curriculum Development.

Woolfolk, A. E. 1987. *Educational psychology.* 3d ed. Englewood Cliffs, NJ: Prentice Hall.

Xin, J. F. 1999. Computer-assisted cooperative learning in integrated classrooms for students with and without disabilities. *Information Technology in Childhood Education Annual 1999*: 61–78.

Yelland, N. 1999. Reconceptualizing schooling with technology for the 21st century: Images and reflections. *Information Technology in Childhood Education Annual 1999*: 39–59.

A Model for the Design and Development of Multimedia Projects

A SCENARIO

Eleni shook her head as she reflected on the multimedia projects her students had recently presented. They certainly had mastered the programs (some used PowerPoint and others created Web pages). They had fun with the technology and enjoyed the opportunity to work together on a team. Eleni was worried, however, that the end products varied tremendously, and she had no idea how to assess the projects. Some of the projects were rich with content; others seemed little more than a series of unrelated images and media elements. Eleni vowed that the next projects her students created would be a little more focused.

At the next district meeting of middle-school teachers, Eleni made a point to ask teachers from nearby schools about their experiences with multimedia projects in the classroom. She spoke to Mr. Impetuous and Mr. Plan from Washington Middle School.

Mr. Impetuous and Mr. Plan were both middle-school teachers who had integrated multimedia projects into their classrooms within the last year. As she listened to them recount their projects, Eleni was amazed by the contrast in their experiences. Mr. Impetuous said that multimedia projects had been disastrous for him. He blamed the results on his students, stating that they were disruptive, unorganized, and noisy. His advice was to continue teaching in a traditional mode (lecture), to maintain maximum control at all times, and to use objective (multiple-choice questions) for assessment. On further investigation, Eleni learned that Mr. Impetuous had provided little or no guidance for his students. He simply introduced them to a couple of computer programs and set them loose to produce a project. There were no agreed-on project goals, no systematic procedure for producing the projects, and no evaluation plan.

21

In contrast, Mr. Plan was extremely positive about his experience and was continuing to expand the integration of multimedia projects into his curriculum. Although he taught basically the same group of students as Mr. Impetuous, Mr. Plan found that his students worked well together and completed their projects on time. Mr. Plan emphasized the need for specific goals and procedures, noting that his students knew exactly what was expected of them. He commented that through the project design and development he had been able to cover the topics in more depth, and the students appeared to understand the material better. Yes, the classroom had been a little noisier than during a lecture, but the students stayed on task and were very enthusiastic about their projects. They (Mr. Plan and his students) had agreed on a rubric for the projects before they started so that everyone knew exactly what was expected and how the projects would be evaluated.

As Eleni returned to her school, ideas on how to improve project-based learning for her students started to form. She began to realize that providing structure and rubrics for projects would not negate students' creativity and innovativeness. From now on, she would be sure that her students realized the importance of the overall process, which includes careful analysis and design, as well as a forum to express their ideas in multiple dimensions.

OVERVIEW

Every teacher knows that good instruction involves careful planning. Whether or not a teacher creates detailed lesson plans, he or she understands the value of preparing the content, sequence, and instructional materials for each lesson. In addition, experienced teachers always have a backup plan (or two) in case the lesson does not progress as expected.

Careful planning is especially critical when integrating multimedia projects in the classroom. Planning saves time, reduces frustration, eliminates fragmented learning experiences, and results in better products. Following a systematic plan is recommended for teachers who are using technology for instruction as well as for students who are creating multimedia projects. This chapter introduces a model for technology projects. It is based on 3Ds and an E: DECIDE, DESIGN, DEVELOP, and EVALUATE. The topics of this chapter include the following:

The DDD-E Model

- DECIDE phase: Planning activities for teachers and students

- DESIGN phase: Determining the program structure and implementation

- DEVELOP phase: Gathering and creating the media elements and facilitating the lesson

- EVALUATE phase: Reflecting on the project and the student achievement

OVERVIEW OF THE DDD-E MODEL

Implementing multimedia projects in a classroom environment is a rewarding, yet challenging, undertaking. A multitude of issues will surface, such as: Which standards can be addressed? How many students should work in each group? Which media components are appropriate? Should the project result in a presentation, a digital movie, or a Web page? How many hours or days should the students work on the project? How should it be evaluated? The questions (and possible answers) are endless.

One way to address the numerous issues involved in designing and developing multimedia projects is to follow a process that outlines the analysis, design, development, and evaluation of the project. The model proposed by this book consists of DECIDE, DESIGN, DEVELOP, and EVALUATE (DDD-E). This model is intended to serve as a general outline for projects, but it can be modified or expanded to meet individual needs. It provides a framework for the phases of multimedia projects but does not negate a constructivist approach to individual project design or development.

Creating a multimedia project is similar to cooking a gourmet meal. First, you must DECIDE exactly which dishes you plan to serve (which will be influenced by who is coming to dinner and which groceries you have in the cupboard). If more than one person is cooking the meal, you also must decide who is going to be responsible for preparing each dish.

Next, the DESIGN of the meal includes locating the recipes and organizing the ingredients. Recipes, like flowcharts and storyboards, provide the structure for the dishes, detailing the required amounts of each ingredient and the sequence of cooking events.

The meal is DEVELOPed by gathering all of the components, mixing everything in the correct sequence, and combining the ingredients. As each individual dish is prepared, the overall meal must be considered. For example, appetizers are usually prepared first and served before the main course.

You EVALUATE throughout the process of making the meal (e.g., licking the spoon and making sure a dish is not burning). Dinner guests provide the final assessment by providing feedback after the meal has been served.

The DDD-E model consists of three main phases (DECIDE, DESIGN, DEVELOP), surrounded by EVALUATE (see Figure 2.1). This chapter provides a general outline of the model. Subsequent chapters (3 through 7) provide in-depth treatments of each phase, with recommendations for classroom implementation and modification.

Each phase in the DDD-E model involves activities for both the teacher and the students. The DECIDE phase focuses on determining the program goals; the DESIGN phase specifies the program structure; and the DEVELOP phase includes producing the media elements and programming the project. The EVALUATE phase occurs throughout the design and development processes. At each phase of the process, the project should be reviewed, and, if necessary, revised. Table 2.1 outlines teacher and student activities for each phase in the DDD-E model. These activities are introduced in this chapter. Detailed descriptions of each are provided in Chapters 2 through 7.

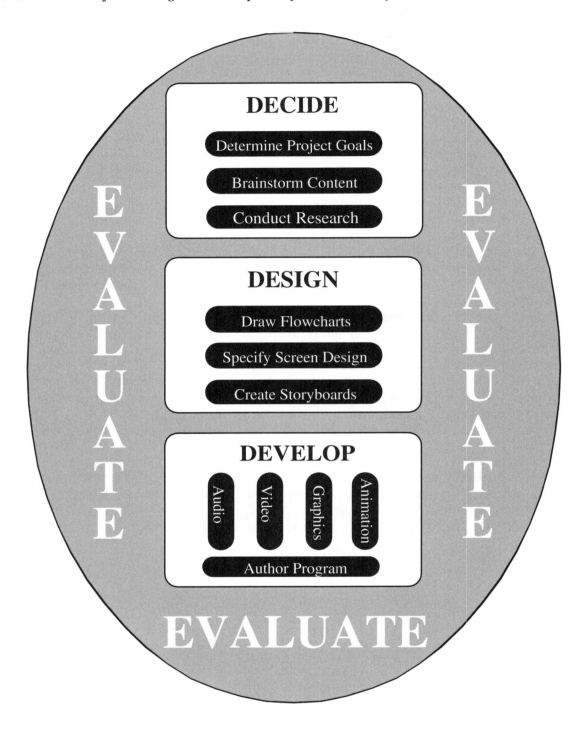

Figure 2.1. The DDD-E model.

Table 2.1.

Teacher and Student Activities in the DDD-E Model

Phase	Activities: Teacher	Activities: Student
DECIDE	PLANNING Identify standards and set instructional goals Decide on a project Assess prerequisite skills Determine assessment techniques ORGANIZING Examine grouping alternatives Create cooperative groups Schedule computer time	Brainstorm content Conduct research
DESIGN	Present design guidelines and templates Conduct formative assessment	Outline content Create flowcharts Specify screen design and layout Write scripts or storyboards
DEVELOP	Manage media production Facilitate multimedia activities Conduct formative assessment	Create graphics Construct animations Produce audio Produce video Author program
EVALUATE	Provide student assessment Reflect on activity and revise for future	Debug program Evaluate peers Conduct self-evaluations

DECIDE

The first phase in a multimedia project is DECIDE. This phase sets the stage for the entire project. The DECIDE phase is influenced by many variables, including the content area, location and number of computers, available software, and students' experiences and expertise. The DECIDE phase includes the following activities for teachers and students.

TEACHERS

- Identify standards and set instructional goals

- Decide on a project

- Assess prerequisite skills

- Determine assessment techniques

- Examine grouping alternatives
- Create cooperative groups
- Schedule computer time

STUDENTS

- Brainstorm content
- Conduct research

Identify Standards and Set Instructional Goals (Teacher)

The first step in the DECIDE phase is to identify the standards and goals that will be addressed with the multimedia project. Standards and benchmarks for students exist at the national level for content areas. Many states and local districts also have standards and/or benchmarks to measure student achievement. Technology can be used as a tool in the classroom to address a multitude of standards and instructional goals—from science to reading. See Chapter 3 for more details.

Decide on a Project (Teacher)

Before assigning a multimedia project, educators need to consider whether it is the most effective way to achieve the desired learning outcomes; alternative approaches might be more effective or efficient.

When assigning a multimedia project, consider the following:

1. *It should be relevant to the student.* Projects are more meaningful if the students can see how the areas of study affect them. In other words, a project about pollution can be introduced by focusing on how pollution has affected the beaches or air quality in the local area.

2. *It should be relevant to the curriculum.* Technology should be used as a tool, not as an end in itself. Therefore, each multimedia project should be closely related to instructional objectives.

3. *There should be sufficient resources.* Some topics do not lend themselves to multimedia simply because there are not enough resources. For example, it may not be appropriate to ask students to create a multimedia project about authors and assign Mark Twain to one group and Catherine Gregory to another. Likewise, it can be frustrating to implement a multimedia project without sufficient hardware and software. Before starting a multimedia unit, review the resources that the students will have available, such as books, clip media, the Internet, and computers. This will help teachers schedule computer time, arrange groups, and provide students with the necessary materials to complete their projects.

4. *There should be sufficient time.* Carefully evaluate the amount of time that can be devoted to project development. Short-term projects with well-defined scope could be completed in three to four hours. Long-term projects, involving research, synthesis of information, and complex production could take several weeks to complete.

Assess Prerequisite Skills (Teacher)

It is crucial that students have the necessary prerequisite skills for using the computer and multimedia tools. Teachers should ensure that students are familiar with basic computer skills (turning on and off the computer, copying files, navigating through folders and directories, and handling the computer hardware) and the skills necessary for creating the assigned multimedia project.

Determine Assessment Techniques (Teacher)

When the project begins, it is important to inform the students about the goals and assessment methods. Students should be aware if "paper" products, such as storyboards or content outlines, will be required, as well as the evaluation instruments that will be used.

Rubrics are common measurement tools for multimedia projects because they provide guidelines for assessment, while allowing room for creativity and subjectivity. In many cases, the teacher and students will work together to outline the requirements and establish the rubrics. Sample rubrics for multimedia projects are included in Chapter 7.

Examine Grouping Alternatives (Teacher)

Many of the multimedia projects will be completed by groups of two to six students. It is important to establish the size and membership of the groups early in the process because the group members will need to work together to brainstorm and research their approach.

There are many alternatives for assigning students to a group, including student learning styles, multiple intelligences, student interests, random assignment, and areas of expertise. Chapter 3 provides detailed information on alternatives in group size, group composition, and group structure.

Create Cooperative Groups (Teacher)

Teamwork and collaboration are important elements and outcomes of multimedia projects. Within each group, the members may take on the roles of a multimedia design and development team. The primary team members are listed in Table 2.2.

The team roles need not be independent of each other. In other words, one student may serve as both the program author and the graphic artist. Likewise, all students can take on all roles and work together for the final product. Chapter 3 provides more information about how to assign student roles.

Schedule Computer Time (Teacher)

It's not necessary to have a room full of equipment to implement multimedia activities; however, one of the first steps is to take an inventory of the hardware and software options that are available at your school or district. Once you know what is available, you can begin to schedule access to computers and other peripherals (see Chapter 3).

A promising trend in this area is the increased access to laptop computers and other wireless devices in many schools. As technology becomes more ubiquitous, multimedia projects can be developed with less and less concern about equitable access for all students.

Table 2.2.

Multimedia Team Members

Team Member	Roles in Multimedia Project
Project manager	• Organize the team members • Set the schedules • Track the progress
Instructional designers	• Determine the screen layout • Create the flowcharts • Specify the project design in the storyboards
Graphic artists	• Create the graphics • Create the animations
Production specialists	• Record and edit the audio
Program authors	• Produce the program • Debug and test the program

Brainstorm Content (Students)

After establishing the design teams, allow students time to explore the project by brainstorming with their group members. There are two aspects of the project that students can explore—content and approach. For example, if a group is creating a program about Florida history, the students may begin by generating ideas about topics. The project might include explorers, soldiers, Indians, resources, and weather, among other things. (Note: Brainstorming is effective only if the students are somewhat familiar with the content.)

After they have exhausted the ideas for content (without criticizing anyone's ideas), they can explore possible approaches. Given the Florida history project, they might suggest making a video about a reenactment of an historical battle, they could collect pictures of the explorers, or they could generate maps showing settlement patterns. Be sure to allow plenty of time for the students to explore the content and approaches thoroughly.

Conduct Research (Students)

Every project should include ample time for the students to research the content. For this step, students should have access to as many resources as possible, including the Internet, books, and journals. It may be necessary to help students get started and to provide a checklist of required components for the project. For example, if the project is focusing on a country, you may require students to include information about the imports, exports, history, geography, politics, culture, and so on. In addition to collecting the research, students should be encouraged to synthesize it and present it in a novel, concise manner.

DESIGN

The DECIDE phase outlines the goals and content of the project. In the DESIGN phase, the project takes form through flowcharts and storyboards. After teachers inventory available hardware and software, present design guidelines, demonstrate flowchart techniques, and provide storyboard templates, students organize the sequence and specify the exact text, graphics, audio, and interactions of the project. It is crucial to emphasize the importance of the DESIGN phase to students. If they do not dedicate sufficient time and energy to this phase, they may end up wasting valuable time during the DEVELOP (production) phase. The DESIGN phase should represent approximately 50 percent of the total time committed to the project.

TEACHERS

- Present design guidelines and templates
- Conduct formative assessment

STUDENTS

- Outline content
- Create flowcharts
- Specify screen design and layout
- Write scripts or storyboards

Present Design Guidelines and Templates (Teacher)

Through the use of examples and nonexamples, teachers can introduce students to design guidelines for text, menus, navigation, color, and other elements. Soon, the students will be critiquing each other and providing insight into effective presentations.

Multimedia projects can be simplistic or complex, depending on the age of the students, the length of the project, and the instructional goals. Templates are useful tools to help students outline and structure their projects—the templates can be used as digital documents (the students fill them in on a computer), or they can be printed and filled in with paper and pencil. Information about guidelines and templates are provided in Chapter 4.

Conduct Formative Assessment (Teacher)

As students begin to design their projects, through the use of content outlines, flowcharts, storyboards, and so on, it is important to provide feedback on their progress. At this point, teachers can provide feedback to students about whether they are staying within the project scope, addressing the project goals, and working well with their team members. Chapter 7 focuses on assessment techniques.

Outline Content (Students)

After the brainstorming and research steps of the DECIDE phase, the students should synthesize, organize, and outline the content for the project. This step helps set the stage for the flowcharts. Many factors influence the content outline, including the intended audience and the time allotted to the project. These and other factors are covered in detail in Chapter 4.

Create Flowcharts (Students)

The flowcharting process illustrates a program's sequence and structure. It is important that students visualize how the various parts of a project fit together. Students should be encouraged to experiment with different ways of presenting content. To help them determine the best options, ask questions such as, "Does one idea logically follow another throughout the program?" "Is there a central point from which all of the other ideas should be linked?" "Can you start with three or four choices and then subdivide the selections?" Be sure to demonstrate different projects with various structures to illustrate the alternatives. Additional information about flowcharts and project structure is provided in Chapter 4.

Specify the Screen Design and Layout (Students)

The storyboards for the project detail all of the text, graphics, and interactions for each screen (page). Before they write the storyboards, work with the students to determine the screen design (the layout or template for each screen). Each screen should contain specific functional areas (such as title, text, graphics, prompts, navigation options, and feedback) to make the program more consistent and easier to follow.

Write Scripts or Storyboards (Students)

After the screen templates and functional areas have been determined, the students can proceed with the scripts or storyboards. Storyboards should contain all the information that will be placed on the screens, as well as information that will help the programmer and production specialists develop the media components. At this point, the students (instructional designers) determine the best way to present the information, how much information goes on each screen, and the like. Sample storyboard templates are provided in Chapter 4.

DEVELOP

After the storyboards are complete, the development process can begin. Depending on the complexity specified in the storyboards, the DEVELOP phase may involve producing audio elements, video segments, graphics, or text. Different members of the project team can develop these components simultaneously, or they can be developed in sequence by all of the members working together. The DEVELOP phase also includes the programming (often referred to as *authoring*) of the program.

As the class approaches the DEVELOP phase, teachers should ensure that they have the knowledge and skills necessary to work with the development tools (such as graphics programs or video editors). They should also emphasize the restrictions or constraints that may apply. For example, if the projects are being created for Web delivery, the file size will be an important factor. Activities in the DEVELOP phase include:

TEACHERS

- Manage media production
- Facilitate multimedia activities
- Conduct formative assessment

STUDENTS

- Create graphics
- Construct animations
- Produce audio
- Produce video
- Author program

Manage Media Production (Teacher)

The configuration and management of a multimedia activity will vary based on the number of available computers (and other hardware), the grouping strategy, and other factors. Chapter 5 addresses various configurations for computer access and outlines the Jigsaw cooperative learning approach, wherein students assume various roles and interact with peer groups.

Facilitate Multimedia Activities (Teacher)

As the students engage in the multimedia activity, the teacher's role becomes that of a facilitator. This includes the following activities:

- Ensuring that all of the necessary equipment, batteries, software, and so on is available
- Reviewing necessary prerequisite skills related to the technology or concepts related to the content
- Circulating the room, assisting students as they need it
- Monitoring the progress of each group or student, ensuring that students stay on task
- Troubleshooting hardware and software issues
- Conducting formative evaluation and providing ongoing feedback to students' progress
- Being aware of the time allotted for the activity in relation to the progress
- Having a backup plan (or two) in case the technology crashes
- Emphasizing the relationship to the lesson's goals

Conduct Formative Assessment (Teacher)

Continuous feedback for students is important throughout the Develop phase. As students create their media elements, teachers should ensure that the elements are appropriate for the content, follow design guidelines, and are stored in the correct file formats. Chapter 7 focuses on assessment techniques.

Create Graphics (Students)

Graphics—pictures, charts, diagrams, and drawings—can play a major role in conveying the content of a multimedia program. After the requirements are specified in the storyboards, students work to create the appropriate graphics. The procedures for creating graphics with software programs, scanners, and digital cameras are outlined in Chapter 5.

Construct Animations (Students)

In some cases, the project may also include animations—graphics that move in rapid sequence to create the illusion of motion. Animations can convey many complex abstractions, such as water moving in a pipe, or they can be used to attract attention to a particular screen or project. Details on animation techniques are provided in Chapter 5.

Produce Audio (Students)

All the sound elements of a program (narration, music, and sound effects) are referred to as *audio*. Students can record the audio elements of a project themselves, or they can incorporate sounds from the Internet or other sources. The procedures and alternatives for audio production are outlined in Chapter 5.

Produce Video (Students)

Students are accustomed to viewing video (television, DVD, etc.). It is now more feasible than ever for students to use camcorders and desktop computers to record and edit video segments. The video clips can then be integrated into a hypermedia or presentation program or used to create a stand-alone video. Many factors must be considered when producing, editing, and implementing video segments; these factors are discussed in Chapter 5.

Author Program (Students)

One of the last steps in the DEVELOP phase is to incorporate all the text, graphics, and other media components into a finished program. Many tools can be used to author a multimedia project, including application software (such as word processors or image programs) hypermedia programs (such as HyperStudio and Ezedia), presentation programs (such as PowerPoint), Web-based editors (such as Netscape Composer), and video editors (such as iMovie and MovieMaker). All of these options are inexpensive; relatively easy to use; and can include text, graphics, audio, and video. Chapter 6 outlines popular programming options for school-based projects. Chapters 8 through 11 focus on sample presentation, hypermedia, Web-based projects, and video projects.

EVALUATE

The evaluation of multimedia projects is both formative and summative. Both the teacher and students conduct formative assessment throughout project development. For example, the teacher should assess the research and brainstorming during the DECIDE phase. She or he should also provide feedback for the students on their flowcharts and storyboards before they begin the development process. Summative evaluation takes place at the end of the project. The steps in the EVALUATE phase include the following:

TEACHERS

- Provide student assessment
- Reflect on activity and revise for future

STUDENTS

- Debug program
- Evaluate peers
- Conduct self-evaluations

Provide Student Assessment (Teacher)

Multimedia projects are a great way to provide alternate assessments for students. Rather than judging their knowledge based on a multiple-choice, A–F grading system, teachers can assess their abilities to construct knowledge and communicate it through a variety of media. The exact method for determining a multimedia project's overall grade will vary. Most important is to provide a meaningful way to communicate the progress to students and their parents. See Chapter 7 for more information on student assessment and assessment techniques.

Reflect on Activity and Revise for Future (Teacher)

Reflection is an important aspect of all multimedia activities—for both students and teachers. Teachers who systematically reflect and modify their lessons will be better prepared to offer a similar, perhaps even more effective, lesson in the future.

Debug Program (Students)

Throughout the project development, students should test and debug the program. This process includes testing the media elements on various computers, locating grammar and punctuation errors, and testing the program for inoperative links. When students complete their projects, student groups should review each others' programs for possible bugs before the projects are submitted for final evaluation.

Evaluate Peers (Students)

Group dynamics are an important part of most multimedia projects. Besides the teacher's assessment, students should be encouraged (or required) to evaluate their peers' projects. Instruments for peer evaluation are included in Chapter 7.

Conduct Self-Evaluations (Students)

It is also important for students to conduct self-evaluations and to report on their progress through journal entries or other assessment tools. For more information on self-evaluations, see Chapter 7.

DDD-E BENEFITS

There are many learning benefits for students who use technology as tools, information vehicles, and context to support knowledge construction, communication, and representation of ideas. Studies have also found that "producing multimedia is a more powerful way of learning than studying already produced materials" (Jonassen, Peck, and Wilson 1999, 102). Participating in the design and development of multimedia programs can improve students' creativity and attitudes and promote a deeper and more sophisticated understanding of the content. Table 2.3 outlines student activities and correlates them to some of the cognitive skills and activities that are involved in each phase of the DDD-E process.

Table 2.3.

Cognitive Skills for Students

Phase	Student Activities	Cognitive Skills
DECIDE	• Brainstorm content • Conduct research	• Formulate questions • Design search strategies • Select and interpret information • Analyze and synthesize information
DESIGN	• Outline content • Create flowcharts • Specify screen design and layout • Write scripts or storyboards	• Organize and structure content • Allocate information to nodes/chunks • Chunk information into logical patterns • Sequence tasks into a timeline • Write meaningful scripts • Convey information through appropriate media • Demonstrate creativity

DEVELOP	• Create graphics • Construct animations • Produce audio • Produce video • Author program	• Translate storyboard information into media elements • Select appropriate media formats • Construct media elements
EVALUATE	• Debug program • Evaluate peers • Conduct self-evaluations	• Produce and verify program • Analyze program effectiveness • Engage in self-reflection

SUMMARY

Careful planning is critical when developing multimedia projects. Models such as DDD-E can help teachers and students structure the development of multimedia projects while encouraging student creativity. The DDD-E model provides a framework for students to work collaboratively in designing and developing their projects and allows opportunities for ongoing evaluation throughout each phase of the DDD-E process. Chapters 3 through 7 focus on each phase of the DDD-E model; Chapters 8 through 11 provide multimedia project ideas based on the DDD-E model.

REFERENCES

Jonassen, D. H., K. L. Peck, and B. G. Wilson. 1999. *Learning with technology: A constructivist perspective.* Upper Saddle River, NJ: Merrill.

Decide

A SCENARIO

Mr. Sandaval had been teaching fifth grade for 12 years and felt unsure about using technology in his classroom. Even though his school had recently purchased mobile computer carts with laptops for every two classrooms, he dismissed the idea of using these new tools because it would take away the time needed to address state content standards. It seemed as though students were being tested every two weeks. Who had time to teach, let alone use technology? Ms. Van Pelt empathized with Mr. Sandaval about his perception of more time spent on testing than teaching but shared with him how her fourth graders were able to use a presentation program to address various fourth-grade content standards. Students were able to finish and present their presentations within two weeks, the typical time they would have spent working on their reports via paper and pencil. "The difference," she noted, "is that technology opens doors to resources and skills my students would not otherwise have. In addition, students are excited about bringing in digital photos, audio, and video to support what they are reporting. Multimedia provides them with a variety of ways to express what they know. My kids are excited about learning and sharing what they know!"

Mr. Sandaval asked Ms. Van Pelt to help him plan a similar project with his students. They looked at Mr. Sandaval's current course of study and decided to focus on standard 5.3 (Students describe the cooperation and conflict that existed among the American Indians and between the Indian nations and the new settlers), number 6: Explain the influence and achievements of significant leaders of the time (e.g., John Marshall, Andrew Jackson, Chief Tecumseh, Chief Logan, Chief John Ross, Sequoyah). Ms. Van Pelt helped Mr. Sandaval determine how to use the available technology resources, ensure that he and his students had the necessary prerequisite skills, decide on methods of assessment, determine how to group his students, and so on.

"Phew!" sighed Mr. Sandaval. "There's a lot more to this than telling the kids to read their textbook and answer a few questions!"

"They'll get a lot more out of it, too, Mr. Sandaval—keep an eye on your test scores! Also, once you've done this a couple of times, assigning multimedia projects will become easy, too!"

Within the next couple of weeks, Ms. Van Pelt asked Mr. Sandaval how things were going. "Great!" he exclaimed. "The kids know more than I do about the program, and they have found some incredible resources to support their learning. Thanks for helping me plan this activity. You helped me make some great decisions! Thanks, too, for helping me teach the students how to evaluate and appropriately use Internet resources. Come back next week to see their presentations. Bring your class!" Ms. Van Pelt accepted the invitation and smiled, knowing both Mr. Sandaval and his students were engaged in a positive learning experience.

OVERVIEW

There are many things to consider before starting a multimedia project. For example, what content standard(s) will be addressed? Is a multimedia project appropriate? Are there the necessary resources to support multimedia projects? These questions and others are addressed in the first stage of the DDD-E process—the DECIDE stage. The DECIDE stage sets the foundation for the remaining stages of the DDD-E process; hence, the planning and organization of the DECIDE phase contribute to the overall success of the students' multimedia projects. The DECIDE stage includes determining the project's goals (deciding on relevant standards and benchmarks), establishing whether multimedia is appropriate, assessing students' prerequisite skills and background knowledge, deciding on assessment techniques, and planning grouping strategies and roles. Much of the teacher's time will be spent on planning and organizing the projects. Students' time will be spent on brainstorming and conducting research. Topics in this chapter include the following:

- Planning multimedia projects

    Identifying standards and setting instructional goals

    Deciding on a project

    Assessing prerequisite skills

    Determining assessment techniques

- Organizing multimedia projects

    Examining grouping alternatives

    Creating cooperative groups

    Scheduling computer time

- Managing brainstorming and research activities

PLANNING MULTIMEDIA PROJECTS

DECIDE is the first phase of the DDD-E process, and it involves a significant amount of planning and organization. Planning includes setting instructional goals, deciding on a project, assessing and developing prerequisite skills, and deciding how the projects will be assessed.

Identifying Standards and Setting Instructional Goals

Educators are responsible for ensuring that students meet specific content standards across a variety of subject areas. District, state, and other tests are used to measure students' progress. Teachers are held accountable for their students' success and are expected to identify state or other standards that their lessons address, as well as to identify learning objectives and outcomes. For many educators, this means strict adherence to textbooks and drill sheets for fear of not addressing a standard. Standards can be met a variety of ways through a multitude of instructional strategies, however, including the use of multimedia projects. In fact, as discussed in Chapter 1, students are more likely to retain what they have learned when constructing knowledge.

Multimedia projects can be used across all subject areas. When deciding to use a multimedia project to address a specific content standard or set of standards, consider the time needed to complete the project, how the standard(s) will be addressed through the project, and the students' ability levels. Consider whether such a project is the most effective way to achieve the desired learning outcomes. Textbooks, worksheets, independent research, field trips, or other hands-on activities may address an instructional goal more effectively. For example, students may more effectively classify objects (e.g., rocks, plants, leaves) in accordance with appropriate criteria by actually touching, handling, examining, testing, and manipulating the objects rather than researching and presenting a multimedia project about them. This is not to say that a multimedia presentation could not assist with students' learning, but the students' time may be better spent with a hands-on science lesson than in the creation of a multimedia project.

When setting instructional goals for multimedia projects, it is critical that the goals reflect the identified content standard(s) and that there is a clear way to assess the students' learning. It is important that students learn something beyond computer skills and that the appearance of the final presentation does not overshadow the project's content. It is easy to become overly involved and influenced by multimedia special effects (such as sound, animation, video, transitions, and so on) and to forget about the purpose of the project. Assessing a multimedia project solely on its looks is comparable to rating a car based on its exterior instead of its engine or judging a cake's taste by its looks. Instructional goals and assessment criteria need to be introduced at the beginning of multimedia projects to ensure that learning outcomes are addressed.

In addition to addressing specific content standards, instructional goals may be designed to:

- Accommodate multiple learning styles and interests

- Encourage cooperative learning and social skills

- Foster active learning by promoting interdisciplinary investigations

- Develop critical thinking, reasoning, problem solving, and metacognitive processes

- Enhance presentation and speaking skills

Instructional goals will vary depending on the ability level of the learner, available resources, and the learner's experience.

Deciding on a Project

After identifying the appropriate content standards and defining the instructional goals, the teacher can select and design a project to meet the desired goals. Assuming it is a multimedia project, the teacher will need to decide whether the instructional goals can best be achieved through a program such as HyperStudio, EzediaMX, the World Wide Web, a desktop video program (e.g., Apple's iMovie or Microsoft's MovieMaker), or a presentation program (e.g., PowerPoint by Microsoft).

Teachers will want to choose multimedia production programs based on the ability level of their students. For example, younger or lower-ability students may benefit from Scholastic Keys, a program that provides a kid-friendly interface for Microsoft Word, Excel, and PowerPoint. Ideas for projects are endless. Table 3.1 presents a variety of projects by subject area.

Table 3.1.

Sample Project Ideas

Subject	Project Ideas
Language arts	Book reports; interactive and multiple-ending stories; poetry collections; news reports; phonemic awareness activities for younger students; famous authors; parodies; mythology; reports on stories from multiple cultures or time periods; word origins; grammar, spelling, or vocabulary activities; rhyming games; story starters; prompted writing; creative writing
Mathematics	Problem-solving adventures; famous mathematicians; number recognition activities for younger students; number systems; geometry concepts; math puzzles and solutions; addition, subtraction, multiplication, or division concepts; history of mathematics; units of measure; currency exchange; stock market; inflation; finance; retailing; advertising; proofs
Science and health	Space exploration; pollution; animals; plant growth; weather; insects; nutrition; inventions and inventors; body systems; dissection; simple machines; chemical properties; ocean life; diseases; light and colors; science magic tricks; drugs, alcohol, or smoking; home remedies; exercise; senses; technology; volcanoes; plate tectonics; natural disasters; diet
Social studies	State or country reports; famous people in history; world wars; Industrial Revolution; Civil War; Holocaust; Gold Rush; geography; Westward Movement; community events and history; family tree; explorers; hobbies and interests; government; careers; cultural holidays, foods, or celebrations; ancient civilizations; American Revolution; national symbols
Fine arts	Famous artists or musicians; film history; cinematography; music history; musical instruments; film or music genre; history of dance; music, movie, or play reviews; opera; music notation; song writing; animation; special effects; music and culture; famous paintings; art styles; famous entertainers

In addition to instructional goals, time is another consideration when deciding on a multimedia project. Students need to be given projects that can be completed within a prescribed time period. For example, if the multimedia project is part of a three-week unit on the California Gold Rush, teachers should limit the size and complexity of the project to what their students are capable of completing in a two- to three-week period.

Available resources affect the amount of time that may be needed to complete a multimedia project. Educators need to assess the number of computers and other resources (such as software, scanners, digital cameras, and so on) available for the project and what additional resources may be needed. This will help teachers schedule computer time, arrange groups, and ensure that the necessary resources are available. For example, teachers may need to plan additional time in the computer lab, borrow computers from other classrooms, have students bring in their own laptops, request Compact Disc Rewritables (CD-RWs) media or Flash (or keychain) drives for their students, or ensure that the necessary software is installed on all of the computers. Once a teacher has gathered all the necessary components, she or he is ready to introduce the project to the class.

Assessing Prerequisite Skills

Once the instructional goals and project have been defined, teachers must ensure that their students have the skills needed to complete the project successfully. These include basic computer operations (e.g., properly turning on and off the computer, saving and printing files, opening and closing programs); the use of the assigned multimedia tools and peripherals; searching, evaluating, and citing Internet (and other) resources; understanding and following fair use and copyright laws; or other background knowledge teachers deem necessary for a particular project. Teachers can assess students' skills and background knowledge from past projects (if available), observations, skills tests and activities, and so on. Necessary skills may be taught as a whole class, in small groups, or by student experts (e.g., peer teaching). Review guides or index cards may be used to help students remember certain aspects of a program or device. It is important that the use of technology does not obstruct the students' learning. Students should be made to feel comfortable with the technology prior to their use of the tool for content learning. Educators may use a jigsaw approach to teach certain elements of a complex program, ensuring that each group has a member who is an "expert" in a particular part of the program. Additional or more advanced skills can be taught as the students design and prepare their projects.

Determining Assessment Techniques

In addition to identifying standards and setting instructional goals, deciding on a project, and assessing students' prerequisite skills, educators need to consider how they will monitor and assess students' work. This is actually a part of identifying standards and setting instructional goals, but its final form cannot be determined until the project has been decided and students have the necessary background knowledge and skills to proceed. The method of assessment will vary according to the type of the project, although a daily log or journal of the students' progress is something that may be applied across all projects. Chapter 7 discusses multiple strategies for assessing multimedia projects throughout each stage (DECIDE, DESIGN, DEVELOP, and EVALUATE) to ensure that instructional goals and standards are being met. Rubrics for formative and summative assessments are included, as are strategies for evaluating individual and group work. Educators may design their own assessment activities, borrow from others, use the examples in this book, or access Web sites such as RubiStar (http://rubistar.4teachers.org) for more ideas and resources for creating rubrics. Deciding on methods of assessment before students start their multimedia projects helps to ensure that students know what is expected of them, that they are on the right track, and that objectives are being met.

ORGANIZING MULTIMEDIA PROJECTS

In addition to planning, the DECIDE phase of the DDD-E process involves organizing the students' learning environment. This includes examining grouping alternatives, creating cooperative groups, and designing computer schedules.

Examining Grouping Alternatives

Depending on the project, students may work collaboratively or cooperatively. Students in collaborative groups work toward the same goal, but they are not necessarily accountable for each other's learning. Success may not depend on the efforts of all group members, allowing some students to loaf while others do all the work. Students in cooperative groups work toward a common goal and are accountable for each other's learning, providing both academic and personal support. Cooperative group members are taught social skills to help them coordinate their efforts, and teamwork is emphasized.

As mentioned in Chapter 1, there are many types of cooperative group methods. These include Student Teams Achievement Divisions (STAD), Teams Games Tournament (TGT), Team Assisted Individualization (TAI), Jigsaw, Group Investigation, and Learning Together. Groups may be heterogeneous or homogeneous. Most research supports heterogeneous groups (Johnson and Johnson 1999a). Heterogeneous groups are usually formed with a mixture of ability, gender, or ethnicity; homogeneous groups consist of students with similar abilities or interests. Johnson, Johnson, and Holubec (1994, 26) state that "[h]eterogeneous groups tend to promote more elaborate thinking, more frequent giving and receiving of explanations, and greater perspective-taking during discussions about material, all of which increase students' understanding, reasoning, and long-term retention." Although heterogeneous groups are recommended, there are some instances when homogeneous groups are advantageous. For example, educators may find homogeneous groups best for specific class topics, the creation of interest groups, or competition within groups (Fuchs, Fuchs, Hamlett, and Karns 1998; Johnson and Johnson 1999a).

Grouping Variables

Both grouping styles (heterogeneous and homogeneous) have advantages and disadvantages, depending on the grouping variable. Grouping variables include (but are not limited to) ability, learning style, intelligence, cognitive preference, gender, and background. Ability grouping is based on high, middle, and low achievement. Learning styles may include textual, visual, tactile, and auditory. Intelligences include linguistic, logical-mathematical, spatial, bodily-kinesthetic, musical, interpersonal, intrapersonal, and naturalist. Cognitive preference defines learners according to how they place themselves on a continuum between "global processing" and "analytical processing." Global individuals tend to be more sensitive to others, better communicators, and more socially oriented. Analytical individuals tend to be more introverted but are better at organizing and analyzing content. The next variable, gender, is self-explanatory. Background may include ethnicity, experiences, age, and likes and dislikes. Table 3.2 presents the advantages and disadvantages of these grouping variables.

In addition to heterogeneous and homogeneous grouping, groups may be established by interest or random assignment. For example, students whose favorite pet is a cat may work together to produce a multimedia project about cats, or students may be randomly assigned to groups by picking topics out of a hat. These grouping methods also have advantages and disadvantages. Interest groups may enhance communication among members and identify common interests and similarities among students. The disadvantage of interest groups is that they are self-selected, which may generate more off-task behavior, result in undesired homogeneous grouping (ability, ethnicity, or gender), and eliminate possibilities for students to expand their circles (Johnson, Johnson, and Holubec 1994).

Random assignment can provide variety in the groups and is perceived as one of the best ways to assign students to groups (Johnson and Johnson 1999a). However, general random assignment may pair incompatible students. As an alternative, teachers may want to use stratified random assignment. This is the process of categorizing select groups (e.g., low-, average-, and high-ability students) and randomly selecting a member from each group to form a mixed team. For example, a teacher may randomly select a low-ability student, an average-ability student, and a high-ability student from predefined groups to serve as a three-member team rather than randomly select three students from one large group. Stratified random assignment may be used to ensure that certain students do not get placed together or that each group has students with one or two characteristics (e.g., reading level, math ability, or computer skills).

Stratified random assignment can be used to create groups of students with preferred intelligence. For example, by using stratified random assignment, the teacher can ensure that each group has one member with high linguistic intelligence, another member with high logical-mathematical intelligence, another member with high spatial intelligence, and another member with high interpersonal intelligence.

Table 3.2.

Advantages and Disadvantages of Various Grouping Variables

Grouping Variable	Type	Advantages	Disadvantages
Ability	Heterogeneous	Best opportunity for peer support and tutoring	Free-rider effect
Ability	Homogeneous	Students tend to bond and communicate more effectively	Low-ability students are often left at a significant learning disadvantage
Learning style, intelligence, or cognitive preference	Heterogeneous	Students are exposed to multiple perspectives and problem-solving methods, stimulating students' learning and cognitive development	May be hard to group if students display a preference for one dominant learning style, intelligence, or cognitive preference; communication skills may be more difficult to develop because of different interests
Learning style, intelligence, or cognitive preference	Homogeneous	Students tend to bond and communicate more effectively	Students' focus and exposure to different perspectives are limited

Gender or background	Heterogeneous	Reduces stereotypes, promotes equality among perceived ability and leadership roles	Teachers may need to ensure that social skills are in place to eliminate preconceived biases
Gender or background	Homogeneous	May benefit specific special interest groups or class topics	May cause unnecessary tension between groups; not representative of the real world

Groups can be teacher-selected or self-selected. Teacher-selected groups allow teachers to decide which students will work together, ensuring balance and the potential for positive relationships. At-risk students can be assigned to a group with supportive students in the class. Teachers can also ensure that students with non-achievement-oriented and disruptive behavior are not grouped together. Self-selected groups are the least recommended (Johnson and Johnson 1999a). Typically, self-selected groups are homogeneous, spawning isolated groups of high achievers, males, minorities, socialites, females, and nonachievers. This leads to more off-task behavior and limited social experiences.

Group Numbers

In addition to grouping variables, the number of students placed in each group can make a difference in the group's success. Group numbers may depend on the students' abilities, number of computers in the classroom, time constraints, project requirements, cooperative group method, and other variables. Most studies on cooperative learning report group sizes ranging from two to six students. Johnson, Johnson, and Holubec (1994) provide the following points about group size:

1. As the size of the group increases, the range of abilities and viewpoints increases. Additional resources (members) may help the group succeed, and varying viewpoints will challenge the students to evaluate more critically their own viewpoints and opinions.

2. The larger the group, the more skillful the members must be at ensuring that everyone remains on task, has a chance to speak, reaches a consensus, understands the material being learned, and maintains good working relationships. Interactions increase as the group size increases, requiring additional interpersonal skills.

3. As group size increases, there is less face-to-face interaction among members and a reduced sense of intimacy. Lower individual responsibility may result, as well as a less cohesive group.

4. If a short period of time is available, smaller groups should be used. Smaller groups can take less time to get organized, and they may operate more quickly.

5. The smaller the group, the more difficult it is for students to avoid their share of the work. Small groups make students more accountable by increasing the visibility of their work.

6. The smaller the group, the easier it is to identify group difficulties, including leadership struggles, unresolved conflicts, and learning difficulties. Problems are more visible and more easily addressed in small groups.

Advantages and disadvantages of various group sizes for multimedia design teams are listed in Table 3.3.

Design teams generally consist of several people, depending on the size of the project and the number of available computers. With large groups, individuals or pairs of students can be assigned specific tasks. For example, following the group's research efforts, one person may be responsible for the graphics, one person may be responsible for the music and narration in the project, two more people may be responsible for completing the storyboards (based on a group-approved template), and two students may be responsible for entering information into the computer. Group members will have additional responsibilities as well; hence, it may not be possible for one member to complete his or her main responsibility until other members of the group complete their parts of the project. Students will need to ensure that everyone stays on task and assists other members.

Table 3.3.

Advantages and Disadvantages of Various Group Sizes in Multimedia Design Teams

Group Size	Advantages	Disadvantages
One	Work at own pace Not dependent on others	Requires more classroom computer access time (every individual will need time on the computer) Does not reflect real-world learning Does not promote learning from different perspectives Does not encourage cooperative problem solving Takes long to complete a project Individual may not be capable of handling all of the project's requirements
Two or three	Learn from each other Share project responsibilities Supports real-world learning, learning from different perspectives, and cooperative problem solving Classroom computer access time is cut in half, as students can work together at the computer	Need to ensure that everyone contributes and has a chance to speak

Four	Learn from each other	Need to ensure that everyone contributes and has a chance to speak
	Share project responsibilities	May be difficult to share computer
	Supports real-world learning, learning from different perspectives, and co-operative problem solving	Requires greater interpersonal skills
	Increases classroom computer access time	
	More talent and resources are available to create the project	
	Projects can be completed in less time	
Five or six	Same as four	Same as four
		Easier for a member not to contribute
		More chance of group disputes, leadership difficulties, and off-task behavior, which may delay project
		Group dynamics may be more appropriate for older, more mature students

Creating Cooperative Groups

The success of cooperative groups depends on positive interdependence, a group goal, and individual and group accountability. Teamwork skills must be taught just as purposefully and precisely as academic skills. For most classroom multimedia projects, teamwork is essential.

Introducing Social Skills

Before placing students into cooperative groups, it is important to determine the goal of the multimedia project and what types of student interactions are desired. In most cases, students will need to be taught or reminded how to work cooperatively. Vermette (1998, 158) suggests the following working relationship skills:

- Acknowledging contributions
- Checking for agreement
- Disagreeing in an agreeable way
- Encouraging others
- Expressing support
- Inviting others to talk
- Keeping things calm and reducing tension

- Mediating

- Responding to ideas

- Sharing feelings

- Showing appreciation

The teacher may want to have groups model or practice these skills, as well as discuss the importance of listening, politeness, and other appropriate communication habits.

Teachers may want to create social skill objectives. These may be defined by monitoring student groups and diagnosing the specific problems students are having working together, or by asking students which social skill would improve their teamwork. Based on the teacher's observation and students' input, a social skill can be taught to help solve the problem.

Placing Students into Cooperative Groups

After social skills have been introduced, decide on the cooperative group method (e.g., STAD, TGT, TAI, Jigsaw, Group Investigation, or Learning Together) that will most beneficial for the students and their assigned multimedia project (see Chapter 1). Depending on the project, desired interactions, and cooperative group method, assess students' strengths and weaknesses, their interests, who they like to work with, and so on. Consider group dynamics and create heterogeneous conditions. Along with the survey found at the end of this chapter (see the Self Survey blackline master), a teacher's own observation and background with his or her students can help facilitate student placement.

Students may be placed in design teams before or after introducing a multimedia project. Teachers may poll student interests before introducing the project or may wait to assess student interest until after the project has been introduced. For example, an informal survey might be created to assess students' interest in certain animals. Based on the survey results, the teacher can heterogeneously group students according to their interests before introducing a multimedia project about animals. Alternatively, the teacher could introduce a multimedia project about animals and let students group themselves according to their interests. Precautions must be taken, however, because of the disadvantages associated with self-selected groups. Hence, some students may choose groups based on the animal's popularity (not their true interest) and friends' choices. In addition, some animals may not draw enough students or they may attract too many students, creating bad feelings and a sense of unfairness if students are assigned to a different animal. Polling students' interests and assigning teams before introducing a project is recommended.

Assigning Roles

Another important aspect of cooperative group learning is role assignment. Assigning roles helps to ensure that all students participate and that no one person dominates a group. Roles may be based on group behaviors, computer tasks, or project assignments. For example, in a group of four students, one person may ensure that everyone gets a chance to speak (turn-taking monitor), one person may record the group's activities (record keeper), one person may ensure that the group's noise level is kept to a minimum (noise monitor), and one person may be responsible for keeping the group on task (task master). These group behavior roles may be rotated on a daily basis. Computer tasks may include keyboarder (enters information into the computer), editor (oversees computer input), and record keeper (keeps track of group's progress). Project assignment roles may include a graphic artist, instructional designer, production specialist, and program author.

Assignment roles may also become the basis for forming the groups. For example, a survey can be used to form the groups according to Gardner's Theory of Multiple Intelligences (see the Self Survey blackline master). Students are placed into teams based on their interests and observed strengths. Each design team might contain one student who ranked high in linguistics (I like to read books, write, and tell stories), one student who ranked high in logic-mathematics (I like math, strategy games, and working with puzzles), and two students who ranked high in spatial skills (I like to draw and I understand things better by looking at a picture). Student "linguistic experts" may take on the responsibilities of the subject matter experts, "spatial experts" may be considered the teams' graphic artists and storyboard designers, and "logical-mathematical experts" may be responsible for the project's flowchart and programming needs. Additional project roles may be assigned according to the students' self-rankings in the remaining areas of the survey: bodily-kinesthetic (I have a hard time sitting still), musical (I am a good singer and I know when music is off key), interpersonal (I get along well with others and I am a good listener), intrapersonal (I am dependable and self-confident), and naturalist (I enjoy the outdoors and can easily identify and classify the things around me).

Scheduling Computer Time

Until one-to-one laptop access and other wireless devices are a standard in all schools, the most challenging aspect of designing and developing multimedia projects may be computer access. Various situations are possible. Computer labs are typically available for one 30- or 40-minute time slot a week. A computer assistant may or may not be available, and stations may range from 10 to 30 or more computers. Classrooms may have one or more computers, with or without a projection system. Some schools have mobile computer carts with laptops available for checkout, increasing the number of computers possible in a classroom. Mobile computer carts may not always be available if other teachers request them, however. There are several advantages and disadvantages for each situation when creating multimedia projects (see Table 3.4).

Most researchers agree that a minimum of three computers in the classroom is needed to ensure that every student gets some time at the computer during a single classroom period (Dublin, Pressman, Barnett, Corcoran, and Woldman 1994; Morrison, Lowther, and DeMeulle 1999). This requires that students work in groups of three or four. While students are waiting for their group's turn at the computer, they work on a related, noncomputer task. For example, students may be engaged in a silent reading activity, follow-up materials about the computer lesson, or another related activity. Teachers should resist teaching a directed lesson when students are actively engaged on classroom computers for several reasons:

1. Students on the computers are missing the lesson.

2. Students near the computers are more likely to be watching their computer classmates rather than the teacher.

3. Some computer programs require sound (interrupting the teacher's directed lesson), and headphones are not always available.

4. The teacher cannot immediately assist students on the computers if he or she is involved in a directed lesson.

5. Students not on the computers may be more concerned about the clock and their turn at the computer than what the teacher has to say.

6. Scheduling may require students to take their computer turn during the middle of the directed lesson, as well as returning students to the directed lesson without having participated in the beginning of the lesson.

Table 3.4.

Advantages and Disadvantages of Computer Situations

Computer Setting	Advantages	Disadvantages
Lab (10 to 15 computers)	• Working in groups, all students have access to the computers at the same time; teacher can facilitate whole-class instruction • Computer coordinator may be available to assist students • Students can take turns working individually on computers with computer coordinator while other students work on noncomputer assignments with teacher • Less cost to secure and network computers	• Usually limited to 30 or 40 minutes a week • Fire drills, assemblies, holidays, may cause lab time to be missed • Computer use is more likely to be an isolated activity than an integral part of the curriculum • Whole school uses the same computers and printers, causing more wear and tear on the systems, more variable problems, and additional soft- ware costs to meet everyone's needs • Instructional time is lost going to and from computer lab
Lab (20 or more computers)	• Same as other lab situation • Individual students have access to the computers at the same time; teacher can facilitate whole-class instruction • Additional computers may be available for multimedia purposes (e.g., making desktop videos)	• Same as other lab situation
1 or 2 computers in the classroom	• Computer available every day for "teachable moments" • If a projector device or large monitor is available, can be used to facilitate whole-class/small group instruction • Some software is specifically designed for whole-class/small group instruction (e.g., Tom Snyder Productions, Inc.) • Software funds can be used to purchase a variety of software that meets students' and teachers' individual needs vs. lab sets that may not be used by all teachers or students • Students may take better care of their "own" classroom computers	• Individual computer time is difficult to manage • Some group computer projects may take an undesirable length of time to complete due to limited access • More cost involved with purchasing computers and printers for every classroom, networking, and securing every room (alarm system)

Three or more computers in the classroom	• Same as other classroom situation • Student groups can have daily access • Computers are more likely to be used as an integral part of instruction and tool for learning	• Requires more classroom space than one or two computers • More cost involved with purchasing computers and printers for every classroom, networking, and securing every room (alarm system)
Mobile computer carts	• Can provide additional access for group projects • Can be removed from classroom and stored in secure location • Provides more flexibility (e.g., can be taken outdoors or on field trips)	• May not always be available • Time needed to move computer cart in and out of the classroom • Computers may be damaged in transit • May have batteries that need to be recharged.

For many teachers, the thought of three or more computers in the classroom may seem unrealistic; however, computer access is improving. The National Center for Educational Statistics (2002) reports that about one in every five students has access to an instructional computer connected to the Internet. More and more schools are purchasing laptop computers for students or requiring or recommending that students bring their own (Carter 2001; Vail 2003). Wireless networks and lower costs have helped make one-to-one access a reality in many school districts. The trend is here, but how soon every teacher will have ample and updated technology in their classrooms is questionable. Change occurs slowly. In the meantime, teachers can place more computers in their classroom to facilitate multimedia projects by borrowing other classrooms' computers or arranging to borrow an additional computer from a computer lab. Parents and businesses may also lend support. Teachers may research organizations such as Share the Technology (http://www.sharetechnology.org) to locate equipment for donation or Computers for Learning (http://www.computers.fed.gov/School/user.asp) to learn how to receive excess federal computer equipment.

To help teachers address the various computer situations possible, computer schedules have been developed to assist teachers in managing multimedia projects in their classroom (see Figures 3.1 through 3.5).

Time	Computer Time	Project Assignments	Four-Computer Classroom Daily Computer Use (Version 1)
9:00 a.m. to 9:30 a.m.	A B C D	E F G H	• 24 to 36 students • 2 to 3 students per group • 20-minute rotation schedule • When students are not at computers, they work on related project assignments. For example, Groups A, B, C, and D have computer time between 9:00 a.m. and 9:20 a.m. Groups E, F, G, and H, and groups I, J, K, and L work on related, noncomputer assignments.
9:30 a.m. to 10:00 a.m.	E F G H	A B C D	

Figure 3.1. Computer schedule for a four-computer classroom (version 1).

Time	Computer Time	Project Assignments		Four-Computer Classroom Daily Computer Use (Version 2)
		1	2	• 24 to 32 students
9:00 a.m. to 9:20 a.m.	A B C D	I J K L	E F G H	• 3 or 4 students per group • 30-minute rotation schedule • When students are not at computers, they work on related, noncomputer project assignments. For example, Groups A, B, C, and D have computer time between 9:00 a.m. and 9:30 a.m. Groups E, F, G, and H work on related assignments.
9:20 a.m. to 9:40 a.m.	E F G H	A B C D	I J K L	
9:40 a.m. to 10:00 a.m.	I J K L	E F G H	A B C D	

Figure 3.2. Computer schedule for a four-computer classroom (version 2).

Time	Computer Time	Project Assignments		Three-Computer Classroom Daily Computer Use
		1	2	• 27 to 36 students
9:00 a.m. to 9:20 a.m.	A B C	G H I	D E F	• 3 or 4 students per group • 20-minute rotation schedule • When students are not at computers, they work on related project assignments. For example, Groups A, B, and C have computer time between 9:00 a.m. and 9:20 a.m. Groups D, E, F, G, H, and I work on related, noncomputer assignments (projects 1 and 2).
9:20 a.m. to 9:40 a.m.	D E F	A B C	G H I	
9:40 a.m. to 10:00 a.m.	G H I	D E F	A B C	

Figure 3.3. Computer schedule for a three-computer classroom.

Time	Computer Time	Project Assignments			Two-Computer Classroom Daily Computer Use
		1	2	3	• 24 to 32 students
9:00 A.M. to 9:15 A.M.	A B	C D	E F	G H	• 3 or 4 students per group • 15-minute rotation schedule • When students are not at computers, they work on related project assignments. For example, Groups A and B have computer time between 9:00 a.m. and 9:15 a.m. Groups C, D, E, F, G, and H work on related, noncomputer assignments (projects 1, 2, and 3).
9:15 A.M. to 9:30 A.M.	C D	E F	G H	A B	
9:30 A.M. to 9:45 A.M.	E F	G H	A B	C D	
9:45 A.M. to 10:00 A.M.	G H	A B	C D	E F	

Figure 3.4. Computer schedule for a two-computer classroom.

Time	Computer Time		Project Assignments				One-Computer Classroom MW/TTH Computer Use
	MW	TTH	MW	TTH	MW	TTH	
9:00 A.M. to 9:15 A.M.	A	E	B F G H	B F G H	C D E	A C D	• 3 or 4 students per group • 24 to 32 students • 15-minute rotation schedule • Groups have computer time twice a week
9:15 A.M. to 9:30 A.M.	B	F	F G H	B G H	A C D E	A C D E	• When students are not at computers, they work on related project assignments. For example, Group A has computer time from 9:00 a.m. to 9:15 a.m. on Mondays and Wednesdays. Groups B, F, G, and H and groups C, D, and E work on related, noncomputer assignments (projects 1 and 3).
9:30 A.M. to 9:45 A.M.	C	G	A D E E	A C D E	B F G H	B F H	• On Friday, students are provided with additional time to complete their related, noncomputer assignments. Groups may send one person to work with other groups to find clip art or research via the computer. For example, one person from each of groups A, B, C, and D may work together on the computer from 9:00 a.m. to 9:30 a.m., and one person from each of groups E, F, G, and H may work together on the computer from 9:30 a.m. to 10:00 a.m.
9:45 A.M. to 10:00 A.M.	D	H	A C E	A C D E	B F G H	B F G	

Figure 3.5. Computer schedule for a one-computer classroom.

Note that four computers in the classroom can provide students with 30 minutes of daily access to computers versus the 30 minutes of weekly access provided by computer labs. Two or three computers in the classroom can provide student groups with 75 to 110 minutes of computer time a week, respectively. One-computer classrooms provide limited group access, but they can be used to facilitate whole-class projects. For example, the class may decide to create a project about African American inventors to present to the community during Black History Month. Students may be placed in groups of three to research a specific inventor and to design a one-card or one-page presentation about their inventor. A template can be designed to assist students with their presentation. Student groups can take turns at the classroom computer (see Figure 3.5) inputting their data while others are finishing their research or working on a related small-group activity. A blackline master for scheduling computer time can be found at the end of this chapter. Teachers who are lucky enough to have one-to-one access in their classroom should not encounter problems scheduling computer time. Schedules may still be needed to share specific peripherals (still and video cameras, scanners, etc.) if these resources are limited or printers and Internet connections if the classroom is not wireless.

MANAGING BRAINSTORMING AND RESEARCH ACTIVITIES

After the preliminary management issues of the DECIDE phase have been addressed, the teacher can provide the students with time to brainstorm and research the topic of their project. This step should be prefaced with the purpose of the students' multimedia projects, and each group should be provided with guidelines and rubrics for their project (see Chapter 7). To solidify the groups, let teams develop their own name or "company" logo.

Brainstorming Activities

After student groups have established their project roles (e.g., graphic artist, instructional designer, production specialist, and program author), behavior roles (e.g., turn-taking monitor, noise monitor, record keeper, task master), and team name, provide students with time to brainstorm. Depending on the ability level and experience of the students, brainstorming may be conducted as a whole class or by individual groups. Teachers may wish to provide students with the BrainStorm or KWL Knowledge Chart blackline masters at the end of this chapter, or rely on brainstorming software such as Inspiration or Kidspiration (see http://www.inspiration.com/index.cfm). For high-ability and experienced groups, provide a rubric of questions or guidelines that covers the assigned instructional content. For example, if students are creating multimedia projects on Egypt, provide them with specific content questions and related pictures to research and include in their presentations. If students are creating a multimedia project about family history, provide them with guidelines as to the type of information that should be included. These guidelines can help focus the students' thoughts as they brainstorm ideas.

For younger and lower-ability students, make sure they have previous background knowledge in the assigned topics. Guide them through a KWL Knowledge Chart—what we know, what we want to find out, and what we learned (see the KWL Knowledge Chart blackline master at the end of this chapter). Each student can participate in the chart activity at his or her desk as the teacher directs the whole class using a transparency of the chart on an overhead projector. Student groups can exchange their thoughts and share their ideas with the class. Following the introduction of the KWL Knowledge Chart, student groups can be assigned a particular outcome on the chart. For example, if the chart is about the solar system, student groups might be assigned to find out what the class wants to know about a particular planet. Group One might answer class questions about Pluto, Group Two might answer class questions about Mercury, and so on. The chart would be completed after the students present their final multimedia projects.

Additional brainstorming techniques include recording students' sensory experiences. For example, many teachers pop popcorn in class to facilitate the student's creative writing skills. Students experience and discuss the sound, smell, taste, texture, and sight of popcorn before they write about it. A similar approach may be taken toward a particular multimedia project. For example, if the goal of the project is to develop and present a persuasive advertisement, such as why a group's hamburger is the best, educators may bring in different hamburgers for the students to sample, as well as let the students view videos of hamburger commercials, examine newspaper and magazine advertisements for hamburgers, inspect the packaging, and so on. As a class, the students can brainstorm and discuss how the hamburgers and their advertisements are the same or different, and what issues (price, taste, nutrition, popularity, or convenience) may affect consumer choice. Following this whole-class experience, students can return to their groups and brainstorm strategies for their projects based on their new background knowledge. Final projects might include a persuasive presentation and samples of the group's hamburger creations.

Research Activities

After students have brainstormed about their topic, the teacher reviews the group's brainstorming chart and asks clarifying questions to ensure that the group is on track. After the group's work is approved, the students can begin researching the different areas of their topic. Students may want to assign each group member a specific task.

Research activities may take place on or off the computer. Computer schedules can be designed that allow student access to CD-ROMs and the Internet to further their research (see Figures 3.1 through 3.5). Students not assigned to computers can conduct research at the school library or in the classroom, using newspapers, textbooks, literature books, magazines, and other resources. High-ability students will need time to organize and synthesize gathered information and assign further research responsibilities. Younger and lower-ability students will need to work together to find the answers to their assigned questions from the KWL Knowledge Chart. Field trips, guest speakers, experiments, and other opportunities may be arranged to assist students with their research. Students can use a bibliography information sheet (see the Bibliography Information blackline master at the end of this chapter) to record and track their sources throughout the DDD-E process.

Students may also have the opportunity to conduct research outside the classroom. Groups may assign members to conduct research via the Internet, locate or create graphics, or develop narration or audio clips on their home computers or in the media center. Students can also create portions of their group's multimedia project at home, provided they have the appropriate software. Many Web tools are free, and HyperStudio has a "Home Use Policy" that permits students to work on their projects at home. Never assume, though, that students have access to home computers or other research materials. It is inappropriate to assign homework if all of the students do not have the skills or resources to complete it.

Each group's record keeper should keep a journal (see the Journal Entry # blackline master at the end of this chapter) of his or her group's progress, including the time spent brainstorming. Journal entries can help students reflect on their work, social experiences, and how they are achieving their goals. Teachers should review journal entries on a daily basis to help students keep focused and to address problems before they get out of hand. Groups can keep their journal entries in a binder and submit the binder with their final project. Groups may spend two to five class periods conducting the initial research for their projects.

SUMMARY

There are many variables to consider when assigning multimedia projects: standards and benchmarks, computer access, student experience, grouping variables, group size, student roles, time needed to complete the project, and so on. The DECIDE phase of the DDD-E process encourages teachers to address these variables before assigning multimedia projects.

After determining the project goals, appropriate background knowledge, guidelines, and rubrics are provided to assist student groups with the brainstorming and research activities. These activities provide the foundation for the next step of the DDD-E process: DESIGN. Journal entries continue throughout the DDD-E process, helping students to reflect on their progress and project goals.

There are multiple stages to creating multimedia projects, but the DECIDE phase is the most critical to their success. The stages that follow (discussed in Chapters 4 through 7) depend on the planning, organization, and research activities conducted in the DECIDE phase; each stage depends on its predecessor. The time needed to complete each stage will depend on the size and complexity of the project, as well as the level and number of students in each group. Well-managed classrooms and organized projects will add to the success of students' multimedia endeavors and learning.

BLACKLINE MASTERS

Several blackline masters are presented in this chapter to assist teachers with the DECIDE phase. These include the following:

- Self Survey: one method of organizing students into groups based on Howard Gardner's Theory of Multiple Intelligences
- Computer Schedule: a template for organizing classroom computer time
- BrainStorm: a webbing activity designed to help students link their ideas
- KWL Knowledge Chart: a chart to help students organize what they know and what they want to find out about a topic
- Bibliography Information: one way to record and identify sources used throughout the DDD-E process
- Journal Entry #: a method of recording and tracking a group's progress.

Blackline masters may be copied for educational purposes. They may also be used to help educators create their own DECIDE activity and organization sheets, such as a modified survey, computer schedule, or bibliography information sheet.

REFERENCES

Carter, K. 2001. Laptop lessons: Exploring the promise of one-to-one computing. *Technology & Learning* 21(10): 39–49.

Dublin, P., H. Pressman, E. Barnett, A. D. Corcoran, and E. J. Woldman. 1994. *Integrating computers in your classroom: Elementary education.* New York: HarperCollins College Publishers.

Fuchs, L. S., D. Fuchs, C. L. Hamlett, and K. Karns. 1998. High achieving students' interactions and performance on complex mathematical tasks as a function of homogeneous and heterogeneous pairings. *American Educational Research Journal* 35(2): 227–67.

Johnson, D. W., and R. T. Johnson. 1999a. Learning together and alone: Cooperative, competitive, and individualistic learning. 5th ed. Needham Heights, MA: Allyn & Bacon.

Johnson, D. W., R. T. Johnson, and E. J. Holubec. 1994. *Cooperative learning in the classroom.* Alexandria, VA: Association for Supervision and Curriculum Development.

Morrison, G. R., D. L. Lowther, and L. DeMeulle. 1999. *Integrating computer technology into the classroom.* Upper Saddle River, NJ: Prentice Hall.

National Center for Educational Statistics. 2002. Students and computer access. [Online]. Available: http://nces.ed.gov/pubs2002/internet/4.asp. Retrieved on December 4, 2004.

Vail, K. 2003. School technology grows up. *American School Board Journal* 190(9): 34–37.

Vermette, P. J. 1998. *Making cooperative learning work: Student teams in K–12 classrooms.* Upper Saddle River, NJ: Prentice Hall.

Self Survey

Rank the following statements according to how well they describe you. Give the statement that describes you the best a "1," the second best a "2," and so on.

Name _____

☐ I like to read books, write, and tell stories.
(linguistics)

☐ I like math, strategy games, and working with puzzles.
(logic-mathematics)

☐ I like to draw and I understand things better by looking at a picture.
(spatial)

☐ I have a hard time sitting still.
(bodily-kinesthetic)

☐ I am a good singer and I know when music is off key.
(musical)

☐ I get along well with others and I am a good listener.
(interpersonal)

☐ I am dependable and self-confident.
(intrapersonal)

☐ I enjoy the outdoors and can easily identify and classify things around me.
(naturalist)

Computer Schedule

		Mon.	Tues.	Wed.	Thur.	Fri.	Sat.
Team Name:	Comp.						
_____	Time						
Team Members:							
_____	Role						
_____	Role						
_____	Role						
	Role						
		Mon.	Tues.	Wed.	Thur.	Fri.	Sat.
Team Name:	Comp.						
_____	Time						
Team Members:							
_____	Role						
_____	Role						
_____	Role						
_____	Role						
		Mon.	Tues.	Wed.	Thur.	Fri.	Sat.
Team Name:	Comp.						
_____	Time						
Team Members:							
_____	Role						
_____	Role						
_____	Role						
_____	Role						

BrainStorm

Create a web or "brainstorm" of your related ideas. Add additional thoughts as necessary.

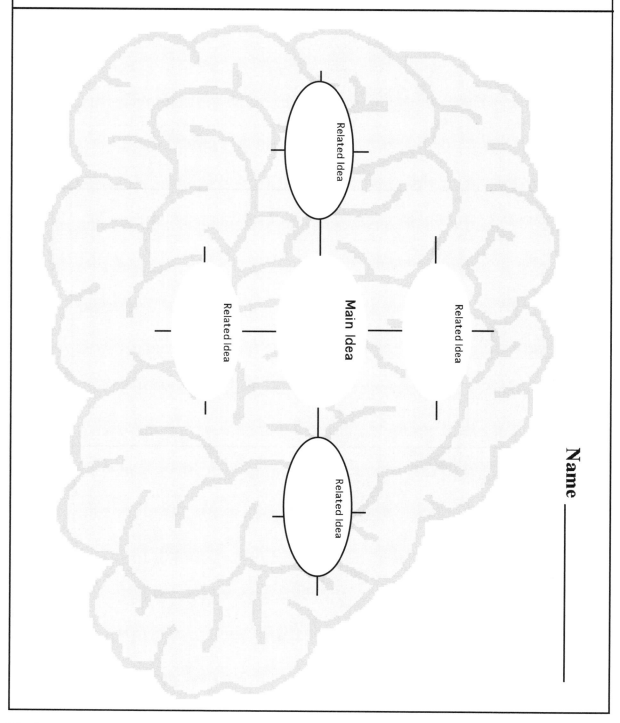

Related Idea

Related Idea

Main Idea

Related Idea

Related Idea

Name _____

KWL Knowledge Chart

	What we know
	What we want to find out
	What we learned

Bibliography Information

Team Name _____

Description	Media Type	Story-board#	Source

May be reproduced for classroom use. From Karen S. Ivers and Ann E. Barron, *Multimedia Projects in Education*. 3d ed. Westport, CT: Libraries Unlimited. © 2006.

Journal Entry

Date _____   Team Name _____

Today's accomplishments: _____

_____

_____

_____

_____

Today's problems: _____

_____

_____

_____

Goals for tomorrow: _____

_____

_____

_____

	1	2	3	
Group dynamics: poor   okay   great   Recorder's initials:

Comments: _____

_____

_____

Design

A SCENARIO

Toli, Sam, and Oma listened as Mr. Gomes discussed the purpose of their project. Each group would conduct research related to the Vietnam War and create a Web site. The presentation needed to include maps of Vietnam, historical information, photographs (from the Web), and an interview with someone who was more than 50 years old (and could remember the war).

After the students were finished with their initial brainstorming and research activities, Mr. Gomes passed out several 3- x 5-inch index cards to each group. Each group was instructed to pretend each card represented one Web page, and outline their content for their project. Quickly, Sam piped up, asking, "If this is a multimedia project, why do we need to write on index cards? I'd rather just start finding the maps, recording the audio, and making the Web pages."

"Yes," agreed Mr. Gomes, "Starting right away on the computer can be very tempting. However, let me show you the results of two projects from last year—one group carefully planned their project and created content outlines and storyboards; the other group did not. Let's see if you can tell the difference."

The first project that Mr. Gomes demonstrated seemed a bit disorganized. Some of the Web pages had titles, some did not; some of the Web pages had a lot of text in a very small font, other Web pages had very little text and used a large font. There was also little consistency in the colors and graphics—it looked like the project was produced by three students who had used completely different approaches.

Next, he demonstrated a project that was obviously well planned. The content was inviting, innovative, and extensive; yet the consistency of the presentation made the program very easy to follow.

"OK, I see your point," Sam said, "But I'll bet the first group finished their project a lot faster!"

"Actually," responded Mr. Gomes, "It took them longer. Because they did not have a good plan, they had many disagreements and failed attempts in the DEVELOP phase of the project. For example, they spent a lot of time locating photographs that weren't relevant, and they recorded their interview over and over again because they had not planned the questions in advance. They learned that the time and energy invested in the DESIGN phase could pay dividends later in the project."

OVERVIEW

The DESIGN phase is extremely important because it produces the blueprint for the entire project in the form of content outlines, screen templates, flowcharts, and storyboards. At the beginning of the DESIGN phase, teachers may want to show examples of well-designed projects as well as poorly designed projects. They should also set the parameters for the project, such as delineating the content, detailing the research requirements, and outlining the media components (number of slides, use of audio, etc.). Student teams should be provided with a list of other requirements or expectations. (See the Project Checklist blackline master at the end of this chapter.)

To assist teachers with aspects of the DESIGN phase, this chapter provides techniques for introducing topics that are important to design; it also presents design guidelines and recommendations for structuring and formatting multimedia projects. The chapter concludes with several blackline masters that are correlated to the activities in the DESIGN phase. Topics that the teacher should present to the students include the following:

- Outlining the content

- Creating flowcharts
    Linear structures
    Tree structures
    Cluster structures
    Star structures
    Flowchart symbols

- Specifying screen design

- Creating storyboards
    General planning sheet
    Detailed storyboards and scripts

- Reviewing design guidelines
    Text
    Menus
    Icons and navigation
    Color

OUTLINING THE CONTENT

In the DECIDE phase, the broad instructional goals are stated for the project, and a brainstorming session helps to determine the possible topics. In addition, research is conducted to further delineate the topics that will be included in the project.

As the students enter the DESIGN phase, the content should be solidified with outlines, flowcharts, and storyboards. Several factors will influence the content, including the timeline, age of students, subject area, and the venue for the project.

When a project is assigned, it is often wise for the teacher to specify the project requirements in terms of content and components. For example, teachers may assign a topic, such as a famous author, and require that the students provide background information on the author's childhood, a synopsis of his or her publications, and the author's impact on society. An Intention Outline or similar template can be used to help students specify the goals and outcomes of the project, its target audience, and an outline of the content (see blackline masters at the end of this chapter).

When the Intention Outlines are complete, the teacher should review them to ensure that the students' goals are clearly stated and aligned with the assignment's instructional objectives, the content outline contains the depth required for the project, and the topics are organized logically.

The students should also determine the primary venue for the project and how the audience might influence the content. Venues might include presentations for classroom peers, school assemblies, community groups, or external audiences via the Internet. If a project is designed for third graders, the content, presentation, and elements will be noticeably different from the content, presentation, and elements of a project designed for adults.

CREATING FLOWCHARTS

After the Intention Outline is complete, students should be encouraged to think through the flow of the project. A flowchart can be used to visually depict the sequence and structure of a program. To introduce the logic of flowcharts, teachers can use exercises such as the Bunny Hop or Medusa's Market (see blackline masters at the end of this chapter). Such exercises encourage students to think through decision points and represent their paths in a logical manner.

There are several common flowchart structures, including linear, tree, star, and cluster. Teachers should demonstrate various projects that use different structures and point out the advantages and disadvantages of each. The Project Structures blackline master at the end of this chapter can be used to help students differentiate among the various options for project flow and choose the appropriate structure for their projects. Students should be encouraged to experiment with different ways of presenting content. Content mapping programs, such as Inspiration and Kidspiration are excellent tools for developing flowcharts.

Linear Structures

Linear structures are appropriate when there is a specific sequence or a step-by-step procedure (see Figure 4.1). For example, a student may create a linear project that details the process required to dissect a frog. Projects designed as presentations (such as those created with PowerPoint) and videos are usually linear in design.

Figure 4.1. Linear structure.

Movement options in a linear structure may provide options for branching forward or backward. Most linear programs also include a method for starting over at the beginning.

Tree Structures

A tree structure is appropriate when the main idea branches into a few other topics, which in turn are further subdivided. Tree structures are common in both Web and hypermedia projects. For example, Figure 4.2 illustrates a tree-shaped project where the user can select any of three states from the Main Menu. When he or she clicks on a state, a submenu appears with state politics and state history.

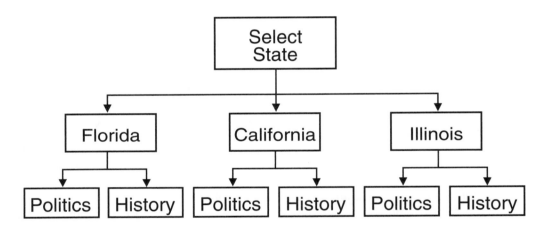

Figure 4.2. Tree structure.

Movement options in a tree structure usually allow users to branch forward and backward, return to the previous menu, or return to the Main Menu.

Cluster Structures

The cluster approach combines tree and linear structures. For example, Figure 4.3 illustrates a Main Menu where the user can select an option, then proceed to a linear presentation about adding or multiplying fractions.

Movement options in a cluster structure allow users to branch forward and backward within the linear segments or return to the Main Menu. In most cases, the linear segments should not contain more than five or six screens.

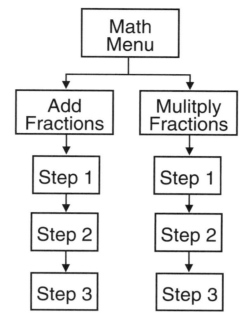

Figure 4.3. Cluster structure.

Star Structures

Star structures are used when one idea or screen branches to several other, single ideas. Many Web pages and hypermedia programs are designed with a star format. For example, a Web page may provide information about a school (see Figure 4.4). From the main page, hyperlinks allow access to other pages with the sports schedule, school address, student activities, and so on. Each of the linked pages branches directly back to the introduction/menu page.

A star structure allows the user to branch out in any direction from the Main Menu. In most cases, the only option thereafter is to branch back to the Main Menu to make another selection.

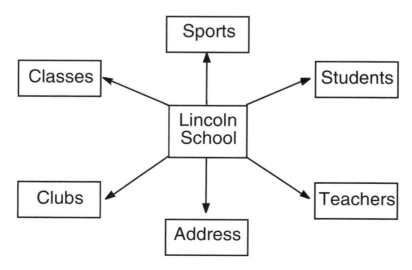

Figure 4.4. Star structure.

Flowchart Symbols

Students should be encouraged to flowchart their lessons after the content outline is complete. There are several standard symbols that are used in flowcharts. For example, a diamond generally represents a decision point, and a small circle serves as a connector from one part of the flowchart to another. These symbols can be created by hand, with rulers, with drawing templates, or with computer programs (such as Inspiration). Figure 4.5 illustrates common flowchart symbols.

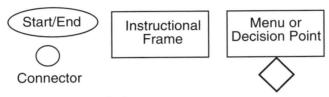

Figure 4.5. Common flowchart symbols.

When creating flowcharts, ask the students to label each element. With proper labeling, they will be able to easily match the flowchart components with the details of the program. Figure 4.6 is a flowchart of a program about Florida that was created with Inspiration. Each symbol in the figure has a short title, and connectors are used to return to the menu.

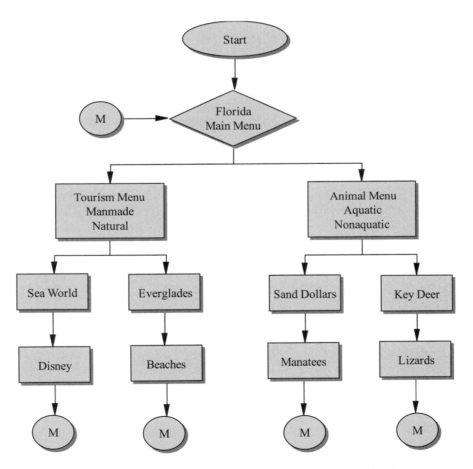

Figure 4.6. Flowchart for project about Florida (created in Inspiration).

Young students can also create flowcharts using the symbol libraries in Kidspiration. For example, the flowchart in Figure 4.7 was created for a third-grade presentation about farm animals.

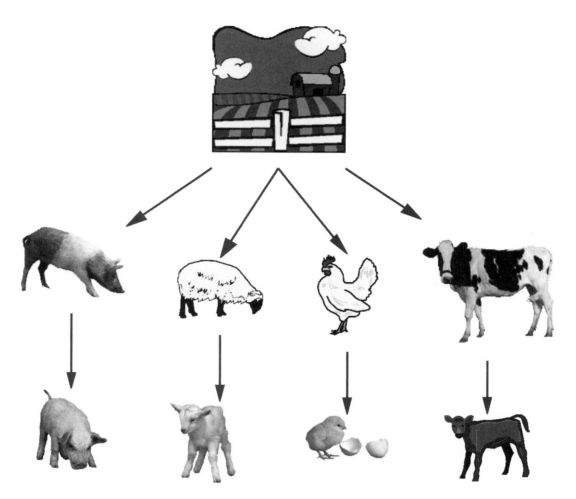

Figure 4.7. Flowchart for project about farm animals (created in Kidspiration).

SPECIFYING SCREEN DESIGN

After the general flow of the project is diagrammed, the students should determine the look and feel of the screens that will be used in the project. This includes defining the color scheme and location of graphics, icons, and other items.

Depending on the intended venue and the method of delivery, the navigation may vary considerably. For example, if the project will be projected for a class presentation, the students will not have to include extensive navigation options, because they will be controlling the navigation. However, if the project is designed for individual use or as an external Web site, there must be sufficient prompts to help users navigate through the project.

For consistency, each screen should contain defined functional areas. The functional areas will vary based on the purpose of each screen (menu vs. presentation) and on the programming tool used (PowerPoint vs. HTML). The primary functional areas for a presentation or instructional screen may include the following:

- *Title.* The title of each screen is usually located at the top or on the left side.

- *Informational/instructional text.* The text should be located in a consistent area of the screen.

- *Graphics.* The graphics can be placed on the side of the text, above it, or below it (see Figure 4.8).

- *Directions or student prompt.* If user input is required, a prompt area should be included.

- *Icons or navigation options.* The navigational options (icons or buttons) are usually located along one of the edges of the screen.

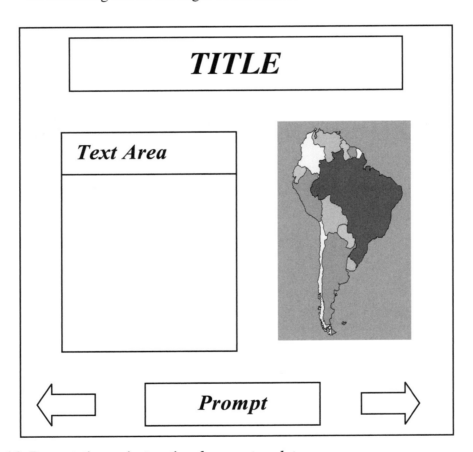

Figure 4.8. Presentation or instructional screen template.

Note that in Figure 4.8 the text is on the left, the graphic is on the right, and the navigation options are on the bottom. This is only one example of the numerous possibilities for instructional templates. For example, the text could be above the graphic, or it might be a text-only screen.

Menu screens and question screens will have slightly different functional areas. For example, Figure 4.9 contains the following areas:

- *Title.* The title of each screen is usually located at the top or on the left side.

- *Directions and Question.* The question should be located in a consistent area of the screen.

- *Answer choices.* The answers choices might consist of textual options or graphical areas.

- *Graphics.* Graphics may be used as part of the question or as answer options.

- *Feedback.* Feedback may appear in a pop-up dialog box or in a consistent location on the screen.

- *Icons or navigation options.* The navigational options (icons or buttons) are usually located along one of the edges of the screen.

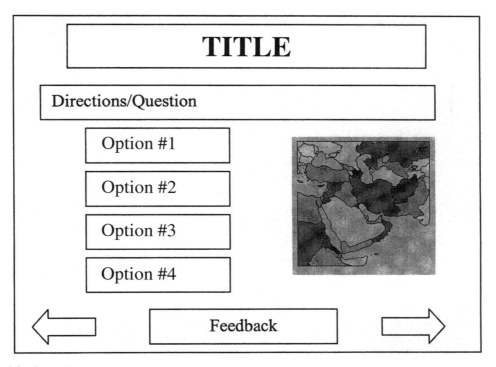

Figure 4.9. Question screen.

The menu template in Figure 4.9 is based on four text options (it is best to provide between three and six menu options). The menu selections can be text or graphics, and they might be arranged horizontally, vertically, or in another pattern. Prompts and Exit options may also be included.

CREATING STORYBOARDS

After the content has been outlined and the screen designs have been determined, the storyboards can be created. Storyboards contain all the information that will be placed on the screens as well as information that will help the programmer and production specialists develop the media components. Storyboards can be thought of as "blueprints" for the program or project. They provide the visual representation of the screen, as well as scripts for the audio, details for the video, and branching information.

General Planning Sheet

Before beginning the storyboards, it may be helpful to have the students fill out a general planning sheet. This sheet provides an opportunity for the students to allocate, or chunk, the information into separate screens without specifying all the details. Figure 4.10 illustrates the manner in which a title screen and instructional screen can be completed. (A Planning Sheet blackline master is provided at the end of this chapter as a tool for students.)

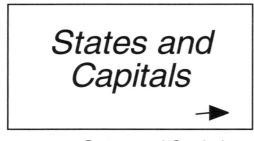

Figure 4.10. General planning sheet.

An alternative to using a planning sheet is to have the students outline their screens on 3- x 5-inch or 5- x 8-inch index cards. Each card can be used to represent one computer screen or page. The students can divide each card into functional areas and place the content (text and graphics) on the screen in the appropriate places. The backs of the cards can be used to provide information for navigation and media elements. An advantage of using this method is that the students can arrange (and rearrange) the cards on a desk in the sequence appropriate for the program, before finalizing the storyboards.

Detailed Storyboards and Scripts

After the general plan is outlined, encourage the students to write detailed storyboards and scripts for the project. Storyboards are more detailed than planning sheets because they contain all the descriptive information required to produce the text, graphics, animations, audio, and video for the project. In addition, the links for each button or interaction are specified. Several storyboard templates are provided at the end of this chapter.

The storyboards should provide all the information that will appear on the final screens. At this point, the students will determine the best way to present the information, how much information goes on each screen, and which media elements are appropriate. Each storyboard should contain a display area, branching information for the programmer (if appropriate), details about the font size and color, and a list of media elements.

Blackline masters are provided at the end of this chapter for creating storyboards for hypermedia, presentation, Web-based, and video projects. These storyboards can be copied and distributed to the students. Advanced students may want to create their own storyboards in a word processor, database, or other application. Storyboard tools and templates are also available on the Web (see the Resources section at the end of this chapter).

Storyboards for Hypermedia Programs

Hypermedia programs, such as HyperStudio or eZedia, usually contain at least three screen types: instructional screens, menu screens, and question screens. Because of their branching ability, questions and other types of interactions are common in hypermedia programs. The feedback for correct and incorrect responses may be provided by branching to a different screen, or a pop-up dialog box might provide the feedback. Note that the Hypermedia Storyboard template provides a large, blank area for the students to diagram exactly how each screen will be formatted, as well as areas to specify the navigation, text, audio, and video components. See Chapter 8 for hypermedia project ideas.

Presentation Programs

Presentation programs, such as PowerPoint, are not designed to provide as much interactivity as hypermedia programs (although the action buttons can provide basic branching capabilities). Presentation programs generally include design templates and backgrounds that have been professionally developed. Figure 4.11 illustrates some of the basic layouts that are provided with PowerPoint. Note that these layouts and templates are generally designed for projecting to a large audience. In most cases, the font is large and the text is presented in bulleted lists. See Chapter 10 for project ideas using presentation programs.

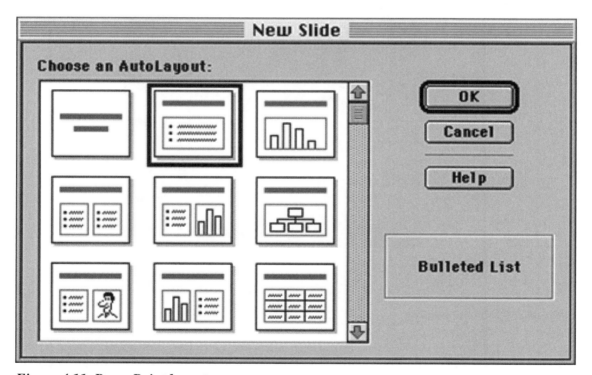

Figure 4.11. PowerPoint layouts.

Web-Based Programs

A wide variety of screen templates are appropriate for Web pages. Because large graphics take longer to transfer over the Internet, it is usually advisable to use text, with small images, graphic banners, or bullets. Navigational links on a Web page should be well defined so users will know where the links will lead.

Although feedback in the form of pop-up windows is possible on Web pages, the programming is more complex. In most cases, school-based Web pages will consist of text and hyperlinks to other pages or media files. Templates and examples of Web-based pages and projects are provided in Chapter 9.

Video Projects

Digital video files can be integrated into hypermedia, presentation, or Web-based programs, or they can be "stand-alone" projects, consisting entirely of video. In either case, the video window may be set within a graphical backdrop that contains control options. For example, Figure 4.12 represents a digital video program that is displayed on a television-like screen. Video storyboards are used to specify the different screen shots (such as close-up, wide shot, over the shoulder, etc.), the audio components, and the actors that will be used in production. Sample video projects are provided in Chapter 11.

Figure 4.12. Video window.

Storyboarding is not an easy task for many students. One way to encourage good techniques is to review and sign off on the storyboards before the students begin producing the projects (see the Storyboard Review blackline master at the end of this chapter). If the students have thoroughly outlined their content and approach via storyboards, their time spent on the computer or with the video camera will be much more efficient. Keep in mind, however, that the level of detail required in storyboards may vary based on the age of the students, the complexity of the project, the time allotted to the project, and other factors.

REVIEWING DESIGN GUIDELINES

As students add details to their storyboards, they will have to make numerous decisions. The following design guidelines can help students specify information related to text, menus, icons and buttons. Guidelines for media elements, such as graphics, animations, audio, and video are provided in Chapter 5. Information about development programs, such as HyperStudio, eZedia, PowerPoint, HTML, Inspiration, and so onare included in Chapter 6.

Guidelines for Text

- Left-justify the text (not centered).
- Use mixed case (not all caps).
- Avoid long lines of text.
- Double space text if possible.
- Keep sentences short and sweet.
- Use active tense.
- Chunk information into short paragraphs.
- Do not blink text unnecessarily.
- Use at least 12-point font size for hypermedia and Web pages.
- Use at least 24-point font size for presentation projects.
- Use generic fonts that are available on all computers.
- Do not place text on a background that has a pattern or graphic.

Guidelines for Menus

- Provide between three and six options on a menu.
- Include an exit option on all menus.
- Clearly state the directions for selecting menu options.
- Include titles on all menus.
- Place menu options in logical sequence.

Guidelines for Icons and Navigational Buttons

- Place icons in consistent locations throughout the program.
- Use common icons (such as arrows) for navigation.

- If an icon is inactive, remove it or make it dim.
- Make icons big enough for users to click on them easily.
- Provide instructions to help users navigate.
- Make permanent buttons small and unobtrusive.
- Place permanent buttons along the edge of the screen.
- Include options for users to back up and exit.

Guidelines for Color

- Use fewer than seven colors per screen.
- Use consistent background colors.
- Use consistent text colors.
- On dark backgrounds, use light text.
- On light backgrounds, use dark text.
- Highlight key words in a contrasting color.
- Do not use red backgrounds.

SUMMARY

The DESIGN phase is crucial to developing a successful multimedia project. Teachers should emphasize the importance of outlining the content of the project and present design guidelines through the use of examples and nonexamples. In addition, teachers can demonstrate the use of storyboards and scripts to help students plan and structure their projects prior to the production of graphics, video, and other media. The blackline masters at the end of this chapter, as well as Internet resources, can assist teachers and students in the design aspects of multimedia projects.

RESOURCES

Flowchart (Studio 1151): http://www.mcli.dist.maricopa.edu/authoring/studio/guidebook/flow.html

Inspiration Software: http://www.inspiration.com/home.cfm

Kidspiration Software: http://www.inspiration.com/productinfo/kidspiration/index.cfm

Multimedia in the Classroom: Design and Development: http://fcit.usf.edu/multimedia/

Multimedia Interface Design: http://ourworld.compuserve.com/homepages/adrian_mallon_multimedia/hci.htm

Storyboard Pro Software (free software and tutorial) from Atomic Learning: http://www. atomiclearning.com/storyboardpro

Storyboarding (by Jane Stevens): http://journalism.berkeley.edu/multimedia/course/storyboarding/

Storyboarding: http://www.emu-continuingeducation.org/courses/EDMT623/storyboard.html

User Interface Design: Tips and Techniques at http://www.ambysoft.com/userInterfaceDesign.pdf

BLACKLINE MASTERS

A variety of blackline masters are presented in this chapter to help teachers and students design a multimedia project. Practice activities are included to help students with flowcharting. The following blackline masters conclude this chapter:

- Project Checklist: a general checklist of expectations for multimedia projects

- Intention Outline: an outline of intent that specifies the goals and content of a project

- Project Structures: illustrations of different flowcharts

- The Bunny Hop: a flowchart sequencing activity

- Medusa's Market: a flowchart sequencing activity

- Planning Sheet: a tool to assist students in planning their storyboards

- Hypermedia Storyboard: a sample hypermedia storyboard template

- Presentation Storyboard: a sample presentation storyboard template

- Web Storyboard: a sample storyboard template for Web projects

- Video Storyboard: a sample storyboard for digital video projects

- Storyboard Review: a preliminary evaluation sheet to help students produce and revise their storyboards

Project Checklist

Team Name _____

Before developing your project at the computer, complete the following:

- ☐ Intention Outline
- ☐ Flowchart
- ☐ Planning Sheet
- ☐ Storyboards

Make sure your project has:

- ☐ a minimum of _____ pages (or cards).

- ☐ a maximum of _____ pages (or cards).

- ☐ a Title page (or card).

- ☐ credits (designers and bibliography information).

- ☐ a Main Menu.

- ☐ appropriate navigation options.

- ☐ text that is easy to read and is accurate.

- ☐ complete sentences with correct punctuation, grammar, and spelling.

- ☐ the assigned media requirements.

_____ Clip Art	_____ Animation	_____ Video
_____ Scanned Image	_____ Digitized Camera Photo	
_____ Original Audio	_____ Clip Sound (digitized)	
_____ MIDI File	_____ Original Graphic	

- ☐ Other: _____

  _____

Intention Outline

Project Title: _____

General Goal: _____

Specific Outcomes: _____

_____

Audience

Who will use this project (e.g., students, teachers, parents)?

Content Outline

I. _____

    A. _____

    B. _____

    C. _____

II. _____

    A. _____

    B. _____

    C. _____

III. _____

    A. _____

    B. _____

    C. _____

Project Structures

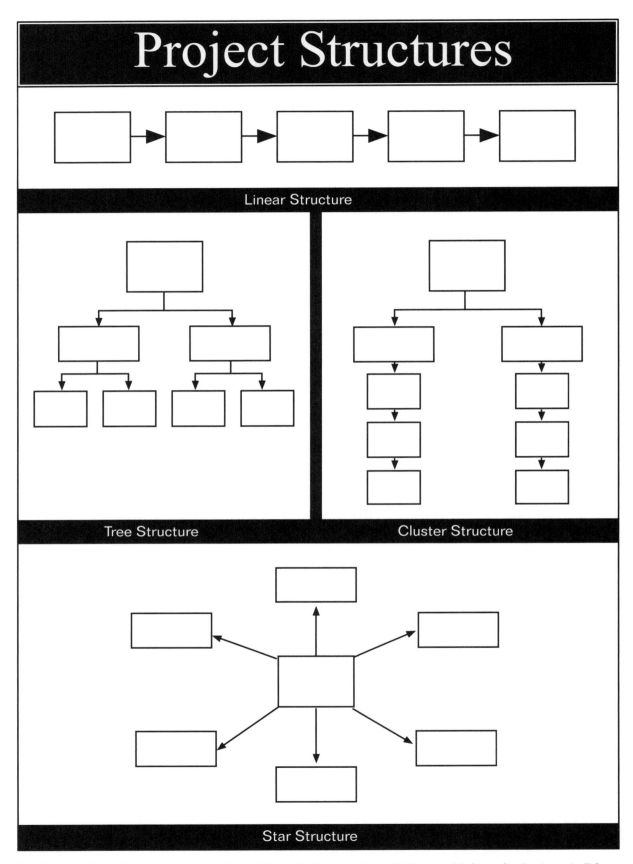

Linear Structure

Tree Structure

Cluster Structure

Star Structure

May be reproduced for classroom use. From Karen S. Ivers and Ann E. Barron, *Multimedia Projects in Education*. 3d ed. Westport, CT: Libraries Unlimited. © 2006.

The Bunny Hop

Benjamin Bunny is helping his friend hide eggs. Help Benjamin figure out what to do by placing a letter in the correct section of the flowchart. Remember that diamond shapes are for asking questions and box shapes are for decisions. Two are already done for you.

_____ A. Wait ten minutes.

_____ B. Hide egg.

_____ C. Is anyone peeking?

_____ D. Continue to hop down the bunny trail.

_____ E. Place colored eggs into basket.

_____ F. Are there eggs in the basket?

_____ G. Hop down the bunny trail.

_____ H. Look for a place to hide egg.

_____ I. Go home.

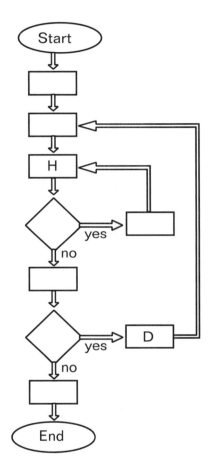

<u>Extension ideas:</u> Create a flowchart for getting ready for school in the morning, cooking your favorite meal, or packing for a vacation.

Answer: E, G, H, C (yes is A), B, F (yes is D), I

Medusa's Market

Medusa needs to go to the grocery store. Help her get into her car and drive to the grocery store's parking lot by placing a letter in the correct section of the flowchart. Remember that diamond shapes are for asking questions and box shapes are for decisions. Three are already done for you.

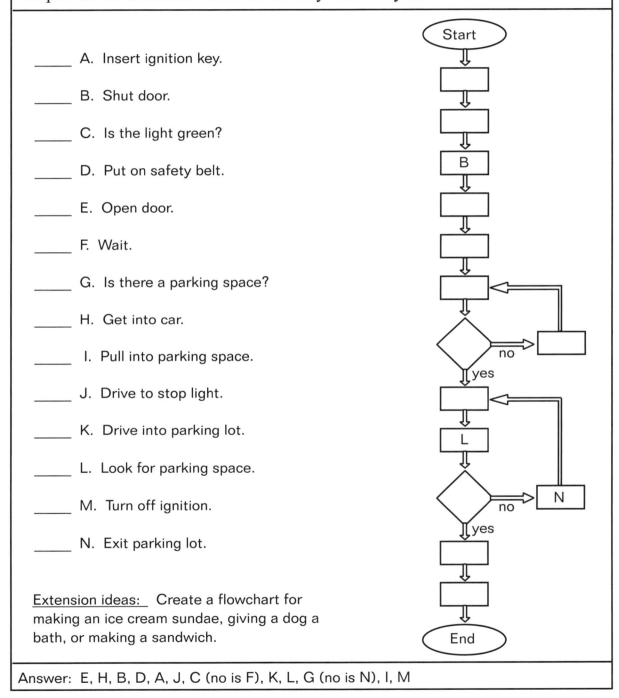

_____ A. Insert ignition key.

_____ B. Shut door.

_____ C. Is the light green?

_____ D. Put on safety belt.

_____ E. Open door.

_____ F. Wait.

_____ G. Is there a parking space?

_____ H. Get into car.

_____ I. Pull into parking space.

_____ J. Drive to stop light.

_____ K. Drive into parking lot.

_____ L. Look for parking space.

_____ M. Turn off ignition.

_____ N. Exit parking lot.

Extension ideas: Create a flowchart for making an ice cream sundae, giving a dog a bath, or making a sandwich.

Answer: E, H, B, D, A, J, C (no is F), K, L, G (no is N), I, M

Planning Sheet

Name of group: _____

Use this sheet to plan the general content of your pages.

Title: _____
Content: _____
Links: _____

Title: _____
Content: _____
Links: _____

Title: _____
Content: _____
Links: _____

Title: _____
Content: _____
Links: _____

Title: _____
Content: _____
Links: _____

Title: _____
Content: _____
Links: _____

Hypermedia Storyboard

Name of group: _____ Storyboard Number: _____

Use this sheet to specify the details of the project.

Navigation

Button: _____ Link to: _____ Action: _____

Button: _____ Link to: _____ Action: _____

Button: _____ Link to: _____ Action: _____

Text

Color: _____ Size: _____ Font: _____

Audio

Source: _____

File: _____

Description: _____

_____

_____

Video

Source: _____

File: _____

Description: _____

_____

_____

Presentation Storyboard

Name of group: _____ Storyboard Number: _____

Use this sheet to specify the details of the project.

Template

Name: _____ Color: _____ Layout: _____

Text

Color: _____ Size: _____ Font: _____

Transition: _____ Build: _____

Audio

Source: _____
File: _____
Description: _____
_____
_____

Video

Source: _____
File: _____
Description: _____
_____
_____

Web Storyboard

Name of group: _____ Storyboard Number: _____

Use this sheet to specify the details of the project.

Navigation

Hyperlink: _____ Link to: _____

Hyperlink: _____ Link to: _____

Hyperlink: _____ Link to: _____

Text and Background

Text Color: _____ Size: _____ Font: _____

Background Color: _____ Background Graphic: _____

Audio	**Graphic**
Source: _____	Source: _____
File: _____	File: _____
Description: _____	Description: _____
_____	_____

Video Storyboard

Name of group: _____ Storyboard Number: _____

Use this sheet to specify the details of the project.

Video Details

Description of Scene: _____
_____

Actors: _____

Lighting: _____ Camera Shot: _____

Scenery: _____

Props: _____

Transition Effect: _____

Audio

Source: _____

File: _____

Description: _____
_____

Special Graphics

Source: _____

File: _____

Description: _____
_____

Storyboard Review

Students included:	Yes	No	N/A
a title screen	—	—	—
a credit screen	—	—	—
directions/information for the user	—	—	—
a main menu	—	—	—
forward and back links	—	—	—
factual and interesting information	—	—	—
consistent and clear layout designs	—	—	—
required media elements	—	—	—
font information for text boxes	—	—	—
font information for titles	—	—	—
background information	—	—	—
_____	—	—	—
_____	—	—	—
_____	—	—	—

Comments:

_____

_____

_____

_____

Developing Media Elements

A SCENARIO

Archy's group was creating a project about Italy. Through their research, they discovered that art and music are very important parts of Italian culture. Rather than making a project with just text, they decided to add some other elements, such as graphics and sound.

After they completed their flowcharts and storyboards, their next step was to create the graphics. The students were using PowerPoint to develop the project, and they were pleased to learn that PowerPoint includes a toolbar with some drawing tools. The PowerPoint tools were easy to use, and they were able to create a few simplistic graphics of Italian architecture. Then they looked at the clip art provided with PowerPoint and found maps and other images that fit their program's theme.

Next, they wanted to include a few Italian poems and translations, as well as an interview with someone who was familiar with Italy. Luckily, Clayton's father was bilingual and had gone to school in Florence, Italy. Clayton took the iPod home and attached a microphone so he could interview his dad and record the Italian poems. The next day, he transferred the audio files to the computer and imported them into a sound-editing program. After working together for an hour, the group was pleased with the edited version of the interview. They were, however, surprised at how large the audio file was when then transferred it to the network.

The group also wanted to find some Italian music for the program. Mr. Thomas suggested that they search on the Internet. The students were surprised when they immediately located a site with hundreds of MIDI songs with very small files. After their experience with the narrated words, they thought that the songs would be very short because the files were small. Instead, they were pleased to find that some of the songs played almost three minutes. "How can this be?" they asked Mr. Thomas. "It's a MIDI file," he explained. "Music stored in the MIDI format has a much smaller file size than the digital audio files that you narrate and record."

The group was almost finished when Clara (who was still searching the Internet) shouted, "Wow! Look what I found! It's a movie of the gondolas in Venice!" Sure enough, she had located a short digital movie. Mr. Thomas showed them how to download it and include it in their program. Even though it was only a few seconds long, it was almost a megabyte in size. Their project was a success, and they were already talking about how they would make their own movie for the next assignment.

OVERVIEW

After the flowcharts and storyboards have been approved, students begin developing their multimedia projects on the computer. The third phase of the DDD-E model is DEVELOP, which includes producing the media components, such as text, graphics, animations, audio, and video. It also covers the programming (or authoring) of the program. This chapter focuses on designing and producing the media; Chapter 6 outlines the tools available for authoring and delivery.

Media elements (graphics, animation, audio, and video) are key components of multimedia projects. They can help bring a presentation to life by providing realism, color, motion, and sound. Used effectively, media elements add many instructional benefits, enhance visual literacy, and address multiple intelligences and learning styles. This chapter outlines the procedures for creating and editing graphics, animations, audio, and video elements. It concludes with classroom management strategies for teachers. Media resources are also provided at the end of the chapter. Topics include the following:

- Graphics

    Creating a graphic

    Importing an existing graphic file

    Scanning graphics

    Capturing digital images with a camera

    Guidelines for graphics

- Animations

    Frame animations

    Path animations

    Guidelines for animations

- Audio

    Digital audio

    Recording audio with computers

    Synthesized speech

    MIDI

    Digital audio file formats

    Using existing audio files

    Guidelines for audio

- Digital video
  - Digitizing video
  - Editing video
  - Constraining the file size of digital video
  - Digital video file formats
  - Using existing video files
  - Guidelines for video

GRAPHICS

The term *graphics* refers to images or any information in the computer that is presented via pictures, drawings, or paintings. As computer display systems evolved to include more and more colors, images became increasingly prevalent. Now, it is rare to find a computer program or multimedia project that does not contain at least a few images.

There are many ways to obtain graphics for a computer project: they can be created from scratch with a computer program; they can be imported from an existing file; they can be scanned from a hard copy; or they can be digitized with a camera. Each method has advantages and disadvantages.

Creating a Graphic

Many graphics creation programs are available, including ColorIt, CorelDraw, Photoshop, and Microsoft Paint. These programs vary in price, sophistication, and many other attributes, but they can all be used to create computer graphics and save them in various file formats. Computer graphics (and graphics creation programs) can be roughly divided into two types: paint (bitmapped) or draw (vector).

Paint (Bitmapped) Graphics

Paint (bitmapped) images are made up of individual pixels (picture elements), which are small dots on the screen. The individual pixels are usually represented as horizontal and vertical lines in a matrix. The small pixels can be arranged to form a graphic—similar to a Lite-Brite toy. In this type of program, the pixels retain their independence. In other words, even if the pixels are positioned to form the appearance of a square, when you zoom in, you can see that the square is made up of tiny, individual pixels (see Figure 5.1).

There are numerous software programs that can be used to create bitmapped graphics; they are often referred to as *paint programs*. Popular examples include Adobe Photoshop and Microsoft Paint. These programs are appropriate when you want to use a brush effect or apply a mixture of colors. With these programs, you can easily add effects such as distortions, textures, or gradients. For example, in Paint's toolbox, the paint tools allow students to create squares, circles, text, and so forth (see Figure 5.2). All of the images created with these tools will be bitmapped and consist of individual pixels. If students want to move a graphic (such as a square) after it has been created, they must use a selection tool (such as the lasso) to select all of the pixels that are to be moved.

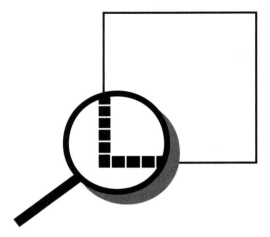

Figure 5.1. A bitmapped graphic is made up of individual pixels.

Figure 5.2. Microsoft Paint toolbox.

Draw (Vector) Graphics

A vector (object-oriented) graphic might look similar to a bitmapped image when it appears on the computer screen, but it is stored in a very different manner. Object-oriented drawings consist of geometric shapes instead of individual pixels. In a vector image, every component of a graphic, such as a circle, square, or line, is defined by a precise mathematical formula. If you were to zoom into the graphic, you would not see individual pixels (see Figure 5.3). This is an important feature in that object-oriented drawings can be enlarged to any size, and they will always look smooth.

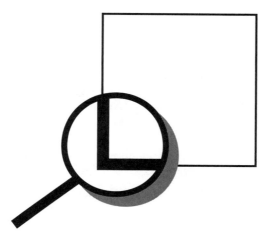

Figure 5.3. Vector graphics do not contain individual pixels.

Object-oriented images are ideal for geometric drawings such as blueprints, charts, or line drawings. Because the images consist of geometric figures, they can be layered on top of each other and still retain their identity. The individual geometric figures can also be moved, copied, or resized without affecting other objects. When an object is "selected," tiny handlebars appear to allow you to change the size of the image. Popular software programs for vector graphics include CorelDraw and Adobe Illustrator. Software applications, such as PowerPoint, Word, and AppleWorks, also contain drawing features that can be used to create vector graphics (see Figure 5.4).

Figure 5.4. Drawing tools in Microsoft Word.

Importing an Existing Graphic File

In some cases, the students may not have the time or software programs required to create their own graphics, and they may find it more expedient to use existing files. Many programs provide a collection of clipart that can be easily imported into the programs. After the clip art is inserted into the program, it can be repositioned and resized. Numerous clipart sites are available on the Internet (see Graphic Resources at the end of this chapter). You can also go to Google (http://www. google.com) and click on "Images" to search the Web for images. Be sure to check for copyright restrictions when using clipart.

Most programs also allow users to import picture files that are not provided as clipart. The key to importing existing graphics files into a program is to make sure that the files are in a compatible format. For example, PowerPoint will open and display graphics files that have the extension BMP, PICT, TIF, GIF, JPG, and others. In contrast, graphics files on the Web are almost always stored in GIF, JPEG, and PNG format. See Table 5.1 for a list of common graphics formats.

If you have a graphic that is not in the appropriate format, you can use a graphic converter program to change the format. For example, if you had a PICT graphic and you wanted to place it on a Web page, you could open it in Adobe PhotoShop and save it as a GIF file. There are also shareware programs, such as Graphic Converter (available at http://www.lemkesoft.de/en/graphcon.htm), that can be used to convert image formats.

Table 5.1

Common Graphic Formats

Extension	Description	Platform	Application
BMP	Microsoft Bitmap	Windows	Windows applications
WMF	Windows Metafile	Windows	Windows applications
PICT	Macintosh Picture Format	Macintosh	Macintosh applications
TIF	Tagged Image File Format	Windows, Mac	Common format for exchanging files between platforms
EPS	Encapsulated PostScript	Windows, Mac	Common for printed documents
GIF	Graphics Interchange Format	Windows, Mac	Common on the Web
JPEG	Joint Photographic Experts Group	Windows, Mac	Common on the Web
PNG	Portable Network Graphic	Windows, Mac	Common on the Web

Scanning Graphics

Many times, students may want to use an image in a multimedia program that currently exists only as a hard copy, such as a photograph or a picture in a book. *Scanners* are computer peripherals used to convert print materials (hard copies) and other objects into images on a computer. Capturing images with a scanner makes it possible to incorporate complex images into multimedia projects.

The typical scanning process is very similar to copying a piece of paper on a photocopy machine. The paper copy is placed on a scanner, a light passes under it, and a bitmapped image is created. The difference is that instead of producing a copy on paper, the image is transferred to the computer screen.

Scanners come with software that offers several settings. These settings can affect the quality of the scanned image and the size of the file. When students scan graphics, caution them to scan only the portion of the picture that they need. Also, they should select a resolution of about 72 dots per inch (dpi) or pixels per inch (ppi). Scanning at a higher resolution for display on a computer screen will result in a very large file.

Another consideration is the setting for the number of colors. Scanners can produce graphics in black and white, shades of gray, or a wide range of colors. However, if the capture is set at "millions" of colors, the file size can be extremely large. After the image is scanned, it should be saved, or exported, in a format that is compatible with the presentation—in other words, if it is going to be used on a Web page, it should be saved as a GIF or JPG file.

Capturing Digital Images with a Camera

A photograph of a person is difficult to draw from scratch on a computer. If your students have a photograph and a scanner, they can scan the image. However, if they do not already have a photo that has been developed on film, they may want to use a digital camera to capture the image.

Digital cameras simplify the capturing process by enabling students to capture still images without film. The procedure for using a digital camera is simple: point and click. Most cameras have a small preview screen, and you can delete the image if you don't like it. The photos are stored on a small memory card within the computer. To transfer the pictures to a computer, simply connect the camera to the computer with a cable, open a graphics program, and download the images onto the computer drive. After the images are downloaded, they can be enhanced, resized, or repositioned and integrated into a multimedia project. Programs such as iPhoto by Apple Computer can be used to create interactive books, galleries, and slideshows of images created with cameras, scanners, or image editors.

Guidelines for Graphics

The following guidelines can help you and your students determine the appropriate use of graphics in multimedia projects.

- Use graphics to enhance the project and illustrate important concepts.

- Do not include graphics that distract from the project.

- If possible, use several simple graphics rather than one complex graphic.

- If complex graphics are required, add arrows or highlight boxes to help focus attention on the relevant areas.

- If graphic icons are used for buttons, or other similar elements, be consistent—always use the same icon for the same function.

- Be consistent when placing graphics—designate one part of the screen for graphics and another part for text, title, and so on.

- Use 256 colors or fewer to help keep file sizes as small as possible.

- Graphics should be created or scanned at 72–100 dpi (if they are going to be displayed on a computer screen).

- Check copyright restrictions on all graphics that will be used outside of the classroom.

- Graphics that are incorporated into Web pages should be less than 50K (total for all graphics on one page).

ANIMATIONS

Animations are graphics that include movement. For example, an animation may be used to depict the flow of electricity, cell division, or a volcano eruption. Animations help convey and reinforce complex concepts. Although animations can add a wealth of information and excitement to multimedia projects, they can also be time-consuming to develop. This section outlines two types of animations (frame and path), presents resources for locating animations, and provides guidelines for the use of animations.

Frame Animations

Frame animations were popularized by movie and cartoon animators who use them to create the illusion of motion. The first Mickey Mouse cartoon was created by drawing many images with very slight differences between the images. When the images are played in rapid sequence (usually 5–15 frames per second), they blend together, and we see Mickey walking and dancing. Likewise, to create frame animations on a computer, you must draw several frames and play them in rapid succession (see Figure 5.5).

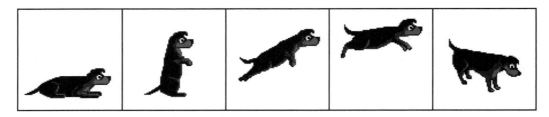

Figure 5.5. Graphics for a frame animation (Addy from HyperStudio).

If you see an animation on a Web page, it is probably a GIF animation, a common frame-based animation format. For example, you might see a small mailbox that opens and closes. If you watch it carefully, you will note that it is made up of three or four images that cycle over and over again. GIF animations are popular because they are small (in file size) and easy to create. You can locate thousands of GIF animations in clipart galleries and on the Web by doing a search.

You can also create your own GIF animations by producing a series of still images that have slight alterations from one image to the next. Then, using image editors or software tools such as GIF Construction Set (http://www.mindworkshop.com/), you can set the play time so that each image will display a split second before the next one appears.

Flash by Macromedia is another popular program for creating animations. Flash is popular for creating Web animations because it uses vector graphics, which are often much smaller than the bitmapped graphics. Flash also offers many sophisticated options, such as key frames and in-betweens. With these features, you can draw a character on frame one, go to frame 10, grab its left arm and raise it. The software will then calculate the arm's motion for frames 2 through 9 and create the individual images.

Path Animations

A path animation involves moving an object on a screen that has a constant background. For example, a title may "fly in" from the left side; an airplane may fly across the page; or a ball may bounce through a scene. Some programs include features that can easily create path animations. For example, PowerPoint provides numerous predesigned animation schemes (such as "fade in and dim" or "boomerang and exit") for the titles and bullets on the slides. The timing, sequence, speed, and direction of these schemes can be easily modified.

PowerPoint also has a path (called motion) animation option, which allows you to specify the path an object (text or graphic) will follow. For example, if you wanted to animate a plane flying across the screen, you would follow these steps:

1. Create a slide and insert a picture of an airplane.

2. Select "Custom Animation" from the Slide Show menu.

3. Highlight (click) the object (airplane) that you want to animate.

4. Click the "Add Effect" button and select "Motion Paths" from the pull-down menu.

5. Select a predefined motion or "Draw Custom Path."

6. Click the mouse and hold it down as you drag the airplane across the screen to define the path (see Figure 5.6).

7. Double-click the mouse when you reach the end of the path.

8. Select "Slide Show" to see the complete animation.

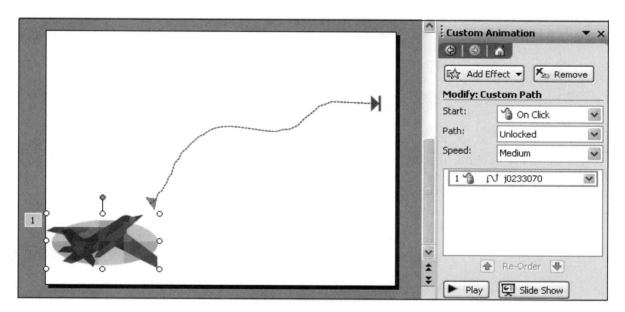

Figure 5.6. Path animation window.

Guidelines for Animation

The following guidelines can help you and your students determine how to use animations appropriately.

- Use animations to illustrate an abstract concept, such as erosion on a river.

- Keep the animation sequences short, or allow users the option to interrupt and proceed with the program.

- Test the animations on various computers to ensure that the speed is appropriate.

- Use path animations to move one or two objects on a screen.

- Use frame animation for more complex sequences involving multiple changes.

- Do not include animations that distract from the content.

- If the animation is designed for the Web, keep the file size small.

AUDIO

Audio refers to sound elements in a program. These elements can include recorded narration, music, and sound effects (such as a bird singing or a telephone dial tone). Audio can assist students' learning, as well as add realism, excitement, and motivation to projects.

Your students can add audio components to their projects in many ways. They can record the audio with a microphone (digital audio); they can use synthesized speech; they can create music with a MIDI input device; or they can use clip audio (elements that are available for free or for sale).

Digital Audio

Audio can be recorded with a computer and stored in a digital format on computer hard drives, networks, CD-ROMs and other storage devices. The audio files can be accessed and played by a computer program. A major advantage of this technology is that teachers and students can record their own voices or sounds and store them on a computer.

Bringing sound into the digital domain of computer bits and bytes requires a sampling process. At small but discrete time intervals, the computer takes a "snapshot" of the sound. This process is called sampling, and the number of samples taken each second is referred to as the sampling rate. The more samples, the better the sound quality. For example, audio sampled 44,000 times per second (44 kilohertz or kHz) will provide better quality than audio sampled 22,000 times per second (22 kHz).

Selecting a sampling rate is based primarily on two factors: the sound quality needed and the storage space available. The two factors are interrelated: the higher the quality, the more space required, and vice versa. For most educational applications, a sampling rate of 11 kHz is sufficient. If storage space is at a premium, even 5 to 8 kHz will provide intelligible narration. For music programs, which require higher quality, higher sampling rates are recommended. Table 5.2 compares the file sizes generated when a one-second audio clip is recorded at various sampling rates.

Table 5.2.

Comparison of File Sizes and Sampling Rates

Sampling Rate	Storage for 1 Second of Sound	Seconds of Sound per 1 MB Storage
44 kHz	44 kilobytes	22 seconds
22 kHz	22 kilobytes	45 seconds
11 kHz	11 kilobytes	90 seconds

Recording Audio with Computers

The recording process for digital audio is not difficult. Macintosh computers have the necessary hardware components built in for recording audio, and most PCs already have a digital audio board installed to record and play audio files. To digitize audio, follow this procedure:

- Plug a microphone into the audio input of the computer or audio board.
- Open an audio recording program. (In PowerPoint, select "Movies and Sounds > Record Audio" from the Insert menu.)
- Select a sampling rate and other parameters if they are available.
- Click "Record."
- Speak into the microphone.
- Select "Stop" when you have recorded the segment you want.
- Test the recording with the "Play" command. If it is acceptable, name the file and save it to the disk.

Digitized sounds can be viewed and edited like text (see Figure 5.7). With the appropriate software program, sounds can be selected, cut, copied, pasted, and mixed with other sounds. Audio editing is a powerful tool that allows you to rearrange sounds or cut out parts you do not need.

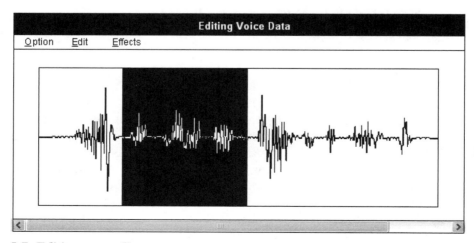

Figure 5.7. Editing an audio wave.

Synthesized Speech

Synthesized speech uses a computer program to translate text into spoken output without any recording process. It simply applies its phonetic rules to pronounce all of the words. The disadvantage of the text-to-speech synthesis method is that it may have an unnatural and mechanical sound. For instance, problems arise with words such as "live" that do not follow consistent rules of pronunciation. Most computer synthesizers cannot accurately differentiate between the use of *live* in these two sentences: "I live in Florida" and "We are using live bait."

Another problem with synthesized speech is that synthesizers do not have the natural inflections of a human voice; they may not "drop off" to indicate the end of a sentence as we do in natural speech. An example of synthesized speech is the Blabber Mouth II feature of HyperStudio. With this feature, students can type in text and select one of many "voices"; the computer then does its best to read the text (see Figure 5.8). Because the only component that the computer has to store is the text, the file size is very small for this type of audio.

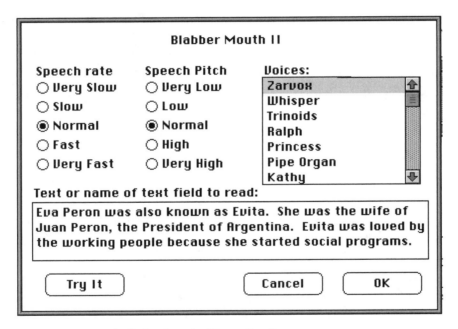

Figure 5.8. Blabber Mouth dialog box in HyperStudio.

MIDI

A synthesizer is a musical instrument or device that generates sound electronically. Synthesizers have existed in various forms for many years, but many of them were incompatible with each other. In the early 1980s, several manufacturers agreed on a hardware standard for the instruments and the MIDI (Musical Instrument Digital Interface) specification was developed.

It is important to note that MIDI music is not sampled and digitized like digital audio files. Instead, MIDI contains information about the sound (such as the note value, the duration, and the pitch), not the sounds themselves. MIDI files provide the instructions on how to reproduce the music. The computer then interprets the MIDI instructions and produces the music using the sounds that are embedded in the sound card, MIDI instrument, or sound module.

An advantage of MIDI technology is that it can produce complex music with very small files. It can play the sounds for stringed instruments, woodwinds, brass, and percussion simultaneously. To produce a MIDI composition, one uses a MIDI input device (such as a keyboard) and software that captures everything as it is played. After the musical information is loaded into the computer, it can be edited or revised in relation to its rhythm, meter, tone, and many other parameters. With MIDI sequencing software, you can experiment with harmonies, record different parts, and play them back as a complete arrangement.

MIDI files are often used in multimedia projects because the file sizes are very small. For example, a file that is less than 10K may play a song that is two or three minutes long. If your school does not have the equipment to record MIDI files, you may be able to locate copyright-free files on the Internet. A list of MIDI sites on the Internet is available in the resources at the end of this chapter.

Digital Audio File Formats

Many file formats are used for digital audio. Some file formats may be recognized by one program and not another. For example, .AIFF formats are common on Macintosh computers, and .WAV is the most common format for Windows computers. Some programs (on either platform) may be able to recognize and play files, such as MIDI; others may not. The following formats are common for audio:

- WAV. The WAV format is the default standard for Windows-based computers. All PC programs can recognize and play this format, and many Macintosh programs can also play the files.

- AIFF. The AIFF format is the default standard for Macintosh computers. All Macintosh programs can recognize and play this format, and most PC programs can also play the files.

- MP3. MP3 stands for Moving Picture Experts Group, Audio Layer III. It is a compression format that can decrease the size of an audio file but maintain a high-quality sound. Although MP3 files can be compressed at different ratios, the standard is about a 10:1 ratio. This enables a three-minute song to be stored on less than 4 MB of disk space. See MP3.com for MP3 players and available files. Many of the small, portable audio players, such as iPods, use the MP3 format.

- RA or RM. RealAudio or RealMedia files can be used to stream audio over the Internet. Streaming audio files are compressed and broken into packets that can be transferred quickly over the Internet (in real time). To play the streaming audio files, a plug-in (a small software program called Real One Player) is generally required at the receiving site.

- ASF (Active Streaming Format). ASF is Microsoft's format for streaming media. It works well with Windows Media Player.

- QT or MOV. Although QuickTime was originally designed for digital video, it can also be used for a combination of audio and video or for audio-only files. A QuickTime player is required for playing QuickTime files on the Web.

- AAC (Advanced Audio Coding). ACC is a compressed audio format used by Apple computer on its iPods.

- SWA. Shockwave Audio is a file format used by Macromedia (the company that produces Authorware, Director, and Flash) to stream audio on the Internet.

- MID or MIDI. A standard for communicating musical information among computers and musical devices.

If you have an audio file that is not in the correct format, there are programs that will convert files from one format to another. For example, Audacity (available at http://www.audacity.com) will convert to and from .WAV, .MP3, and .AIFF.

Using Existing Audio Files

The fair use portion of the copyright law is generally interpreted as allowing students to use copyrighted music in a classroom situation to fulfill an instructional objective (such as an assignment to create a multimedia project). If the students want to use music on their Web site, however, they must have the rights to record and play the music files. Recording a song from the radio and adding a link to it from a Web site would definitely violate copyright laws.

Numerous shareware sound files are available on the Web, including archives of Macintosh audio files (.AIFF format), audio files for Windows computers (.WAV format), and files designed to play on both Macintosh and Windows (MP3, MIDI, etc.). Prior to incorporating these files into a Web page or an application that will be distributed beyond the classroom, you should carefully read the permission statements. If a permission statement is not associated with the file or Web site, send an e-mail message to the site administrator to request permission.

Guidelines for Audio

There are many situations when audio is appropriate in a multimedia program. For example, if the program is designed for nonreaders or if it contains music, then audio is definitely required. In addition, audio is a great way to teach someone a different language or to include sound effects (such as heartbeats). However, audio files can be quite large, and students should be cautioned to use them only when necessary. The following guidelines should be considered for audio.

- Use audio only when it is appropriate to the content.

- Record audio at the lowest acceptable sampling rate to minimize file space.

- Use synthesized speech for programs that require a lot of spoken words.

- If possible, use MIDI or MP3 for music—the files are much smaller than digital audio stored in WAV and other formats.

- Do not add audio that will distract from the screen display.

- Check copyright restrictions if the audio will be played outside the classroom environment.

- If your software program does not recognize the audio file format, locate an audio converter program to change the file format.

DIGITAL VIDEO

Digitized video refers to motion sequences that have been recorded with a computer and saved as a computer file. Digital video has the potential to add realism to multimedia projects. Students can record school assemblies, document field trips, or create commercials—the possibilities are endless!

Digitizing Video

Video can be recorded in digital format. Digital camcorders provide an easy, inexpensive method for capturing video. After video is recorded onto the digital tape cassette in the camera, simply attach a cable (called a firewire cable) to the camera and import the video into a computer. Digital video software, such as iMovie, Final Cut Pro, Premier, or Movie Maker, provide easy-to-use controls for importing the video (see Figure 5.9).

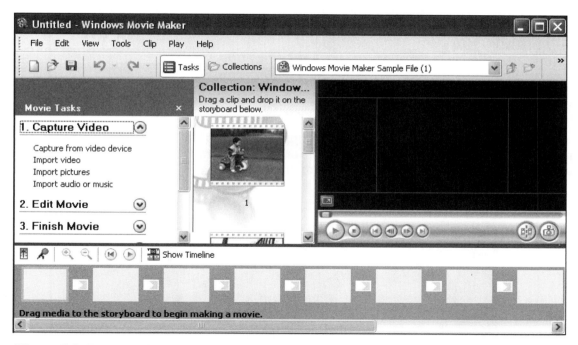

Figure 5.9. Import video controls in Movie Maker.

If you do not have a digital video camera, video can be converted (digitized) through a special card in the computer. Video-digitizing cards (or peripherals) convert the electronic signals of regular (analog) video into digital bits of information for each pixel of the computer screen. The conversion process makes it possible to use a camera, videotape, or broadcast television as a computer input device and to display the video on a standard computer monitor.

Editing Video

In many ways, editing digital video files on a computer is similar to editing videotapes. Individual clips are appended together to make up a movie. The difference is that the clips are digital files stored on hard drives rather than on a strip of magnetic tape. In fact, editing digital video is often referred to as nonlinear editing—it's a process of assembling video clips, still images, and audio into a finished presentation without linear tape.

Digital video editors allow students to sequence video clips, add audio, overlay titles, and experiment with transitions. Through these programs, students can manipulate the video files and other media to tell a story or teach a concept. When the project is complete, they can export it to videotape, save it as a stand-alone computer file, create a DVD, or integrate it into another application, such as PowerPoint.

Although the features and interfaces vary, all of the editing software provides basic functions for editing video. The process consists of these general steps:

1. Import the video and other media into the editing software.

2. Edit the video clips to the desired length.

3. Place the video clips on a timeline in the desired sequence.

4. Add transitions, such as dissolves and cuts between clips.

5. Add title slides and other media elements.

6. Combine the clips into one movie file.

7. Save the movie file in the desired format.

8. Export the movie file to videotape, Web server, DVD, or CD-ROM.

For example, Figure 5.10 shows the editing window in iMovie. Note that the clips that have been imported are displayed on the right. A large preview window (on the left) is used to edit individual clips, and the timeline appears at the bottom of the screen.

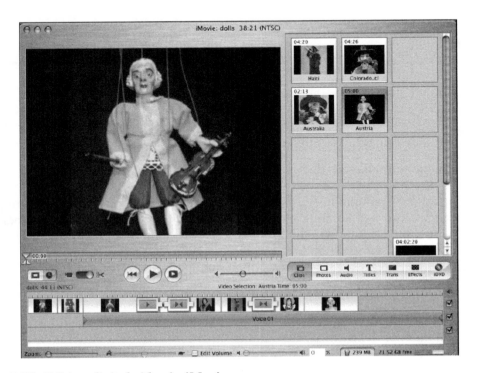

Figure 5.10. Editing digital video in iMovie.

Constraining the File Size of Digital Video

If you are capturing video segments, you will discover very quickly that the files generated by digital video can be huge. A five-minute sequence of "raw" digital video can be up to 5 GB is size—that's gigabytes! To constrain the size of digital video files, you can adjust several factors, including the size of the video window, the frame rate, and the compression technique.

Size of Video Window

Three basic display sizes are used for digital video, although other sizes are possible. A full screen on a computer display that is set for digitized video is usually 640 pixels by 480 pixels; one-quarter of a screen is 320 times 240; and one-sixteenth of a screen is 160 times 120. The file sizes are proportional—an image saved in full screen will result in a file that is four times bigger than one for a quarter screen.

Frame Rate

The standard display rate for video on a videotape or television is 30 frames per second (fps). In many cases, however, digital video will be captured or recorded at a slower rate. Frame rates of 10 to 15 frames per second (fps) are common with digital video. Table 5.3 illustrates how these factors (size and frame rate) affect the size of the video file. Note that the file sizes listed in the chart represent only one second of digital video!

Table 5.3.

File Sizes of One Second of Motion Digital Video with Full Color

Screen Size and Rate	15 fps	30 fps
Quarter screen	1.1 MB	2.3 MB
Full screen	4.5 MB	17.0 MB

After the video segments or single images are captured, editing software (such as iMovie, Movie Maker, FinalCut Pro, and Adobe Premier) can be used to edit the sequences, add special transitions, and construct a movie. Developing digital movies requires a computer with a very large hard drive.

Digital Video File Formats

Video file formats define the contents of a video file, such as how many video or audio streams it contains, the resolution, and the compression types. Digital video is generally recorded in the DV (digital video) format—and the files are very large. There are several common file formats that are used to compress and play digital video, including QuickTime, AVI, AFS, RM, and MPEG.

QuickTime (MOV and QT)

QuickTime, developed by Apple Computer in the early 1990s, was the first popular program to "put it all together" for desktop digital video. QuickTime provides both editing and playback interfaces for synchronized video and audio. QuickTime works well on both Macs and PCs, and it provides good compression, resulting in smaller file sizes.

Windows (AVI, AFS, WMF, WMV)

Shortly after Apple released QuickTime, Microsoft introduced a similar, but incompatible, product called Video for Windows, which uses an .AVI file extension. Since then, Microsoft has introduced other file formats, including .ASF (Advanced Streaming Format), .WMF (Windows Media Format), and .WMV (Windows Media Video).

Real (RA and RM)

Real Networks (and their predecessors) were the pioneers in streaming technologies when they introduced Real Audio in 1995. Since then, the Real formats (RA for Real Audio and RM for Real Media) are widely used for streaming media on both Macs and PCs. The advantage of Real is that their plug-ins are widely available and widely used. The compression is very good, and the quality is excellent.

MPEG (MPG and MP3)

MPEG is a file format as well as compression technique, and it is popular for high-end video applications. MPEG-2 is the format that is used to create DVDs. MP3 is an audio-only offshoot of MPEG. Using MP3, files for individual songs can be compressed down to sizes that are quite reasonable to send through standard Internet connections or to store on small MP3 players, such as iPods.

Using Existing Digital Video Files

If you do not have the inclination, equipment, or time to produce your own digital video movies, you may be able to obtain appropriate files through the Web or archives on a CD-ROM. Be sure you check the copyright restrictions, especially for applications that will be used or accessed outside the classroom.

Several video sites on the Web provide a collection of clips in various formats. These files can be downloaded to your computer. However, before downloading the movies, always check the permission statements, send an e-mail, or call the owner to find out whether you have the rights to use these movies in your projects. A resource list for video is included at the end of this chapter.

Guidelines for Video

Digital video files are generally very large; therefore, you must assess carefully whether you want to use video in a multimedia project—especially one for the Web. The following guidelines should be considered for video:

- Use digital video only when absolutely necessary.

- Keep the window size as small as possible (about one-quarter screen) to help improve performance.

- Check the size of the video files after they are recorded, especially if you are going to transfer them to a floppy diskette or via the Internet.

- Make sure there is adequate lighting when recording digital movies.

- Use a tripod for shooting video to minimize extra motion and achieve better compression.

- Shoot close-ups because the video will be viewed in a small window on the computer.

- Experiment with different compression options to obtain the best quality at the smallest file size.

- Check copyright restrictions on video segments, especially for material that will be used outside the classroom.

SUMMARY

Graphics, animations, audio, and video files can add life and interest to multimedia projects. They can also be used to illustrate and convey abstract concepts, and they can enhance students' visual literacy and their ability to think, learn, and communicate through visuals and other media. Designing and developing media files allow students to be creative and to investigate the presentation of information from several perspectives. Most students are enthusiastic about working with sound, graphics, and video.

Creating media files also presents some challenges for educators and students. The media files can be stored in many formats, and problems may arise when students have media files ready to incorporate into a project, but the program will not "see" or open the files. In addition, recording and editing usually require additional software and hardware, which may be in limited supply in classrooms.

This chapter presented a wide array of options for incorporating graphics, animations, audio, and video files. Although each software program will incorporate the media elements in a slightly different manner, almost all software programs (including basic word processors) now have the ability to add graphics, sound, and video. The potential is limited only by the imagination (and hardware) available to the students.

RESOURCES

Graphics and Animation Resources

Adobe (PhotoShop, Acrobat, Illustrator, Premier): http://www.adobe.com

Barry's Clip Art Server: http://www.barrysclipart.com/

ColorIt! By MicroFrontier: http://www.microfrontier.com/products/colorit40/

Corel (CorelDraw): http://www.corel.com

Digital Photography Exhibit: http://gcc.bradley.edu/exhibit/

Flags of the World: http://fotw.vexillum.com/flags/

Free Clipart from FCIT: http://etc.usf.edu/clipart/index.htm

GIF Construction Set: http://www.mindworkshop.com/

Graphic Converter: http://www.lemkesoft.de/en/graphcon.htm

LView Pro: http://www.lview.com/index1024.htm

Macromedia (Flash, FireWorks, DreamWeaver): http://www.macromedia.com

Media Links Free Graphics Page: http://www.erinet.com/cunning1/tiles.html

NASA Images: http://www.nasa.gov/multimedia/imagegallery/index.html

Scanning 101: http://webmonkey.wired.com/webmonkey/geektalk/97/41/index3a.html?tw=design

Scanning Tips: http://www.scantips.com/basics01.html

Audio Resources

Audio: http://www.comlab.ox.ac.uk/archive/audio.html

Audacity: http://audacity.sourceforge.net/

Classical MIDI Archives: http://www.classicalarchives.com/

GoldWave: http://www.goldwave.com

Harmony Central: http://www.harmony-central.com/MIDI/

MIDI Farm: http://www.midifarm.com/

U.S. Presidents of the 20th Century: http://www.lib.msu.edu/vincent/presidents/

Worldwide Internet Music Resources: http://www.music.indiana.edu/music_resources/

Video Resources

Adobe (Premier): http://www.adobe.com

Apple Computer (iMovie, iPhoto, FinalCut Pro): http://www.apple.com/ilife/

Library of Congress, Motion Pictures: http://lcweb2.loc.gov/ammem/browse/ListSome.php?format=Motion+Picture

Microsoft (Movie Maker): http://www.microsoft.com

Movie Sounds Page: http://www.moviesounds.com/

NASA Video Gallery: http://www.nasa.gov/multimedia/videogallery/index.html

Develop: Multimedia Development Tools

A SCENARIO

Arthur, John, Sara, and Rosita were just starting to design their group project about the War for Independence. They were tasked with conducting research related to the war and interviewing some contemporary soldiers to compare some of the battle weapons and tactics from 1776 with today's army. Ms. Martinez, their sixth-grade teacher, had already outlined the parameters and told the students that they could create their project in PowerPoint, iMovie, or Composer. Each of these formats was familiar to the students because they had used them for developing projects in the past.

They knew PowerPoint was a presentation program that could be used to produce a linear slide show-type report, but it also featured Action Buttons that could be used to add branches from one screen to another. Although iMovie did not provide the same level of interactivity as PowerPoint, it could be used to compile an impressive array of graphics, video clips, transitions, and sound. Netscape Composer was used to author Web pages with hyperlinks, graphics, text, and media elements. The hard part was deciding which tool would be the best for their project about the War for Independence.

Rosita suggested that they use PowerPoint because it was the easiest tool and because she liked the colorful templates that were provided for backgrounds. Arthur argued that iMovie would be best because they could easily incorporate the music from the era, student reenactments of historic events, and video clips downloaded from the Web. They could also make DVDs to take home and show their parents. Sara and John both liked the idea of linking together Web pages for the project and uploading them to the Web server at the district office.

As the students worked through the DECIDE phase of the project, conducting their brainstorming and research activities, it became clear that the Web was the best authoring environment. They were amazed at how many excellent sites existed that focused on the independence of the United States. By developing their project for the Web, they would be able to include links to these sites as a part of the project, as well as to include a streaming video of the interview with the soldier. They could also solicit feedback from students in other countries, especially the United Kingdom, to examine a different perspective about the war.

OVERVIEW

After the media elements are created, they are brought together into a final project with a software program, often called a *development program* or *authoring tool*. There are many affordable software programs that can be used to author and present a multimedia project.

This chapter provides an overview of programs that are commonly available in school environments, such as word processors, presentation programs, concept mapping applications, and hypermedia software. It also presents information on developing multimedia Web pages with HTML and Web editors, along with digital video editors, such as iMovie and MovieMaker. All of these options are inexpensive; relatively easy to use; and can include text, graphics, audio, and video.

This chapter includes the following:

- Multimedia documents and slide shows

    Word processors

    Image programs

    Presentation programs

- Hypermedia software

    HyperStudio

    eZedia

    Flash

- Web page production

    Text editors

    Web templates

    Application programs

    Web editors

- Digital video editors

    iMovie

    Microsoft MovieMaker

- Selecting a development tool

- Facilitating multimedia production in the classroom

MULTIMEDIA DOCUMENTS AND SLIDE SHOWS

Almost all application programs (such as word processors, image editors, and presentation software) can incorporate multimedia components. Most of these programs are inexpensive and available in school environments. With these tools, students and teachers can combine video, audio, text, and graphics to create multimedia documents or develop multimedia slide shows.

Word Processors

Word processors, such as Microsoft Word and AppleWorks, are important tools for all classrooms. In addition to enhancing students' writing abilities, word processors can be used to create multimedia documents, Web pages, and slide shows. Audio segments, as well as images and animations, can be embedded in documents. In addition, some word processors, such as AppleWorks, allow students to save the document as a slide show. As illustrated in Figure 6.1, students can create pages with text, images, sound, and so on, and then set the sequence and timing of the pages for a slideshow.

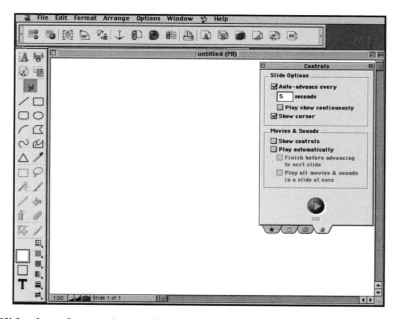

Figure 6.1. Slide show feature in AppleWorks.

Presentation Programs

Presentation programs, such as PowerPoint by Microsoft Corporation and Podium by Apple Computer, are popular because they are inexpensive, easy to learn, easy to use, and can incorporate multimedia elements such as graphics, digital video, and digital audio. Presentation programs generally include a variety of predesigned templates with colorful backgrounds and preformatted fonts to make the presentations look professional. These templates are very useful for novices who are developing their first multimedia projects. Some templates have a particular theme (such as a beach or party); others are more generic. Advise the students to select a design template that offers high contrast between background and text so the words will be easy to read. Presentation software also includes a wide array of clip art and media elements to incorporate into projects.

As the term *presentation* implies, presentation programs are often used for projects that will be presented to a large group, rather than projects designed for individual use. Linear projects, such as lectures and multimedia reports, where one screen automatically follows another, are easy for teachers and students to develop with presentation software. However, the current versions of PowerPoint also include "action buttons," where hotspots can be created on a screen to branch to a specified slide, Web address, or file (see Figure 6.2). By incorporating action buttons, students can add interactivity, such as menu options and questions.

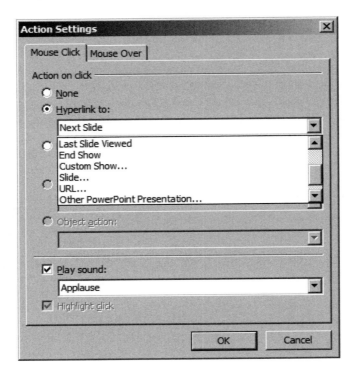

Figure 6.2. Features of action buttons in PowerPoint.

Image Programs

Image programs, such as KidPix and iPhoto are excellent tools for creating multimedia projects. KidPix is an easy-to-use image program that is designed for K–8 grades. It provides tools for creating and modifying images, and it can be used to inspire creativity and allow students to learn via visual elements. After creating or selecting their images in KidPix, students can also create a slideshow with the built-in tool. After the slides are created, they can be displayed as a slide show or saved as a QuickTime movie.

A very popular program for combining images is called iPhoto (part of the iLife suite by Apple Computer). iPhoto allows students to import, organize, edit, and share photographs and other graphics. In addition, students can add titles, transitions, and sounds. The images can be displayed in a slideshow, Web page, book, or movie (see Figure 6.3).

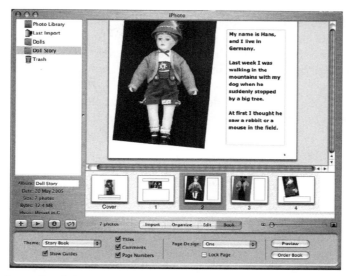

Figure 6.3. Creating a book in iPhoto.

HYPERMEDIA PROGRAMS

Hypermedia programs are designed so that information stored as text, graphics, audio, video, or animations can be accessed in associative, nonlinear ways. For example, the opening screen of a hypermedia application might contain a menu with four options. Buttons (areas) on the menu can be activated, allowing students to select one of the options and branch to the corresponding screen, audio file, video file, or animation. Hypermedia applications are often used for stand-alone projects (as opposed to class presentations) because they enable users to make their own choices and follow their own paths.

HyperStudio

Although the concept of hypermedia has existed for many years, it has become much more popular because of inexpensive programs such as HyperStudio. HyperStudio is a popular hypermedia program because it is easy to use and runs on both Macintosh and Windows computers. The basic structure of HyperStudio consists of stacks and cards (a file is referred to as a *stack,* and a computer screen is called a *card*). Each card can contain text items, buttons, graphics, and other multimedia elements (see Figure 6.4).

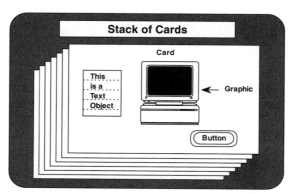

Figure 6.4. Structure of HyperStudio.

Text objects are similar to miniature word-processing blocks and are designed to contain text of various styles and sizes. *Buttons* are designated areas of the screens that can initiate an action, such as moving (branching) to another card or playing an audio, video, or animation. Graphics can be created with paint tools within the HyperStudio, or they can be imported from clip art or other graphics programs.

With HyperStudio, a series of pull-down menus and dialog windows are used to develop the applications. HyperStudio is an impressive package that provides built-in links to audio CDs, digital movies, and digitized audio. Animation tools, Web tools, and testing functions that can track correct and incorrect answers are also available.

eZedia

EZedia produces two hypermedia programs that are cost-effective for schools: eZediaMX and eZediaQTI. eZediaMX (see Figure 6.5) features a drag-and-drop environment, making it easy to add graphics, sound, movies, and text. You can also add navigation between frames, files, applications, and Web sites through linked media in the eZediaMX project. With eZediaMX, users can create digital portfolios, multimedia presentations, electronic slide shows, and interactive CD-ROMs projects. eZediaQTI is designed for the Web. Its drag-and-drop features make it easy to create Web sites, online presentations, interactive movies, and Internet banners. HTML programming knowledge is not required. Both programs allow students to create projects with various forms of interactivity (branches, quizzing, etc.). EzediaMX files are saved as a .zoi file for playback with eZedia Player; EzediaQTI files can be exported as QuickTime movies or HTML files.

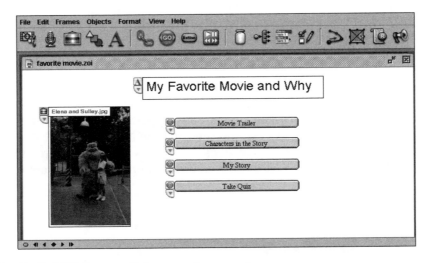

Figure 6.5. eZediaMX drag-and-drop environment.

Flash

Flash is a Macromedia product that has been rapidly gaining popularity in schools. Although originally designed to create animated Web pages, new versions of the product have broadened its application. For example, in addition to creating Web-friendly animations, it is a great tool for creating audio-enhanced and interactive presentations. Finished projects can be stand-alone, or they can be embedded into Web pages, presentation software, or other applications.

The workspace in Flash in called the Stage (see Figure 6.6). Flash has a tool palette that can be used to add text, shapes, and color to the Stage. The Stage is associated with a Timeline, which is made up of frames, much like a movie. This makes it relatively easy to create animations. For example, a circle can be drawn on the Stage in frame one of the Timeline, and a rectangle may be drawn on the Stage at frame 20 of the Timeline. Returning to frame one and selecting "tween" under the Properties option automatically puts the animation in place, moving and morphing the circle to a rectangle as it is "played" on the Timeline.

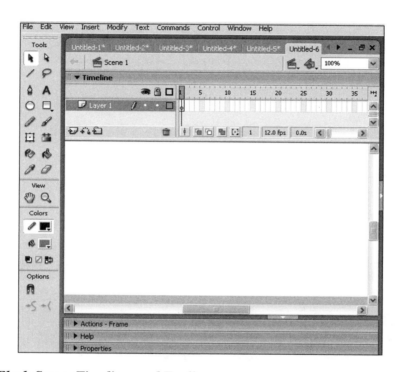

Figure 6.6. Flash Stage, Timeline, and Toolbar.

It is possible to have multiple Timelines in Flash, called layers. This allows the creator to control animations independently. Interactivity is possible with buttons, behaviors, and ActionScripts. Behaviors are predefined actions—ActionScript (Flash's programming language) that has been written for the creator. Creators may also write their own ActionScripts, enabling creators to design individualized, sophisticated, and controlled interactions between users and the program. Finished projects are saved as movies and are viewable through browsers with the Flash plug-in.

WEB PAGE PRODUCTION

Access to the Internet and the World Wide Web is becoming more and more common for schools. This access provides a new environment for publishing multimedia projects. With a simple word processor, students can easily create Web pages that can be viewed by people throughout the world. Even if a school is not connected to the Internet, it is possible for students to use Web technology to publish documents that are available on school networks or stand-alone computers.

All Web pages are derived from text files that are interpreted and displayed by Web browsers (such as Netscape or Internet Explorer). For example, when the text file displayed in Figure 6.7 is displayed through a browser, the student will see the Web page illustrated in Figure 6.8.

```
<HTML>
<HEAD>
<TITLE>Geography Home Page</TITLE></HEAD>
<BODY>
<IMG SRC ="geo.gif">
<BR>
<H2>This page provides links relevant to Freshman Geography</H2>
<P>
Click to see a <A HREF="CA.mov">movie</A> about Central America.
<BR>
<HR>
<UL>
<LI><A HREF="http://www.geo.gov/">Geography sites</A>
<LI><A HREF="http://www.chs.edu/assign/">Assignments</A>
<LI><A HREF="http://www.chs.edu/reports/">Student reports</A>
</UL>
<HR>
</BODY>
</HTML>
```

Figure 6.7. Text file (HTML) for a Web page.

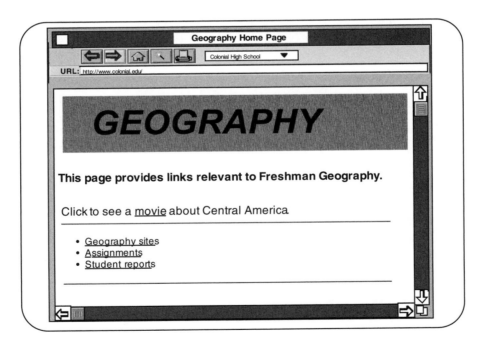

Figure 6.8. Web page created from code in Figure 6.7.

The text files used in Web documents adhere to a specific format called the *HyperText Markup Language* or HTML. HTML files use *tags* (words embedded between the < and > characters) to define how information is formatted on the screen. For example, in the line <B>**This is bold.**</B>, the first tag turns the bold attribute on, and the second one (the one with the /B) turns off the bold attribute. A few common style tags are illustrated in Table 6.1.

Table 6.1.

HTML Quick Reference Guide

	Tag	Definition
Essential Parts	<HTML> <HEAD> <TITLE>...</TITLE> </HEAD> <BODY>...</BODY> </HTML>	These tags represent the template or "skeleton" of an HTML document. HTML tags identify the beginning and ending of the document; HEAD tags contain the TITLE tags, which identify the page's bookmark name; and BODY tags contain the text, pictures, headings, etc. of the document.
Formatting Text: Headings	<H1>...</H1> <H2>...</H2> <H3>...</H3> <H4>...</H4> <H5>...</H5> <H6>...</H6>	HTML has six levels of headings that are displayed in bolder and separate type than the regular body text. Level 1 is the largest heading; Level 6 is the smallest heading.
Formatting Text: Physical Styles	<B>...</B> <I>...</I> <U>...</U> <TT>...</TT>	Physical style tags tell browsers how to display text. For example, text within the tags <B>...</B> will be **bold-face**; text within the tags <I>...</I> will be *italicized*; text within the tags <U>...</U> will be <u>underlined</u>; and text within the tags <TT>...</TT> will be a `typewriter font`.
Formatting Text: Paragraphs	<PRE>...</PRE> <P>...</P> 	A variety of tags are used to format paragraphs. <PRE>...</PRE> displays text with its original carriage returns and spacing (preformat); <P> ...</P> identifies a paragraph; and inserts a carriage return. does not have an ending tag.
Making Lists	<UL> <LI>first item <LI>second item <LI>third item </UL>	<UL>...</UL> creates an unordered list. <LI>tags are placed within the <UL>and </UL> tags to identify each item in the list. Ordered lists that display numbers are created by using <OL>and </OL> instead of <UL>and </UL>. <LI>tags are placed within the <OL> and </OL>tags, also.
Displaying an Image	<IMG SRC = "image.gif" ALT = "alternative text"><HR>	Place the name of the image in "image.gif" and "alternative text." <HR> displays a horizontal line.
Creating Hyperlinks	<A HREF = "http://whereto.com"> location</A> <A HREF = "MAILTO :name@my.domain"> e-mail address</A>	Place the location's address in "http://whereto.com" and link information in "location." The MAILTO link sends an e-mail message. Insert your e-mail address in both locations.
Playing Movies and Sounds	<A HREF="file_ name">instructions </A>	Place the name of the sound or movie in "file_name" and directions (such as "click here") in "instructions."

About 50 tags are commonly used for HTML. Some define the text styles; some are used to embed audio or video links; and others format the bullets, colors, and similar elements. Excellent HTML tutorials are available online. They are listed in the references at the end of this chapter.

Creating a Web page may appear to be intimidating, but many elementary school students are developing are doing it every day. In some cases, they learn a few basic HTML tags and then gradually expand their "vocabulary" as they become more experienced. In other cases, they do not learn HTML at all; instead, they use a word processor or Web editor that allows them to create Web documents without typing in any command codes.

There are several ways to create a Web page, including:

- Create an HTML page "by hand" with a text editor.

- Use a template (such as TeacherWeb).

- Use an application program, such as Microsoft Word or PowerPoint, and Save As . . . Web Page.

- Use a Web editor, such as Microsoft FrontPage, Netscape Composer, or Macromedia DreamWeaver.

Creating a Web Page with a Text Editor

One of the least expensive methods for creating Web pages is to use the free text editors that come with a computer, such as *SimpleText* on a Macintosh and *NotePad* on a Windows machine. An advantage of creating HTML in these simple text editors is that they save the files in text-only format—exactly the format needed for the final files.

To create HTML files in a text editor, you must type in all of the required codes (as illustrated in Figure 6.7). Then, save the file with an .htm or .html extension. Note that the images and media elements will be separate files (usually saved in the same directory). When you are finished, test the file by displaying it through a Web browser.

Keep in mind that no matter how a Web page is created, it is stored in HTML code. Even though there are many other options, it is wise to understand at least the basics of HTML—that way you and the students will be able to make minor changes to Web pages no matter how or where they were created.

Creating a Web Page with a Template

Another way to create Web pages is to use a template. These templates use online forms—you simply fill in the forms, and a Web page is generated. Several Web sites (especially designed for teachers) provide free templates. These sites will also host your pages—they store them on their Web server, so you don't have to worry about uploading or storing them on a local Web server.

The following Web sites offer templates for teachers:

TeacherWeb (http://teacherweb.com/) provides a very straightforward design. Options are available to create school Web sites with areas for a calendar, announcements, links, frequently asked questions, and assignments.

SchoolNotes (http://www.schoolnotes.com/) allows teachers to create notes for homework and class information and post them on the Web.

Myschoolonline.com (http://myschoolonline.com/golocal/) is a large online network dedicated to children's learning.

Classroom.Tripod.com (http://classroom.tripod.com/) has homepage-building tools to help you to create the classrooms of the future.

Creating a Web Page with a Word Processor and Other Application Programs

Web pages have become so popular that many of the standard word processing programs, spreadsheets, presentation programs, and desktop publishing tools include an option to save the file as a Web page (in HTML format). These programs offer a very fast, efficient way to create Web documents from existing documents. For example, students could write stories in Microsoft Word, then use the "Save As . . . Web Page" to convert it into HTML. At that point, it can be uploaded to a Web server and accessed via a Web browser. Application programs are a great way to get started on large, text-intensive projects.

Creating a Web Page with a Web Editor

Several Web editors are available that provide users with a *WYSIWYG* (what you see is what you get) environment. Some of the most popular programs include Microsoft FrontPage, Netscape Composer, and Macromedia DreamWeaver. Netscape Composer is a free download, and DreamWeaver, and FrontPage are relatively inexpensive.

These programs allow users to type text on their Web pages just as they would in a word processing program. Styles, such as bold, are added by highlighting the text and selecting a style on the menu bar. Users do not see the HTML code; it is generated "behind the scenes" and is interpreted by the Web browser. It is possible to insert graphics, include lists, create tables, and insert forms with these programs as well (see Figure 6.9).

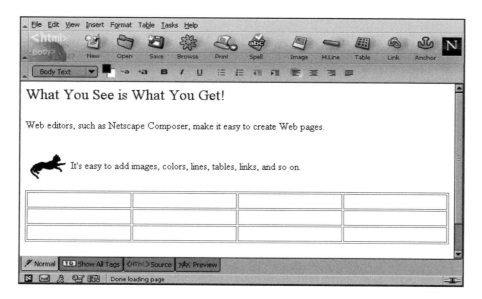

Figure 6.9. Netscape Composer Interface.

After a Web page is created, it (and all relevant media files) must be uploaded to a Web server so the rest of the world can see it. To upload files to a Web server, you may need special permissions and passwords. Most webmasters/administrators are extremely cautious about granting permission to upload files because of the prevalence of hackers and viruses. You may be asked to send the files to the administrator, and he or she will place them on the server.

DIGITAL VIDEO PROGRAMS AND EDITORS

Producing a video project involves a great deal of planning, organizing, and creative energy. As illustrated in Table 6.2, the phases in a video production project are often referred to as pre-production, production, and post-production. The video files can be used in a stand-alone mode (as a videotape, for example), or they can be integrated into a hypermedia, presentation, or Web program.

Table 6.2.

Phases of Digital Video Projects

Pre-Production	Production	Post-Production
• Select project idea/goal • Outline project • Write scripts and storyboards • Assign roles • Design sets (if necessary)	• Shoot video • Record audio • Create graphics • Digitize all analog elements	• Import video into editing software • Edit video clips • Add transitions • Add title slides • Combine the clips into movie file

In the past, editing the video clips into a finished movie was a very complex process that involved high-end, expensive equipment, consisting of multiple videotape players, recorders, and control devices. Thanks to advancements in hardware and software, it is now possible to do very sophisticated editing with a classroom computer. Popular video-editing programs include iMovie and Final Cut Pro by Apple Computer, Windows Movie Maker by Microsoft, and Premier by Adobe. Web sites for these products are provided at the end of this chapter.

SELECTING A DEVELOPMENT TOOL

Each of the development tools described in this chapter has features that are useful for student-created multimedia projects. The following guidelines may help determine which type of tool is best for a particular situation.

- If cost is a factor, application programs or Web pages may be the least expensive. Schools can purchase programs such as PowerPoint at minimal cost; Web pages can be created in text editors or Web creation programs that are free.

- For maximum interactivity, hypermedia programs may be the best. Hypermedia programs are designed to contain hyperlinks to graphics and media elements. In addition, they usually contain question formats and scoring techniques.

- For ease of use, application programs are the best. See Table 6.3 for a comparison of the development tools presented in this chapter.

- Do not use Web programs if a large amount of audio and video is incorporated into the project. The bandwidth (speed) of the Internet is a major constraint in the amount of audio and video that can be added to Web pages.

Table 6.3.

Comparison of Development Tools

Attribute	Application	Hypermedia	Web Pages	Digital Editors
Learning curve	Low	High	Medium	High
Cost	Low	Medium	Low	Low
Amount of interactivity	Low	High	Medium	Low
Amount of multimedia	Medium	High	Low	High

FACILITATING MULTIMEDIA PROJECTS IN THE CLASSROOM

As the students enter the DEVELOP phase of the project, they compile the media elements based on the information in their flowcharts and storyboards. At this point, the teacher's role is that of a facilitator. This includes the following activities:

- Ensuring that all of the necessary equipment, batteries, software, and so on are available

- Reviewing necessary prerequisite skills related to the technology or concepts related to the content

- Circulating the room, assisting students as they need it

- Monitoring the progress of each group or student, ensuring that students stay on task

- Troubleshooting hardware and software issues

- Conducting formative evaluation and providing ongoing feedback to students' progress

- Being aware of the time allotted for the activity in relation to the progress

- Having a backup plan (or two) in case the technology crashes

- Emphasizing the relationship to the lesson's goals

Multimedia activities in the classroom can be exciting, effective, and motivating. Unfortunately, they also offer opportunities for students to be distracted, off-task, and disruptive. Students may misbehave because they become bored, frustrated, or misdirected. However, several techniques can assist in keeping students on task and engaged with the activity and the lesson's goals, including the following:

- Present clear goals and expectations

- Provide adequate structure

- Keep students actively involved

- Assign "Tech Buddies"

- Be flexible

- Teach, model, and enforce time management

Present Clear Goals and Expectations

For some teachers, the thought of having students working cooperatively with multimedia leads to nightmares, as they imagine chaos in the classroom. However, if students are engaged, the discipline problems can actually decrease or disappear entirely! Begin by developing a set of expectations that you and the students can live with—rules that are enforceable. These expectations might include issues such as how to handle the equipment; an appropriate volume level for voices; strategies for seeking help (such as placing a paper cup on the monitor), and so on. Be patient and consistent—you'll be amazed at how engaged the students will become with their activities!

Provide Adequate Structure

Whether your students are first graders or seniors in high school, you must provide a clear framework for them. In other words, "set the stage" at the beginning, telling the students the procedure, exactly what is required (such as writing storyboards), how the activity will be assessed (if you have a rubric, share it with them or let them help you create one), and how much time is allowed for each phase of the activity. If students are working in groups, the roles of the team members should be clear, as well as how the group will be assessed (individually or collectively).

One way to provide structure and assign computer use is by using a Jigsaw cooperative learning approach. For example, each team's graphic artists can work with the graphic artists from other teams to select and review each other's media needs on the class computers. If there were eight groups of students, one person from each group could be designated as the group's graphic artist. These students would form their own group (eight students) to help create and research each other's graphics on the classroom computers. Similarly, the programmers from each group could work together to produce the templates for the projects.

Keep Students Actively Involved

The saying "Idle hands are the Devil's workshop" is very true: if students are waiting for their turn with a camera or computer, they may well look for other diversions. Multimedia activities must be designed to keep all students engaged at all times—no small order! When designing a multimedia project for groups using limited resources, always include supplemental activities that can be completed without hardware. For example, if students are waiting to use a computer, they can conduct research through traditional means (books), work at a learning center that has related manipulatives, evaluate their peers' projects, or write the script for a project.

If limited peripherals (such as a scanner, camera, and so on) and software are available, you may rotate student groups so that they are assigned a different "station" each day. For example, a scanner might be attached to Computer One; Adobe Photoshop might be installed on Computer Two; a video editor might be installed on Computer Three; and Computer Four may have a connection to the Internet. Rotating assignments allows student groups to plan their time using a scanner, a single copy of Adobe Photoshop, or other limited resources. Students may also use a sign-up sheet to use a particular computer, a digital camera, camcorder, or other equipment.

Assign Tech Buddies

Many teachers have found that assigning tech buddies helps to reduce the amount of questions and off-task behavior. By working together, tech buddies can help each other solve problems and troubleshoot. This approach has also been referred to as the "Ask Three Before Me" rule—students must ask three classmates for assistance before seeking the teacher. Student involvement provides valuable assistance for the teacher and helps build students' self-esteem.

Be Flexible

Teachers should accept the fact that technology may not fit neatly into traditional paradigms. For multimedia to foster collaboration, cross-discipline explorations, and complex problem solving, the school schedules may have to be adjusted—some activities may require 30 minutes; others three hours. In addition, Murphy's Law may strike at any time; always have a backup plan (or two).

Teach, Model, and Enforce Time Management

At first, this may seem to be a direct contradiction of the previous guideline ("Be flexible") . Flexibility and time management are both important—for example, suppose you have restructured your class schedule to allow three hours for a cross-curricular, multimedia activity. The students, however, are being very creative, and they are experimenting with every font that PowerPoint allows. The three hours are almost over; one group is finished; one is almost done; and the other three groups would need an additional two hours! Possible solutions to this dilemma include setting a kitchen timer to allow specific amounts of time for substeps. For example, you could announce, "You will have 45 minutes to select your background, fonts, and clipart for the project" (assuming that the planning of the project was previously completed). If various groups and students must share computers, logs with "time in" and "time out" are also helpful, along with a strict rotational schedule (refer back to "Scheduling Computer Time" in Chapter 3).

SUMMARY

The final step in the development process is to combine the text, graphics, and media elements with a development tool. There are many alternatives on the market. This chapter focused on several inexpensive options for schools: application programs, hypermedia, Web pages, and digital movies. As you are planning the curriculum tools for your classroom, consider these tools and others that will allow your students to produce and deliver their products in a timely fashion.

RESOURCES

HTML Tutorials

A Beginners Guide to HTML: http://archive.ncsa.uiuc.edu/General/Internet/WWW/

An Interactive Tutorial for Beginners: http://www.davesite.com/webstation/html/

Bare Bones Guide to HTML: http://werbach.com/barebones/

Writing HTML: http://www.mcli.dist.maricopa.edu/tut/

Applications and Hypermedia

eZedia: at http://www.ezedia.com/

HyperStudio: at http://www.hyperstudio.com/

HyperStudio Showcase: at http://www.hyperstudio.com/showcase/index.html

iLife: at http://www.apple.com/iLife/

KidPix: at http://www.riverdeep.net/products/kid_pix/kpd4.jhtml

Macromedia (Flash and DreamWeaver): at http://www.macromedia.com

Microsoft (MovieMaker and FrontPage): at http://www.microsoft.com

Multimedia Authoring Web: http://www.mcli.dist.maricopa.edu/authoring/

PowerPoint in the Classroom: at http://www.actden.com/pp/

Digital Video Information on the Web

Adobe Premier: http://www.adobe.com/products/premiere/main.html

Desktop Video (About.com): http://desktopvideo.about.com

DV Magazine: http://www.dv.com

Desktop Video Handbook: http://www.videoguys.com/dtvhome.html

Digital Video Primer: http://www.adobe.com/motion/events/pdfs/dvprimer.pdf

Final Cut Pro (Apple): http://www.apple.com/finalcutpro

No Strings Attached: http://etc.usf.edu/wireless/default.htm

3Video Guide: http://pblmm.k12.ca.us/TechHelp/VideoHelp/VideoGuide.html

Evaluate

A SCENARIO

Mrs. Jenkins worked with her teacher partner, Ms. Tinder, to plan a multimedia project with her students. Mrs. Jenkins was unclear how she would assess the students if they worked in groups and was concerned about adequately evaluating all of their work and documenting that it met state standards. She thought about creating a rubric for evaluating the project once it was complete, but how would she ensure students were making appropriate progress as they went through the steps of creating their projects?

It seemed as though each of these stages should be evaluated so that students knew they were on the right track. Ms. Tinder confirmed Mrs. Jenkins' belief about multiple stages of evaluation, emphasizing the importance of ongoing, formative assessment. Through experience, Ms. Tinder learned that guiding and assessing students' work through each stage of project development saved time, ensured students were meeting project goals, and provided Ms. Tinder with feedback toward her instruction, allowing her to provide additional assistance if necessary.

Ms. Tinder provided Mrs. Jenkins with several sample rubrics she could use at each stage of the multimedia project. At first, Mrs. Jenkins was a bit overwhelmed, but when Ms. Tinder explained that the rubrics were not completed all at once, Mrs. Jenkins felt empowered knowing that she could assess her students at each stage of the multimedia project. Ms. Tinder showed her how to apply the results of each rubric to a final rubric at the end of the project. She also instructed Ms. Jenkins on how she could assign individual and group grades. Mrs. Jenkins organized the rubrics by stages. Ms. Tinder reminded her to share the rubrics with her students before each stage so they knew what to expect. She encouraged Mrs. Jenkins to allow her students to offer input and suggestions for the rubrics as well.

OVERVIEW

To ensure multimedia projects are purposeful, educators need to identify the projects' specific objectives and how these relate to district or state standards. In addition, teachers must correlate the objectives with specific assessment measures to ensure students are learning what has been specified in each objective. Assessment criteria can be clarified and categorized using rubrics. Rubrics can provide feedback about the effectiveness of instruction and provide benchmarks for measuring and documenting students' progress. In addition, rubrics let students know what is expected of them. They serve as a grade contract. Based on the expectations outlined in a rubric, students can plan their time accordingly. For example, if video is not a requirement for a multimedia project, students should not spend time incorporating it into their project unless it is appropriate or they have extra time on their hands. Rubrics can help students set their priorities and better manage their projects, as well as help teachers assess students' progress throughout the development of the multimedia projects.

Poor learning experiences can be avoided through well-planned and frequently assessed projects. Formative assessment provides constructive feedback at each phase of the DDD-E process. Without it, students may encounter unnecessary obstacles, extra work, frustration, unfinished products, and fragmented learning. Ongoing assessment helps educators teach for understanding and ensures that students are ready to move on to the next step of a project. This chapter defines several assessment techniques and their relationship to multimedia projects. In addition, it provides information on creating rubrics and provides sample rubrics for each phase of the DDD-E process. Topics include the following:

- Alternative assessment techniques
    The role of multimedia in alternative assessment

- Assessment strategies
    Creating a rubric
    Using rubrics
    Additional rubric options

- Assigning grades

- Reflections and future goals

ALTERNATIVE ASSESSMENT TECHNIQUES

There are a variety of ways to evaluate students' learning. Most schools use standardized tests, but critics claim that these only measure how well a student learns without considering whether he or she can apply what was learned. For example, a student may perform well on a simple mathematics test but still be unable to make correct change. Or a student may score well on a written driving test but still be a poor driver. Proponents of alternative assessment claim that people's capability is found in their ability to produce or perform, not on how well they answer questions on multiple-choice, true or false, or other traditional forms of tests (Ahn 2004; Culbertson and Jalongo 1999; Mabry 1999). Researchers note that traditional tests tend to reveal only what a student can recall or recognize and often focus on low-level knowledge objectives (Alleman and Brophy 1999; Mabry 1999).

Alternative assessment is assessment in some form other than the true or false, multiple-choice, matching, and fill-in-the-blank responses often associated with standardized tests. Performance-based assessment, authentic assessment, and portfolio assessment are forms of alternative assessment. Many of these terms overlap and are used interchangeably. They are defined as follows.

Performance-based assessment requires teachers to evaluate a student's knowledge and skills by observing the student do something (e.g., participating in a debate, playing an instrument, dribbling a basketball) or create something that results in a tangible product (e.g., a model or drawing, a computer program, a blouse).

Authentic assessment includes performance tests, observations, interviews, exhibitions, and portfolios. The goal of authentic assessment is to involve students in activities that better represent what they are likely to face outside the school setting. The context, purpose, audience, and constraints of the task *must* connect to real-world situations and problems. For example, students might be asked to identify the chemical composition of a given solution by conducting various analyses, or they might take samples from local rivers and lakes and identify pollutants. Both tasks would be performance-based, but the latter would be considered authentic because it involves and addresses a real-world problem.

Portfolio assessment is a systematic collection of a student's best work and may include narrative descriptions, records of observation, test results, student reflections or self-evaluations, and so on. Portfolios show growth over time, focusing on a student's progress rather than on a finished product. A portfolio provides a broad view of a student's achievements. E-portfolios (electronic portfolios) may be used to blend technology, accountability, and assessment. Ahn (2004) describes an e-portfolio in which specific learning standards were outlined, allowing students to showcase their exemplary work.

Based on the needs of the learner, alternative assessment techniques have the advantage of providing teachers and parents with directly observable products and clear evidence of students' performance. Assessment results are both meaningful and useful for improving instruction. The following guidelines may be used for creating, monitoring, and implementing alternative assessment in the classroom:

- Plan assessment alongside instruction, not as an afterthought. Your assessment plan should represent what is valued instructionally.

- Ensure that assessments benefit all learners and inform teaching practices.

- Make expectations clear.

- Collect examples of alternative assessments and activities and modify them for your students.

- Include peer assessment techniques. This can enhance students' evaluation skills and accountability.

- Use assessment results to develop learner profiles.

The Role of Multimedia in Alternative Assessment

Creating multimedia projects provides ample opportunities for performance-based assessment, authentic assessment, and portfolio assessment. Table 7.1 identifies project ideas for each of these assessment techniques. Evaluating students on their performance places greater emphasis on comprehension, critical thinking, reasoning, problem solving, and metacognitive processes (Jonassen 2000; Mabry 1999).

Table 7.1.

Multimedia Project Ideas for Various Assessment Techniques

Assessment Technique	Relationship to Multimedia Projects
Performance-Based Assessment	Multimedia projects can be used to demonstrate students' proficiency in specific computer skills; they also serve as a forum for demonstrating and presenting the students' knowledge and skills. For example, using a variety of media elements, students may create a project that demonstrates their knowledge of the water cycle, different body systems, plate tectonics, or other topic.
Authentic Assessment	Multimedia projects may be designed to support classroom presentations, similar to what students are likely to encounter as professionals. In addition, students may create projects that are designed to gather data for analysis (such as a Web page that collects information from users).
Portfolio Assessment	A multimedia database or e-portfolio can be designed to house digitized samples of a student's work. This includes reading samples (a recording of a student reading aloud), handwriting samples, homework, writing samples, artwork, and performances. Items may be entered into the computer by keyboard, a scanner, microphone, video, or digital camera. Students may also create multimedia resumes.

In addition to evaluating students on the final outcome of their performance, it is important to assess students' progress through each step of the DDD-E process. To create successful multimedia projects, assessment must be ongoing. It begins with the DECIDE process and ends with an evaluation of the final product.

ASSESSMENT STRATEGIES

Checklists, narrative or anecdotal approaches, and rubrics are different ways to evaluate a student's performance. Checklists indicate whether certain elements are present; narrative reports consist of a teacher's written notes or documentation of students' progress; and rubrics are used to evaluate designated performance criteria with a rating scale. Each of these can be used to guide students through each step of their project. In addition to teacher observations and anecdotal notes, daily journals (see Chapter 3) can help teachers diagnose each group's progress, problem-solving skills, and social skills. Checklists and rubrics help students know what is expected, leaving the teacher more time to advise and assist students with specific questions.

Creating a Rubric

Before developing a rubric, you must ask yourself the following questions:

- What state or district standards am I addressing?

What knowledge, skills, or concepts am I trying to assess?

- At what level should my students be performing?

- What criteria should I use to judge students' performance?

After identifying the standards and instructional goals, consider the qualities that need to be displayed in a student's work to illustrate proficient or "top level" performance of these goals. For example, "the student lists and describes the contributions of four people associated with the California Gold Rush." After developing the criteria for the highest level of performance, define the criteria for the lowest level of performance. For example, "the student is unable to list or describe the contributions of anyone associated with the California Gold Rush." After developing the high- and low-level criteria, compare and contrast the two to arrive at the middle level of performance. For example, "the student correctly identifies and describes the contributions of two people associated with the California Gold Rush." If additional distinctions are necessary, make comparisons between the existing criteria to arrive at other score levels.

Moskal and Leydens (2000) discuss the validity and reliability of rubrics. Validity includes the following:

- Content-related evidence—the extent the assessment instrument reflects students' knowledge in a particular content area

- Construct-related evidence—the extent the assessment instrument measures students' reasoning, problem-solving, or other processing skills

- Criterion-related evidence—the extent the assessment instrument identifies how well a student's performance can be generalized to other, more relevant activities (e.g., how well the student will perform outside of school or in a different situation)

Moskal and Leydens (2000, 4) note that "Since establishing validity is dependent on the purpose of the assessment, teachers should clearly state what they hope to learn about the responding students (i.e., the purpose) and how the students will display these proficiencies (i.e., the objectives)." They list three steps for evaluating the appropriateness of scoring categories to a stated purpose:

1. State the assessment purpose and objectives.

2. Develop score criteria for each objective.

3. Reflect on the following:

   - Are all of the objectives measured through the scoring criteria?

   - Are any of the scoring criteria unrelated to the objectives?

Teachers should avoid making vague statements such as, "The student covers the topic completely and in depth." What does this mean? What are the criteria for such an accomplishment? What has the student learned? In addition to validity issues, vague or general statements reduce the reliability of the rubric.

Reliability refers to the consistency of assessment scores. Two forms of reliability are interrater reliability and intrarater reliability. Interrater reliability is based on how well or how closely different evaluators or "raters" assess the same scores. If evaluators come to the same conclusion, then the assessment has "interrater reliability." It is important to have set criteria to guide the rating process. Intrarater reliability focuses on outside factors that may influence the scoring of students' work. For example, a rater's fatigue level, mood, or bias may influence the scoring process if the criteria are too subjective. By establishing a description of the scoring criteria in advance, well-designed scoring rubrics address this concern (Moskal 2003; Moskal and Leydens 2000).

When designing a rubric, consider the age and ability level of the students. Note the simplicity of the primary rubric at the end of this chapter (see the Primary MM Rubric blackline). Encourage student input. This allows students to work toward individual goals and to create their own learning experiences. Keep rubrics short, simple, and to the point. Categorize topic areas or provide separate rubrics for each area, depending on the project's sophistication. For beginning projects, focus on only a few outcomes.

Numbers or words (e.g., deficient, novice, apprentice, intermediate, proficient) may be used as a scale to evaluate learning outcomes. It is important that the criteria for each rating is established and listed on the rubric. For example, expanding on the Gold Rush example given earlier, a student would be given a score of "four" if she were able to list and describe the contributions of four people associated with the California Gold Rush, a "three" for three people, a "two" for two people, and a "one" for one person. A score of "zero" would be assigned if she were unable to do the task. Listing the criteria on the rubric or having it readily available for students provides them with clear expectations and performance standards.

In addition to content, teachers may assess students' multimedia projects according to required media elements, design, and so on. These would be considered in the construction of the rubric as well and are discussed in more detail under "Using Rubrics."

Resources for Creating and Finding Sample Rubrics

Sample rubrics can be found on the Internet at a variety of Web sites. In addition, there are online tools available to help teachers construct their own rubrics. Examples include the following:

Kathy Schrock's Guide for Educators: Assessment and Rubric Information
http://school.discovery.com/schrockguide/assess.html
> Lists multiple links to rubric resources, articles, examples, and more.

Midlink Magazine Teacher Resource Room: http://www.ncsu.edu/midlink/ho.html
> Provides links to rubrics, evaluation resources, and downloadable rubric templates.

Rubistar: http://rubistar.4teachers.org/
> Provides sample rubrics for a variety of topics, as well as an online rubric generator where teachers can create or customize their own rubrics. Both English and Spanish versions are available.

Rubrics for Web Lessons: http://edweb.sdsu.edu/webquest/rubrics/weblessons.htm
> Provides additional information on authentic assessment and rubrics, as well as links to rubric examples.

Rubrics allow teachers to clarify criteria in specific forms and make project assessment more objective and consistent. In addition, rubrics allow students to begin their projects with clear and consistent guidelines by which they will be evaluated. Students know what is expected of them and their peers. Rubrics are useful for providing feedback and documenting students' progress. Identifying what students should know and how you will know when they know it is key to creating valid and reliable rubrics.

Using Rubrics

To help students understand how rubrics will be used to evaluate their multimedia projects, review several existing projects. These may be teacher-created for demonstration purposes, samples included with the multimedia program, projects from previous classes, or examples downloaded from the Internet. Review projects that are comparable to your students' ability levels. Encourage students to discuss what they like and dislike about the projects, the projects' strengths and weaknesses, and what they might do to make the project better. Decide what criteria might be used to evaluate the projects. Review sample projects before the DESIGN stage.

As mentioned, rubrics ensure that the students and teacher understand how the project will be evaluated. It is important to provide students with a list of evaluation criteria and standards for the assigned multimedia project at the onset of their projects. Students will know what is expected of them and may put more effort into their projects because of it. Encourage students to use the rubrics to guide them during the learning process and to explain the rubrics to their parents.

Rubrics can be designed to address each step of the DDD-E process and the desired outcome or focus of the multimedia projects. Steps include the following:

- DECIDE—Brainstorming and researching

- DESIGN—Planning and designing

- DEVELOP—Gathering and creating media

- EVALUATE—Evaluating final projects

Figure 7.1 depicts the evaluation stages of the DDD-E process. Note that the teacher reviews daily journals every day to ensure the groups' progress and to help the teacher facilitate instruction. With the exception of the daily journal, each item in Figure 7.1 is included as a blackline master at the end of this chapter. The daily journal entry sheet is in Chapter 3. Additional checklists can be found in Chapter 4.

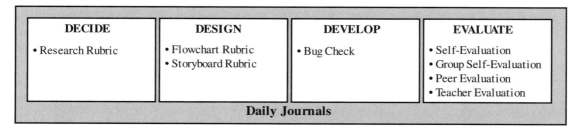

DECIDE	DESIGN	DEVELOP	EVALUATE
• Research Rubric	• Flowchart Rubric • Storyboard Rubric	• Bug Check	• Self-Evaluation • Group Self-Evaluation • Peer Evaluation • Teacher Evaluation
Daily Journals			

Figure 7.1. Evaluation stages of the DDD-E process.

DECIDE. Assessment begins with the groups' original idea and their ability to define the major sections of their reports, as well as how these sections relate to each other. Students should be able to articulate their research question, explain why it is important, and discuss how they intend to pursue it. Following the students' initial research, the teacher may decide to collect, review, and discuss each group's brainstorming or KWL Knowledge Chart (see Chapter 3), as well as their research findings. Teachers can check the accuracy of the information, ensure that students are using a variety of resources, and verify that the students are addressing the stated questions. Note that the defining criteria for each score need to be defined by the teacher (and students, if they helped create the rubric). A sample Research Rubric blackline master appears at the end of this chapter.

DESIGN. After their research has been verified, students need to map and define their ideas through flowcharts. After reviewing the flowcharts, the teacher should meet with each group to discuss the anticipated links, sequences, and section relationships identified in their flowcharts. Assessment may be based on the flowchart's structure, links, clarity, symbols, and labels. Note that the defining criteria for each score need to be defined by the teacher (and students, if they helped create the rubric). See the Design Rubric blackline master at the end of this chapter for an example.

Storyboard production can begin after the flowcharts have been approved. Storyboards help students plan how their computer screens will look and relate to each other. Students should make their storyboards as clear and complete as possible. This allows the teacher to provide guidance before the students invest a great amount of time in the final production phase. Teachers may want to provide students with a list of design guidelines (see Chapter 4). The Flowchart Rubric blackline master at the end of this chapter can be used as an example. Again, the defining criteria for each score need to be defined by the teacher (and students, if they helped create the rubric). The final production phase takes place on the computer after the groups' storyboards have been approved.

DEVELOP. In the DEVELOP phase, students construct their final product to meet the standards and criteria set at the beginning of the assignment. Before students submit their projects for final evaluation, projects should go through a review and debugging phase. This is best performed by their peers. Students can check each other's projects to see if they meet the required criteria, as well as check for programming, spelling, and punctuation errors. A Bug Stops Here blackline master is available at the end of the chapter.

EVALUATE. Self-, peer, and teacher evaluations occur after the projects are complete. These evaluations provide students with multiple levels of feedback. Self-evaluation encourages students to reflect on what they learned as well as how it was learned. In addition, it provides students with the opportunity to elaborate on what went well and what they might have done differently. Peer evaluation offers students another audience for their projects. It allows students to measure the extent to which they were able to successfully explain their work and ideas to their peers. In addition, peer evaluations allow students to practice their evaluation skills, provide ideas and constructive feedback, and help each other with the projects. Peer evaluations may also be used within groups (intragroup evaluation) to evaluate each member's cooperative efforts. (See Group Self-Evaluation blackline master at the end of this chapter.) Teacher assessment provides ongoing support and guidance, as well as a final evaluation of the project. The teacher's evaluation should reflect the criteria established during the beginning stages of the project.

The project's final evaluation may be based on one or more of the following: content learning, technology skills, design skills (see Additional Rubric Options section), as well as media appropriateness, social skills, or self-reflection—depending on the purpose of the project. The depth and scope of the evaluation should be consistent with the students' age and ability level. Sample evaluation forms are reproduced at the end of this chapter.

Additional Rubric Options

Depending on the project's goal and the students' ability level, teachers may wish to employ multiple rubrics to evaluate various outcomes. For example, a content rubric may be used to evaluate the students' understanding of a particular topic, as well as how well they communicated their knowledge. A technical rubric may review defective links, inoperative media (e.g., video or audio clips), and so on. A design rubric may critique the clarity and consistency of the layout, purpose of the media and navigation options, contrast between text and background, text readability (including fonts, sizes, colors, and styles), types of feedback, and whether the students followed their storyboards and flowchart. A presentation rubric may provide students with feedback on their speaking skills, appearance, organization, professionalism, ability to capture and hold the audience's attention, and so on.

One or more of these rubrics may be provided to the students and attached to the teacher's final evaluation form to aid in the summative evaluation of the students' projects. Examples of each of these rubrics are available at the end of this chapter.

ASSIGNING GRADES

Groups may receive a grade based on the combined, averaged scores of the teacher and peer evaluations (see Figure 7.2). Sample teacher and peer evaluation forms appear at the end of this chapter.

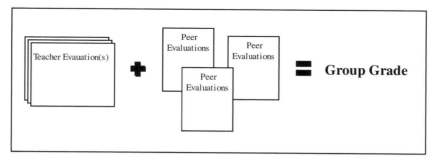

Figure 7.2. Assigning group grades.

Teacher evaluation forms may include an overall rating of a group's journal entries and bibliography information, as well as the average rating of the group's storyboard, design, content, and mechanics rubrics. For example, using the sample teacher evaluation form located at the end of this chapter, a group may have averaged a rating of 2 on their storyboards, design, and technical rubrics, and the teacher may have rated the group's content, journal entries, and bibliography information as 3s (see figure 7.3). The teacher's evaluation equals 15 points, or an average score of 2.5.

Teachers may choose to insert their own categories for final evaluation. In addition to the sample form presented in Figure 7.3, a blank form is included at the end of this chapter.

Using the Peer Evaluation blackline master, students can evaluate each other's projects. The sample form available at the end of this chapter provides space for students to comment on a project's content and design. It also asks that students rate the project on a scale of 0 to 3. Teachers can evaluate the students' comments and weight them appropriately, transferring the students' average rating to the final grades evaluation form (see Final Grades blackline master). For example, if three groups evaluated a project, and groups one and two gave the project a 3 and group three gave the project a 2, the average score transferred to the final grades sheet would be 2.67. Figure 7.4 shows the final grade sheet with transferred scores from the teacher's evaluation and average peer evaluation. In this example, the group grade equals 2.59, the average of the teacher and peer evaluations. The letter grade depends on the teacher's grading scale.

Teacher Evaluation

CRITERIA	0 to .99	1 to 1.99	2 to 2.99	3
Storyboards (see Storyboard Rubric)			2	
Design (see Design Rubric)			2	
Content (see Content Rubric)				3
Technical (see Technical Rubric)			2	
Daily journal entries				3
Bibliographical information				3

Good job! You effectively organized your project and demonstrated excellent teamwork! You averaged 2.5 on your project.

Total __15__

Figure 7.3. Sample teacher evaluation form.

Final Grades

CRITERIA	0 to .99	1 to 1.99	2 to 2.99	3
Group Self-Evaluations				
Self-Evaluation				
Peer Evaluations			2.67	
Teacher Evaluation			2.5	

Group Grade __2.59__   Individual Grade _____

Figure 7.4. Final grade sheet with two transferred scores.

Individual grades may be based on the combined and averaged scores of students' self-assessment, the group's self-evaluations, and the group grade (see Figure 7.5). This ensures individual accountability within groups. Sample self-evaluation and group self-evaluation forms appear at the end of this chapter.

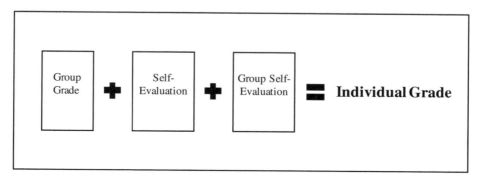

Figure 7.5. Assigning an individual grade.

Using the Self-Evaluation blackline master, students reflect on what they have learned. The teacher uses the student's comments to rate the evaluation on a scale of 0 to 3 and adds his or her rationale for the score on the back of the evaluation. For example, if a student is specific and notably reflective on each of the questions, the teacher may score the evaluation a 3. This score is transferred to the final grade sheet.

The Group Self-Evaluation blackline master provides group members with the opportunity to rate the participation and contributions of their teammates, as well as themselves. The average score of each student is transferred to his or her final grade sheet. For example, if Samantha received ratings of 3, 2, and 2 from her teammates and rated herself a 3, her average group self-evaluation score would be 2.5. The average of the self-evaluation, group self-evaluation, and group grade determine an individual's final grade. In Figure 7.6, the self-evaluation and group self-evaluation scores have been transferred to the final grade sheet, along with the scores from figure 7.4. The final individual grade equals 2.70: the average of the group self-evaluation (2.5), self-evaluation (3), and the group grade (2.59). Again, the letter grade depends on the teacher's grading scale.

Teachers are encouraged to make their own evaluation forms designed to meet the needs and ability levels of their students. Teachers can determine the point scale (0–3, 5–10, etc.) and decide how to weigh the various scores for final evaluation. This chapter provides several examples of various rubrics; teachers may pick and choose those that are applicable to their students and multimedia projects. Additional forms for specific projects are included in Chapters 8, 9, 10, and 11.

REFLECTIONS AND FUTURE GOALS

Learning does not end with a grade. Teachers need to provide time for students and themselves to reflect on what went well and how they would change or improve upon the assignment in the future. Students have an opportunity to assess their own learning and contributions on the self-evaluation form, but their feedback about the learning experience may help teachers improve the organization, management, timelines, and so on, for the next project. Teachers are encouraged to solicit feedback from students, having them write or discuss what helped them complete the project, where they may have encountered confusion or frustration, and what changes would they recommend for the next project. Student feedback as well as the teacher's own reflections and analyses of student learning should be used to improve future learning experiences associated with the development of multimedia projects.

Final Grades				
CRITERIA	0 to .99	1 to 1.99	2 to 2.99	3
Group Self-Evaluations			2.5	
Self-Evaluation				3.0
Peer Evaluations			2.67	
Teacher Evaluation			2.5	
Group Grade __2.59__			Individual Grade __2.70__	

Figure 7.6. Final grade sheet with transferred scores.

SUMMARY

The multifaceted nature of multimedia project development encourages many types of assessment. Assessment is ongoing and determines whether a group is ready to proceed to the next stage of development. Checklists, rubrics, and other assessment tools ensure that students know what is expected of them. In addition, rubrics allow teachers to clarify criteria in specific forms, and make project assessment more objective and consistent. Teachers need to ensure the validity and reliability of their assessment tools, including rubrics.

The DDD-E model poses several levels of assessment. In the DECIDE stage, students should be able to articulate their research question, explain why it is important, and discuss how they intend to pursue it. Next, they should demonstrate their ability to gather, organize, and synthesize information through brainstorming activities and research. In the DESIGN stage, students need to display how they intend to map and link their ideas together. In addition to examining the project flowcharts, students can explain the anticipated links, sequences, and section relationships identified in their flowcharts with the teacher. Afterward, students can begin producing their project's storyboards. The completed set is assessed by the teacher before the students continue to the DEVELOP stage. The DEVELOP stage includes review and debugging by the students' peers. Final projects include self-, peer, and teacher evaluations. Daily journal entries (see Chapter 3) that assess the group's progress and ability to work together can be collected and submitted with the group's final project. Groups may receive a grade based on the combined scores of the teacher and peer evaluations, and a final individual grade may be based on students' self-assessment, group self-evaluations, and group grade. Rubrics ensure that both students and teacher understand how each step of the project will be evaluated. At the end of the project, student feedback, teacher reflection, and analyses of student learning can be used to improve future multimedia project assignments and learner outcomes.

BLACKLINE MASTERS

This chapter includes an assortment of blackline masters designed to help teachers and students review and evaluate multimedia projects. Blackline masters include the following:

- Research Rubric: used in the DECIDE phase to ensure that students are ready to move on to the DESIGN phase

- Flowchart Rubric: a form used to evaluate a group's flowchart before the students proceed to the storyboard stage of the DESIGN phase

- Storyboard Rubric: a final evaluation form for a group's storyboards; a storyboard checklist is provided in Chapter 4

- The Bug Stops Here: a review sheet used to help students debug projects during the DEVELOP phase, before the projects are submitted for final evaluation

- Self-Evaluation: one way in which students can reflect on their participation and learning at the end of a multimedia assignment

- Peer Evaluation: one way in which student groups can evaluate other groups' work

- Group Self-Evaluation: a sample of how students may evaluate their own group's performance (intragroup evaluation)

- Teacher Evaluation: a sample of how teachers may evaluate a group's project

- Blank Evaluation: a template for creating your own rubrics

- Content Rubric: a sample rubric for evaluating the content of a project (Note: Educators will need to fill in the objectives and list the performance criteria.)

- Technical Rubric: a sample rubric for reviewing defective links, inoperative media (e.g., video or audio clips), the use of technology (scanners, digital camera, video camera)

- Design Rubric: a sample rubric for evaluating a project's design

- Presentation Rubric: a sample rubric for evaluating project presentations

- Primary MM Rubric: a simple rubric designed for young children

- Final Grades: an accumulating score sheet for determining an individual's final grade, as well as a group grade

REFERENCES

Ahn, J. 2004. Electronic portfolios: Blending technology, accountability and assessment. *Technological Horizons in Education Journal* 31(9): 12, 16, 18.

Alleman, J., and J. Brophy. 1999. The changing nature and purpose of assessment in the social studies classroom. *Social Education* 63(6): 334–37.

Culbertson, L. D., and M. R. Jalongo. 1999. But what's wrong with letter grades? Responding to parents' questions about alternative assessment. *Childhood Education* 75(3): 130–35.

Jonassen, D. H. 2000. *Computers as mindtools for schools: Engaging critical thinking.* 2d ed. Upper Saddle River, NJ: Prentice Hall.

Mabry, L. 1999. *Portfolios plus: A critical guide to alternative assessment.* Thousand Oaks, CA: Corwin Press.

Moskal, B. M. 2003. Recommendations for developing classroom performance assessments and scoring rubrics. *Practical Assessment, Research & Evaluation,* 8(14). Retrieved January 29, 2005, from http://PAREonline.net/getvn.asp?v=8&n=14.

Moskal, B. M., and J. A. Leydens. 2000. Scoring rubric development: validity and reliability. *Practical Assessment, Research & Evaluation* 7(10). Retrieved January 29, 2005, from http://pareonline.net/getvn.asp?v=7&n=10.

Research Rubric

CRITERIA	0	1	2	3
Clarity of research question	There is no research question stated.	Question is vague and hard to understand.	Question is somewhat clear, but could be more precise.	Question is clear and specific.
Supportive answers	There are no answers to the stated question.	Few of the answers support the research question.	Most of the answers support the stated question.	The answers directly support the stated question.
Resources	No or only one reputable resource is used.	Two reputable resources are used.	Three reputable resources are used.	Four or more reputable resources are used.
Accuracy	Information is lacking and is inaccurate.	The information contains more than one inaccurate statement.	The information contains one inaccurate statement.	The researched information is accurate.
Bibliographical information	Information is lacking and is inaccurate.	The information contains more than one inaccurate statement.	The information contains one inaccurate statement.	The information is correct.
Brainstorm (or KWL Knowledge Chart)	Activity was not started.	Activity is missing more than one required element.	Activity is missing one required element.	The information is complete.
				Total _____

Flowchart Rubric

CRITERIA	0	1	2	3
Structure	The flowchart is incomplete or missing.	The flowchart does not have any structure.	Structure is not aligned with the project's goals and content.	Structure is aligned with the project's goals and content.
Branching	There is no branching.	Branching is incomplete.	Branching is complete, but it is not clearly depicted.	Branching is complete and clearly depicted.
Labels	None of the elements of the flowchart are labeled.	More than one of the elements is not labeled.	All elements are labeled, but not easy to understand.	Each element is clearly labeled and easy to understand.
Symbols	No symbols are used.	More than one incorrect symbol is used.	One incorrect symbol is used.	All symbols are correct.
Ease of use	Flowchart cannot be followed.	Flowchart is difficult to follow; it's easy to get lost.	Flowchart is somewhat easy to follow; it could be clearer.	Flowchart is easy to follow and understand.
				Total _____

Storyboard Rubric

CRITERIA	0	1	2	3
Screens	More than two of the required screens are not included.	Two of the required screens are not included.	All but one of the required screens are included.	All required screens are included.
Links	No links are indicated or described.	More than one link or description is incomplete.	One link or description is incomplete.	All links are indicated and described.
Content	Content is missing or incomplete.	Content is complete, but inaccurate.	Content is complete, but difficult to read and understand.	Content is complete, factual, interesting, and easy to understand.
Layout	The design is inconsistent in more than one area.	The design is inconsistent in one area.	The design is consistent, but not clear.	The design is consistent and clear.
Media elements	Media elements are not included.	Some of the media elements are included and described.	All media elements are included, but not all are described.	Required media elements are included and described.
Font, background, and transition	Font, background, and transition information is incomplete.	Two of the requirements are incomplete.	One of the requirements is incomplete.	All font, background, and transition information is provided.
				Total _____

The Bug Stops Here

Name of group being reviewed: _____

Project title: _____

Reviewed by: _____

Spelling Corrections

Word	Page		Word	Page
_____	_____		_____	_____
_____	_____		_____	_____

Punctuation and Grammar Corrections

Problem	Page	Problem	Page
_____	_____	_____	_____
_____	_____	_____	_____
_____	_____	_____	_____

Link and Media Corrections

Problem	Page	Problem	Page
_____	_____	_____	_____
_____	_____	_____	_____
_____	_____	_____	_____

List design and content comments on back.

Self-Evaluation

Name of group: _____

Project title: _____

Group member: _____

How did you contribute to the project?

What did you learn about your topic in the process of developing this project?

What did you learn about multimedia development in the process of developing this project?

What did you learn about yourself in the process of developing this project?

Teacher's Rating: _____ (Comments on back)

Peer Evaluation

Name of group being reviewed: _____

Project title: _____

Reviewed by: _____

Content

What did you learn about this topic that you did not know before?

In terms of content, what are the strengths of this project?

How might the presentation of information be improved?

Design

What are the strengths in the design of this project?

What improvements in the design would you suggest?

On a scale of 0 to 3 (3 being the highest),
how would you rate this project? _____

Group Self-Evaluation

Name of group being reviewed: _____

Project title: _____

Group member: _____

What were your group's strengths?

What were your group's weaknesses?

What are some of the things that you learned about working with others?

What would you do better the next time your group works together?

On the back of this form, list yourself and your group members. Rate yourself and each of your group members' level of participation in the project. 0 = not enough, 1 = fair, 2 = a lot, 3 = did most of the work. Explain your ratings.

Teacher Evaluation

CRITERIA	0 to .99	1 to 1.99	2 to 2.99	3
Storyboards (see Storyboard Rubric)				
Design (see Design Rubric)				
Content (see Content Rubric)				
Technical (see Technical Rubric)				
Daily journal entries				
Bibliographical information				
			Total _____	

CRITERIA	0	1	2	3
			Total _____	

Content Rubric

CRITERIA	0	1	2	3
Objective:				
Objective:				
Objective:				
Structure: Begins with an introduction, uses students' own words, and ends with a conclusion.	Does not use students' own words.	Uses students' own words, but intro and conclusion are missing.	Uses students' own words, but intro or conclusion is missing.	Meets all of the require-ments.
Flow: Chunks information in a meaningful way, text is easy to follow and understand.	Information is scattered and difficult to understand.	Information is somewhat organized, but difficult to understand.	Information is somewhat organized and easy to understand.	Meets all of the require-ments.
Mechanics: Spelling, grammar, and punctuation are correct.	More than four spelling, grammar, or punctuation mistakes are made.	Three or four spelling, grammar, or punctuation mistakes are made.	One or two spelling, grammar, or punctuation mistakes are made.	Meets all of the require-ments.
				Total _____

Technical Rubric

CRITERIA	0	1	2	3
Navigation links	More than two of the links do not work correctly.	Two of the navigation links do not work correctly.	One of the navigation links does not work correctly.	All links work correctly.
Menu links	More than two of the menu links do not work correctly.	Two of the menu links do not work correctly.	One of the menu links does not work correctly.	All links work correctly.
Media elements	More than two of the media elements are not working.	All but two of the media elements are working.	All but one of the media elements are working.	All media elements operate correctly.
Text boxes	More than four text boxes aren't "read-only" or locked where appropriate.	All but three or four text boxes are "read-only" or locked where appropriate.	All but one or two text boxes are "read-only" or locked where appropriate.	All text boxes are "read-only" or locked where appropriate.
Use of different technology tools (e.g. digital camera, scanner, video camera, microphone, etc.)	Project is lacking more than two of the necessary tools.	Project incorporates all but two of the necessary tools.	Project incorporates all but one of the necessary tools.	Project incorporates all of the necessary tools.
				Total _____

Design Rubric

CRITERIA	0	1	2	3
Continuity	Project does not follow storyboards or flowchart.	Project follows some of the storyboards.	Project follows the storyboards but not the flowchart.	Project follows the storyboards and flowchart exactly.
Layout	The layout is not clear and is inconsistent.	The layout is clear but is inconsistent.	The layout is somewhat clear and is consistent.	The layout is very clear and consistent.
Purpose of media elements	More than two media elements are not meaningful.	All but two of the media elements are meaningful and add to the project.	All but one of the media elements are meaningful and add to the project.	All media elements are meaningful and add to the project.
Text clarity	Text is not easy to read and doesn't contrast with the background.	The text is not easy to read but contrasts with the background.	The text is easy to read but doesn't contrast with the background.	All text is easy to read and contrasts with the background.
Navigation buttons	None of the navigation buttons are easy to understand.	Some of the navigation buttons are easy to understand.	Most of the navigation buttons are easy to understand.	Navigation buttons are clearly marked and identified.
Feedback	Feedback is not consistent or appropriate.	Feedback is consistent but not appropriate.	Feedback is not consistent, but it is appropriate.	Feedback is consistent and appropriate.
				Total _____

Presentation Rubric

CRITERIA	0	1	2	3
Clarity	Presenter(s) did not speak clearly and did not speak loud enough.	Presenter(s) spoke loud enough, but did not speak clearly.	Presenter(s) spoke clearly but not in a loud enough voice.	Presenter(s) was articulate and spoke in a loud enough voice.
Attire	Presenter's attire was not appropriate.	Most of the presenter's attire was appropriate.	Presenter's attire was appropriate, but not well kept.	Presenter(s) was well groomed and dressed for the presentation.
Professionalism	Presenter(s) was rude and disrespectful.	Presenter(s) seemed indifferent and not attentive to the audience.	Presenter(s) acted professional most but not all of the time.	Presenter(s) was polite, professional, and attentive to the audience.
Organization	Presenter(s) was very disorganized, distracting the presentation.	Presenter(s) was somewhat organized but needs to improve a lot.	Presenter(s) was well organized most of the time.	Presenter(s) was well organized throughout the presentation.
Appeal	Presenter(s) did not captivate or hold my attention.	Presenter(s) held my attention for a short period of time.	Presenter(s) held my attention for most of the time.	Presenter(s) captured and held my attention the whole time.
Outcome	I did not learn anything from this presentation.	I did not learn that much from this presentation.	I learned a lot, but I feel more could have been presented.	I learned a lot from this presentation; it was very thorough.
				Total _____

Primary MM Rubric

The project starts with a title screen.

Directions are provided.

Enough information is provided.

The information is correct.

There are no spelling or punctuation errors.

____ pictures and ____ sounds were used.

The screens are linked together so the project makes sense.

Final Grades

CRITERIA	0 to .99	1 to 1.99	2 to 2.99	3
Group Self-Evaluations				
Self-Evaluation				
Peer Evaluations				
Teacher Evaluation				

Group Grade _____   Individual Grade _____

May be reproduced for classroom use. From Karen S. Ivers and Ann E. Barron, *Multimedia Projects in Education*. 3d ed. Westport, CT: Libraries Unlimited. © 2006.

Multimedia Projects: Hypermedia

A SCENARIO

Nick, Nora, Samantha, and Tom enjoyed working together on multimedia projects because they enjoyed learning from each other. Where one might feel unsure about something, another would be there to clarify the task at hand and support the others in their learning. Each felt that he or she had particular strengths and something to contribute to the project. Nora oversaw the development of graphics, Nick led the design of the flowcharts and storyboards, Tom provided leadership in the organization and text editing, and Samantha helped the team put all the project's pieces together using the assigned authoring tool. Each student took pride in teaching teammates his or her own specific skills, and they all tutored each other throughout the design and development of the project. In addition to design and development skills, the multimedia projects focused on a variety of subject areas. Tom dreaded the thought of creating a project that focused on chemical elements, but Samantha was quick to remind him that they all had different strengths and would support each other through the project. She recalled the multimedia project that involved interviewing members of the community, and how awkward and misplaced she had felt. She had been glad her teammates were there to support and encourage her. Thanks to her teammates, she now feels more comfortable conducting interviews.

Mrs. Jewel, their instructor, read similar comments from other students as she reviewed their class journals. Their comments and reflections confirmed her decision to incorporate multimedia projects throughout her curriculum. The students' teamwork and social growth were encouraging, and they continued to perform well, if not better, academically. By integrating multimedia projects throughout the curriculum, Mrs. Jewel allowed her students to share their strengths in subject areas as well as in multimedia production.

OVERVIEW

Ideas for multimedia projects are endless, limited only by the imagination of teachers and students. Multimedia projects can be integrated across the curriculum, and they can help students share their knowledge in many ways. In addition to engaging students as they learn specific content standards, multimedia projects may be designed to focus on specific student skills (learning how to use a particular authoring tool), selected media formats (animation), or social skills (cooperative learning).

As with any other curricular unit, planning is an essential part of successful multimedia projects. Limited computer resources may require educators to facilitate several activities at once. This idea is not new; many educators find themselves managing multiple activities in the classroom on a daily basis. For example, during a social studies unit on the Gold Rush, some students may be panning for gold, others may be working on a model of a mining camp, some may be working on written reports, and more may be weighing and evaluating the value of gold nuggets. During multimedia projects, the only difference is that some students may be working on computers while others are working on noncomputer-related activities. The computer provides the students with yet another mode of learning—one that provides new insights into organizing, synthesizing, evaluating, and presenting information. This chapter presents several ideas for multimedia projects that can be created with hypermedia tools such as eZediaMX by eZedia, HyperStudio by Sunburst, Flash by Macromedia, and others. The tool is not as important as the process. A lesson description, the DDD-E process, and ideas for concurrent activities are provided for each project.

SAMPLE PROJECTS

The following projects address various areas of the curriculum and can be created with most authoring tools. Students should be familiar with the chosen tool before engaging in the multimedia project. The sample projects are designed for classrooms with four computers and 32 students; however, adjustments can be made to meet other conditions. Design teams consist of four students and periods may consist of 30 to 45 minutes. See Chapter 3 for computer scheduling options.

All About Me

Lesson Description: This project is designed for beginners, to provide them with the opportunity to focus on planning, design issues, and the authoring tool. It also addresses standards related to reading and writing. The content of the project is information about the students. Each student team creates an eight-screen (or card) project consisting of the following screens: title, information, main menu, student 1, student 2, student 3, student 4, and credits. (All About Me blackline masters are provided at the end of this chapter.)

DECIDE. Assign student teams as described in previous chapters. As a class, brainstorm what makes people interesting, what information students might find in an autobiography, and other related questions. Generate a class list of 10 items (e.g., name, date and place of birth, hobbies, and favorite books, among other things). Assign each student the responsibility of providing information about himself or herself for each of the 10 items.

DESIGN. The next period, provide student teams with a copy of a flowchart (see the All About Me: Flowchart blackline master). Discuss the flowchart's layout and how the screens will be connected. Next, distribute copies of the All About Me: Storyboard Templates (see the blackline masters at the end of this chapter). Explain how the students should complete the storyboards, and how they will use them to create the computer screens of their multimedia projects. Discuss design issues (e.g., contrasting background and text, consistency) and, if possible, show some sample All About Me projects. These sample projects may be created by the teacher or be projects from previous classes. Use the projects to show good and bad examples of design, and let the students discuss what they observe. For example, a bad example might have navigation icons in inconsistent places on the screens, unreadable text, links that do not work, and spelling mistakes. Following the class discussion, provide students with a list of design guidelines (see Chapter 4) and a checklist of expectations (see All About Me: Project Checklist blackline master). During the next period, students work on their team's storyboards, including the storyboards about themselves. Each self-storyboard should contain a paragraph describing the 10 items that the student has answered about him or herself. Teams' storyboards should be assessed and approved by the teacher before students are allowed to work on the computers. Students can track their progress by using the journal entry forms discussed in Chapter 3.

DEVELOP. After the students' storyboards have been approved, teams take turns at the computer stations. If teams are not working on the computers or on their storyboards, the students can be doing the following:

- Reading an autobiography or biography of a famous person of their choice and working with a Venn diagram to compare differences and similarities between the person they are reading about and themselves

- Creating a self-portrait using pastels, papier-mâché, clay, or other medium

- Creating a three-dimensional, life-size body cutout of themselves using two sheets of butcher paper and paper scrap stuffing

- Using a life-size cutout of a member of their team to study and illustrate the skeletal system, muscles, and so on

- Researching, gathering, and organizing information for a class newspaper or magazine that describes what occurred during the year most students were born

- Researching information about their place and date of birth, hobbies, or the like for a possible extension activity that adds more cards or screens to their project

- As students complete their multimedia projects, another team reviews the project for problems or errors (see Chapter 7). The corrected project, along with the group and self-evaluations and journal entries, is submitted to the teacher. It may take students four to six periods to finish their project

EVALUATE. In addition to the teacher's evaluation, peers may be asked to evaluate each other's projects (see the All About Me: Teacher Evaluation and All About Me: Peer Evaluation blackline masters). The students receive a group grade based on the teacher and peer evaluations. Students receive an individual grade based on their group, self, and intragroup evaluations. The two grades can be averaged for a final score. A class Jeopardy game or quiz may be provided to see how well students know their classmates.

Pollution Solution

Lesson Description: This project focuses on the students' ability to research, synthesize, and present information about the hazards of pollution. Other topics are possible, based on the grade level and science standards that need to be addressed. In this example, students are required to use a variety of media formats to help them emphasize the importance of finding solutions to pollution. For instance, they may incorporate digitized photographs and video segments into their projects to illustrate the outcomes of pollution or animations that illustrate a recycling process.

DECIDE. Assign student teams as described in previous chapters. As a class, brainstorm what students already know about pollution and what they want to learn about pollution (see the KWL Knowledge Chart in Chapter 3). For example, they may know that pollution is harmful, but they may not know the extensive effects of pollution on the environment, what regulations are in effect to help stop pollution, what causes smog, how and what items are recycled, the dirtiest cities in the world, and steps they can take to help stop pollution. Assign or have each group select a different topic to research. Distribute and explain the BrainStorm activity sheet and the Bibliography sheet (see Chapter 3). Before groups brainstorm and begin research about their specific topic, stipulate that groups need to incorporate photos, video segments, or animations to illustrate their points. Ask the students why pictures are important when discussing a topic like pollution. Discuss (or demonstrate) how a picture of dead fish in a river has a stronger impact on people than the text "dead fish in a river" has by itself.

DESIGN. Students may take two or three class periods to research their specific topic. As students are finishing their research, discuss the concept of flowcharts and storyboards. Students need to examine their research findings and organize the information by chunks and meaningful links. Students may want to use index cards to create and manipulate a rough draft of their flowchart and storyboard ideas. Discuss the design issues explained in Chapter 4. View sample projects that contain video, animations, and photographs and have students discuss what makes the projects effective or ineffective. Provide groups with a list of design guidelines; a storyboard template (see Chapter 4); and the journal entry form, project checklist, and bibliography sheet available in Chapters 3 and 4. Explain each form. In addition, provide groups with the storyboard, design, content, and technical rubrics available in Chapter 7. Groups should keep these forms in a binder. Multiple copies of the journal entry form and the bibliography form should also be available. Students may take three to five class periods to complete their flowchart and storyboards.

DEVELOP. After the students' flowchart and storyboards have been approved, teams take turns at the computer stations (see Chapter 3 for a computer schedule). If teams are not working on the computers or on their storyboards, students can be doing the following:

- Creating a brochure that lists local recycling centers and ways that people can help stop pollution

- Writing and illustrating a creative story, performing a skit, or creating an audio story (with sound effects and music) about a superhero who helps prevent pollution, a boy (or girl) who always threw trash on the ground until the ground fought back, a container's question as to whether there is life after trash, and other ideas

- Working on a classroom mural of the trash collected from the school yard

- Creating and videotaping a show where the students demonstrate or create products made from other things, such as birdfeeders made from pinecones, peanut butter, and bird seed

- Writing a poem or song about pollution

- Creating and solving math problems related to money earned by recycling

- Developing quiz questions about their project for other students

As students complete their multimedia projects, another team reviews the project for problems or errors (see Chapter 7). The corrected project, along with the project's rubrics, group and self-evaluations, bibliography sheets, and journal entries, is submitted to the teacher.

EVALUATE. Following the teacher's evaluation of the projects, peers need to evaluate each other's projects, too (see Chapter 7). The students receive a group grade based on the teacher and peer evaluations. Students receive an individual grade based on their group, self-, and intragroup evaluations.

When the grading is complete, a main menu can be developed that links the projects together (see Figure 8.1). Students can view the entire multimedia presentation and answer each other's quiz questions for additional content evaluation. The remaining column on the KWL Knowledge Chart can now be completed.

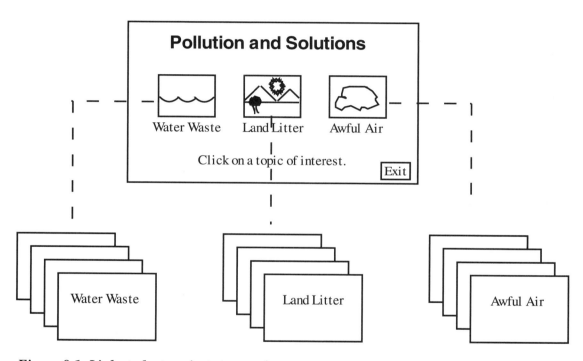

Figure 8.1. Link student projects to a main menu.

Community Concerns

Lesson Description: This project focuses on the students' ability to develop and issue a survey, organize and interpret the collected information, discuss issues with members of the community, and participate in an authentic learning experience. Students are required to research and address community concerns by reading the local newspaper, watching the local news, and interacting with members of the community. Findings are presented in a multimedia project. Authentic learning experiences are the result of conducting interviews, making video recordings and audio tracks of community members, and compiling the data. Multiple standards across different subject areas can be addressed through this and similar activities.

DECIDE. Assign student teams as described in previous chapters. As a class, discuss the concept of a community and what issues their community may be facing. Topics may include the homeless, curfews, the elderly, crime, education, and other concerns. Assign or have each group select a different topic to research. Explain that their research should include local newspaper articles and television news, as well as interviews with community members. Distribute the BrainStorm activity sheet (see Chapter 3) to help students organize the possibilities of their topic. During the next two or three class periods, discuss how to construct a survey and, if possible, distribute sample surveys. Students should think about questions that are important to their particular topic. For example, students researching the concerns of the elderly may ask the elderly questions regarding health care, social security, transportation, recreation services, and family concerns. This student group may contrast and compare answers they receive from the elderly with answers they receive from other age groups. During the interviews, students should ask permission to record, video, or photograph the person being interviewed. All of the data are accumulated, synthesized, and evaluated. Students can keep track of their sources using the Bibliography sheet in Chapter 3. The teacher should approve the surveys before students begin their interviews. Provide the students with an additional week to conduct the interviews and finalize the results.

DESIGN. Discuss the concept of flowcharts and storyboards. Students need to examine their research findings and organize the information by chunks and meaningful links. Students may want to use index cards to create and manipulate a rough draft of their flowchart and storyboard ideas. Discuss the design issues explained in Chapter 4. View sample projects that contain audio tracks, video, and photographs, and have students discuss what makes the projects effective or ineffective. Provide groups with a list of design guidelines, a storyboard template (see Chapter 4), and the journal entry form and project checklist available in Chapters 3 and 4. Explain each form. In addition, provide groups with the storyboard, design, content, and technical rubrics available in Chapter 7. Groups should keep these forms in a binder. Multiple copies of the journal entry form and the bibliography form should be available. Students may take three to five class periods to complete their flowchart and storyboards. Remind students to complete daily journal entries (see Chapter 3).

DEVELOP. After the students' flowchart and storyboards have been approved, teams take turns at the computer stations. If teams are not working on the computers or on their storyboards, students can be doing the following:

- Proposing a club or fundraising campaign that supports their specific topic

- Developing quiz questions about their project for other students

- Working on a class model of their community

- Creating a travel brochure about the benefits of their community

- Writing letters to their local representatives about their findings and concerns

- Composing letters to classes in other communities, encouraging them to conduct the same surveys and share their results (e-mail or regular mail)

- Researching and constructing models or pictures of historical places, events, or people tied to their community

- Creating an interesting facts or trivia game about their community to play with other students

As students complete their multimedia projects, another team reviews the project for problems or errors (see Chapter 7). The corrected project, along with the project's rubrics, group and self-evaluations, bibliography sheets, and journal entries, is submitted to the teacher.

EVALUATE. Students may choose to share their projects with local community members. Peers and teachers can also evaluate the projects. Students may receive a group grade based on the average score of their peer, teacher, and community evaluations. Individual grades are calculated by the group grade, self-, and intragroup evaluations.

All That Jazz

Lesson Description: This project focuses on the students' ability to research, synthesize, and present information about different styles of music. In addition to standards related to reading and writing, students have the opportunity to address standards related to the historical and cultural context of music. Students are required to incorporate audio clips of a selected music style into their projects to help teach other students about music. For example, students creating a project about ragtime could include audio clips of "The Entertainer" and the "Maple Leaf Rag" while discussing the contributions and history of Scott Joplin. Each team chooses or is assigned a specific music style and generates a multimedia project that reports assigned information about that style. Educators may choose to impose a specific layout and style for student storyboards and flowcharts; hence, the projects will contain the same topics and can be connected at the end of the project.

DECIDE. Assign student teams as described in previous chapters. As a class, generate a list of different types of music (e.g., rock and roll, ragtime, classical, jazz, country western). Discuss what students already know about certain types of music and what they would like to learn about the types of music (see the KWL Knowledge Chart in Chapter 3). For example, they may know that Elvis Presley is considered the King of Rock and Roll, that Beethoven wrote classical music, and that ragtime was popular during the 1920s. Students may want to learn the origins of country music or find out more about New Age music. In addition to their topics of interest, ask students to research the following information: the music's history and peak(s) of popularity; at least three musicians and their history and contribution to the music style; and additional music titles and interesting facts. Randomly assign or let students choose a music style from the list. Distribute the BrainStorm activity sheet from Chapter 3. To adhere to a specific project format, explain that each group's BrainStorm sheet should contain the following information: the music type should be placed in the Main Idea bubble and Related Idea bubbles should contain music history, musicians, music titles, and interesting facts. Students can create additional Related Idea bubbles for other topics. Branches from the Related Idea bubbles will contain more specific information about the topic. Allow students three to five periods for research, reminding them that audio clips are required for the project. Assist students with their research by bringing in a variety of music recordings on CD, cassettes, albums, or audio clips.

DESIGN. As students are finishing their research, discuss the concept of flowcharts and storyboards. As a class, discuss how the gathered information might best be organized, chunked, and linked together. Create a flowchart for everyone to follow (see Figure 8.2).

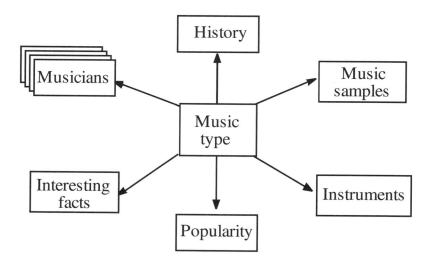

Figure 8.2. Sample flowchart.

Next, discuss the design issues explained in Chapter 4. View sample projects that contain music clips and have students discuss what makes the projects effective or ineffective. Discuss storyboard designs and decide on a standard layout for everyone to use. Distribute the journal entry form and project checklist available in Chapters 3 and 4. Explain each form. In addition, provide groups with the storyboard, design, content, and technical rubrics available in Chapter 7. Students may take three to five class periods to complete their flowchart and storyboards.

DEVELOP. After the students' flowchart and storyboards have been approved, teams take turns at the computer stations. Ensure students are familiar with various audio formats and compression techniques (see Chapter 5). If teams are not working on the computers or on their storyboards, students can be doing the following:

- Writing a persuasive report for a future debate explaining why their music style is the best

- Developing quiz questions about their project for other students

- Developing a board game about the life of a composer

- Reading a biography of a composer and designing a diorama depicting and explaining an important event in the composer's life

- Learning and interpreting the lyrics to a particular song

- Creating a watercolor or acrylic painting that depicts the mood or feelings associated with a particular piece of music

- Learning to play a music selection

- Creating a composition of their own

As students complete their multimedia projects, another team reviews the project for problems or errors (see Chapter 7). The corrected project, along with the project's rubrics, group and self-evaluations, bibliography sheets, and journal entries, is submitted to the teacher.

EVALUATE. Both students and teachers evaluate the projects. The students receive a group grade based on the teacher and peer evaluations. Students receive an individual grade based on their group, self-, and intragroup evaluations. When the grading is complete, a main menu can be developed that links the projects together. The remaining column on the KWL Knowledge Chart can now be completed. Teachers may want to create a quiz or short essay exam that assesses students' knowledge of the presented projects.

Sherlock Project: A Problem-Solving Adventure

Lesson Description: This project focuses on the students' ability to solve problems, research, and develop interdependent clues to produce a multimedia project that demonstrates their processing skills. In addition, graphics and pop-up text boxes can be required components of the project. Students are required to create a mystery that is solved by finding and deciphering the various clues within the project. For example, a group may use the theme of a haunted house and tell the story of how the only way out of the house is to enter the correct combination into the passageway door. Throughout the project, students create mathematical and logic problems that will help users determine the correct code. For example, in the first room of the house, the following clue could be discovered when users click on a ghost (see Figure 8.3):

It happened on a scary night,
One I know was full of fright;
Yet Joey Jones, as calm as could be,
Said, "Divide 800 by the answer in three."

A text box may appear or the clue may be recorded audio, or both. Room three's clue might appear when users click on a book (see Figure 8.4):

Weary travelers visit here;
Guess how many times a year? $(7 * 8) - (10 + 21)$

By combining the clues in rooms one and three, the answer to room one is 32. Room six's clue may indicate that this is the first number in the combination. For example, upon visiting room six, the users may find the following scrawled on the wall (see Figure 8.5):

Room 1 = 1st number to combination

Projects can be made much more complex and sophisticated by integrating current areas of study, incorporating outside research into the answers to the clues, making answers to clues dependent on more than one other clue, and incorporating different media that become part of the clues. To begin, limit students to six clues in the puzzle.

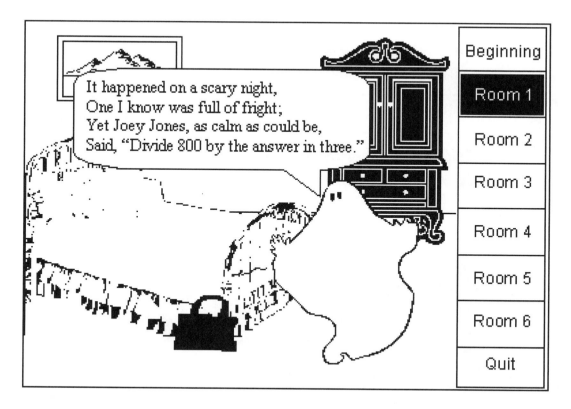

Figure 8.3. Sample screen design for room one.

Figure 8.4. Sample screen design for room three.

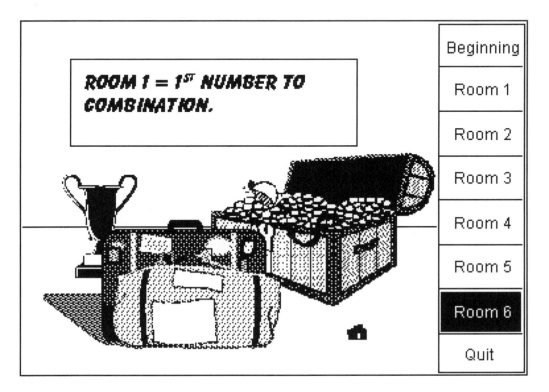

Figure 8.5. Sample screen design for room six.

DECIDE. Assign student teams as described in previous chapters. As a class, discuss the various strategies students can use when solving a math problem, as well as the basic problem-solving steps: (1) understanding the problem, (2) devising a plan, (3) carrying out the plan, and (4) looking back. Discuss the importance of gathering all information before coming to a conclusion about a problem. Illustrate this by distributing one puzzle clue to each student group (see the Introductory Puzzle blackline master at the end of this chapter). Ask the students if they can solve the puzzle. Obviously, they cannot, because they each hold only one piece to the puzzle. Randomly select groups to read their puzzle pieces aloud, while everyone else takes notes. Inquire whether students can solve the puzzle after each clue. Note that some clues may not make any sense until other clues are read and that some clues are interdependent (they rely on other clues for additional information). Some clues may have to be repeated. After all of the clues are read, discuss the answer and how students arrived at it. Reflect on the interdependent puzzle pieces and the importance of gathering and understanding all the clues.

Explain that students are going to create a multimedia project based on the puzzle example. Their project should contain a theme (e.g., a haunted house, a pirate's treasure, outer space, the jungle) and their clues should be hidden (pop-up text boxes) or part of the graphic environment. Users should experience traveling from room to room or place to place.

Let student teams brainstorm about a specific theme and a mystery to go along with it. For example, using an outer space theme, the story might involve the crash of a spaceship on an unknown planet; the clues might spell the name of the planet or give its position from the sun. Or, using a pirate theme, the story might involve the location of a buried treasure; the clues could provide the x and y coordinates to a location on a treasure map. After a theme and a story have been decided, students can discuss the solution to their mystery and create clues that users will need to solve the mystery. Remind students to make some of their clues interdependent. Provide students with two or three periods to complete this first step.

DESIGN. Once student teams have finished their puzzles, review the concepts of flowcharts and storyboards. Each clue should have its own storyboard and the flowchart should show the navigation possibilities throughout the project. Clue cards or screens may be linked to a central location, be accessible from every clue card, or found attached to another clue card. Discuss the design issues explained in Chapter 4. If possible, view sample problem-solving projects for additional design ideas. Provide groups with a list of design guidelines, a storyboard template (see Chapter 4), and the journal entry form and project checklist available in Chapters 3 and 4. Explain each form. Also provide groups with the storyboard, design, and technical rubrics available in Chapter 7 and the puzzle rubric blackline master at the end of this chapter. Groups should keep these forms in a binder and complete daily journal entries.

DEVELOP. After the students' flowchart and storyboards have been approved, teams take turns at the computer stations. If teams are not working on the computers or on their storyboards, students can be doing the following:

- Working on problem-solving puzzles provided by the teacher or brought in by other students

- Creating a record-keeping sheet for users to keep track of their notes as they attempt to solve their completed project

- Researching and contributing to a class book on mathematical magic tricks

- Reading and acting out a mystery on video

- Playing problem-solving games like Master Mind and chess

- Researching and reporting on famous (fictional or nonfictional) detectives

- Writing a mystery and creating puppets for its production

As students complete their multimedia projects, another team reviews the project for problems or errors (see Chapter 7). The corrected project, along with the project's rubrics, group and self-evaluations (see Chapter 7), and journal entries, is submitted to the teacher. Provide the students with at least 10 class periods on the computer to finish a 10-card or screen project, especially because some of the students will spend their development time creating and researching different pictures for their project's theme. Clip art libraries should be made available to the students.

EVALUATE. Following the teacher's evaluation of the project, peers need to evaluate each other's projects as well (see Chapter 7), remembering that specific content may or may not be an integral part of the project. Emphasis should be placed on the clarity of information, sophistication of the puzzle, use of graphics, and overall design. For alternative evaluation forms, see the puzzle rubric and Peer Puzzle Evaluation blackline masters at the end of this chapter. Each Sherlock project should be shared and solved by the different groups.

SUMMARY

The possibilities for multimedia projects are endless, and emphasis on student learning outcomes can be placed in a variety of areas. This chapter presented sample multimedia projects that focus on different areas of the curriculum and learning outcomes. It also provided a variety of ongoing activities for students not working on computers. Extension activities for the projects presented in this chapter include sharing projects with peers over the Internet or with the school and community at local conferences. Projects may also be recorded to CD-ROMs for student distribution and archival purposes.

BLACKLINE MASTERS

This chapter contains variations of several blackline masters presented in other chapters. This provides teachers with additional ideas for creating their own checklists and evaluation forms that are specific to the students' projects and ability levels. Specific forms have been designed for the All About Me and Sherlock projects. References are also made to the checklists and evaluation forms in other chapters. Blackline masters in this chapter include the following:

All About Me: Flowchart: a flowchart for All About Me projects

All About Me: Storyboard Template: an alternative storyboard layout

All About Me: Project Checklist: a specific checklist for All About Me projects

All About Me: Teacher Evaluation: a simplified evaluation sheet for All About Me projects

All About Me: Peer Evaluation: a specific evaluation sheet for All About Me projects

Introductory Puzzle: a story problem containing independent clues

Puzzle Rubric: one way of evaluating problem-solving adventure projects

Peer Puzzle Evaluation: an alternative peer evaluation form for problem-solving adventures.

All About Me: Flowchart

```
                    ┌─────────┐
                    │  Start  │
                    └─────────┘
                         │
                         ▼
                  ┌─────────────┐
                  │  Title card │
                  └─────────────┘
                         ▲
                         ▼
                  ┌─────────────┐
                  │ Information │
                  └─────────────┘
                         ▲
                         ▼
                  ┌─────────────┐        ┌─────────┐
                  │  Main Menu  │───────▶│  Exit   │
                  └─────────────┘        └─────────┘
                         ◇
```

| Student 1 | Student 2 | Student 3 | Student 4 |

Credits

All About Me: Storyboard Template

Background: _____

Border: _____

Pictures: _____

	Font	Size	Style	Justification	Color
Title					
Text					

Button	Go to	Transition	Other

All About Me: Project Checklist

Team Name _____

Before developing your project at the computer, complete the following:

☐ Flowchart   ☐ Storyboards

Make sure your project has:

☐ A minimum of _____ pages (or cards).

☐ A maximum of _____ pages (or cards).

☐ A Title page (or card).

☐ An Information page (or card).

☐ A Main Menu.

☐ A page (or card) with a paragraph description for each member in your group.

☐ A Credits page (or card).

☐ Appropriate navigation options.

☐ Text that is easy to read and is accurate.

☐ Complete sentences with correct punctuation, grammar, and spelling.

☐ The assigned media requirements:

_____ Clip art

_____ Original drawings (use of paint tools)

_____ Audio

☐ Other: _____

All About Me: Teacher Evaluation

CRITERIA	0	1	2	3
Continuity	Project does not follow storyboards or flowchart.	Project follows some of the storyboards.	Project follows the storyboards but not the flowchart.	Project follows the storyboards and flowchart exactly.
Content and mechanics	Project does not contain paragraphs about each team member.	Project contains paragraphs about each team member, but there are many errors.	Project contains paragraphs about each team member, with one or two errors.	Project contains paragraphs about each team member, without any errors.
Media elements	None of the media elements have been incorporated.	Two or more media elements don't work, or few are incorporated.	All media elements are incorporated, but one does not work.	All media elements are incorporated and work.
Navigation buttons	None of the navigation buttons are functioning correctly.	Some of the navigation buttons are functioning correctly.	Most of the navigation buttons are functioning correctly.	All navigation buttons are functioning correctly.
Design	None of the design guidelines were followed.	Some of the design guidelines were followed.	Most of the design guidelines were followed.	All design guidelines were followed.
Daily journal entries	Journal entries are missing for three or more days.	Journal entries are missing for two days.	Journal entries are missing for one day.	No journal entries are missing.
			Total _____	

All About Me: Peer Evaluation

Name of group being reviewed: _____

Project title: _____

Reviewed by: _____

What are the strengths of this stack?

How might the presentation be improved?

What improvements in the design would you suggest?

On a scale of 0 to 3 (3 being the highest), how would you rate this project? Why?

Introductory Puzzle

Help Mr. Alfonzo calculate the average number of pages read in one week by a group of his students: Fred, Ethel, Lucy, Ricky, Wilma, and Betty.

Both Fred and Ethel read two books with 70 pages each. In addition, Fred read a 20-page book about frogs.

Lucy read the same frog book as Fred, the same cat book as Barney, and half of the dog book that Ricky read.

Ricky read a 20-page book about dogs.

Barney read a 60-page book about cats and two 30-page books.

Both Wilma and Betty read the same books as Ethel.

Answer: 115 pages. [Fred: (2x70) + 20 = 160; Ethel: 2x70 = 140; Lucy: 20 + 60 + (20÷2) = 90; Ricky: 20; Wilma: 140; Betty: 140] Divide total pages by 6.

Extension Activities:
- Calculate each student's average number of pages read in one week.
- Determine the range, mode, and medium of the group. Compare and contrast this to the group mean.
- Track and calculate the average number of pages read in one week by individuals and the class. Compare this with other classes and age groups.
- Create a bar graph that illustrates the favorite genre of the class. Compare this with other classes and age groups.

Puzzle Rubric

CRITERIA	0	1	2	3
The project presents users with the goal(s) and objectives of the puzzle.	Project does not have goals or objectives stated.	Project presents a goal, but no objectives.	Project presents objectives, but no clear goal.	Project presents clear goals and objectives for the puzzle.
The group uses several interdependent clues.	The project does not have interdependent clues.	The project has one interdependent clue.	The project has two interdependent clues.	The project has three or more interdependent clues.
The group includes all of the necessary info to solve the puzzle, and the design of puzzle is appealing.	Not enough information is included, and the design is not appealing.	Not enough information is included, but the design is appealing.	Enough information is included, but the design is not appealing.	Enough information is included, and the design is appealing.
The puzzle challenges the user's thinking skills, yet it isn't too difficult to complete.	The puzzle is too simple.	The puzzle is too difficult to complete.	The puzzle is somewhat challenging, but not challenging enough.	The puzzle is challenging, but not too difficult to complete.
It is easy to navigate through the puzzle - buttons are easy to understand and work.	Buttons are not easy to understand and some do not work.	Buttons are easy to understand, but some do not work.	Buttons are not easy to understand, but they all work.	Buttons are easy to understand, and they all work.
				Total _____

Peer Puzzle Evaluation

Name of group being reviewed: _____

Project title: _____

Reviewed by: _____

What are the strengths of this stack?

How might the presentation be improved?

Explain why you were able or unable to solve the puzzle.

On a scale of 0 to 3 (3 being the highest), how would you rate this project? Explain your answer.

Multimedia Projects:
Web Pages

A SCENARIO

The students in Mr. Cuban's class had been using the Web to gather information all year. They found it particularly helpful during the research phase of their multimedia projects. It seemed that there was up-to-date information on just about everything on the Web—although they had learned that not all of it was accurate. For the next multimedia project, Mr. Cuban wanted his students to focus their projects on local, Florida animals, such as manatees, alligators, armadillos, and key deer. The projects would be designed for the Web, and, after they were edited, they would be placed on the school's Internet server and be available worldwide.

The first step was to learn a little HTML (the language of the Web). Mr. Cuban showed his students some sites on the Web that provided HTML tutorials, and they found it very easy to learn a few of the commands and to type them into the text editor. Even linking to other Web pages and graphics was very easy. After they mastered the basics of HTML, he introduced them to Netscape Composer (a free, graphical editor for creating Web pages). Here, they learned how to add some of the more advanced features, such as tables and forms.

As the students worked through the DDD-E process, they were glad that they understood the basics of design and evaluation. They conducted research and located resources (such as sounds and photos) on the Web. They also took a field trip and interviewed park rangers. While there, Kevin captured a short video segment of a key deer. Throughout the process, they were reminded that the projects should be accessible for everyone on the Web—even with a "slower" modem. Therefore, they were careful about the file size of their photos and the length of the audio and video.

When the projects were ready for testing, Mr. Cuban uploaded the files to a Web server, and each student contacted a friend or relative for an online review. Although they had worked hard on all their projects this year, this one seemed even more important because it would have a worldwide audience (and their parents could view it)! When the projects were finished, the students added their school's e-mail address for feedback in the footer of each page. They also added a counter on the page so they could track how many people were using their site to learn about Florida's animals.

OVERVIEW

The World Wide Web is a powerful resource for K–12 education. Never before has the educational community had such an inexpensive, easily accessible method of communicating and distributing information. It opens doors to multicultural education, establishes real-world learning experiences, promotes higher-order thinking skills, and helps increase motivation and writing skills.

The Web offers a wonderful environment for students to create and publish multimedia projects. These projects can reside on a local hard drive (for individual use), they can be shared on an intranet (for internal viewing only), or they can be placed on the Internet (for the whole world to see).

There are many reasons for students to create Web sites. Besides sharing their artwork and stories with others, students can collect data for original research projects and produce reports that are linked to authentic, dynamic information sources. They can also post school news for the community, establish online homework assignment centers, create subject guides with links to the Internet, or produce interactive lessons or WebQuests (see http://www.webquest.org/).

The projects outlined in this chapter are examples of school-based activities that involve Web-based development. The first project centers on a personal homepage for students. In this project, they can concentrate on the development process rather than on obtaining the content. The second project (School Newsletter) and third project (Our Town) require that the students interact with others to acquire the information needed.

The Web is also a great place for students to publish reports on a variety of topics that they can share. By creating a Web-based report, they can include links to resources available at other sites. The "Sailing the Internet with Magellan" project is an example of a report that incorporates many sites but also includes original material that has been synthesized by student groups.

The final project in this chapter focuses on creating instructional materials to be distributed on the Web. Similar to interactions designed in hypermedia programs, students can provide information on a Web page and then embed questions to test the knowledge of the users.

SAMPLE PROJECTS

The following projects can be created with tools ranging from text editors and word processors to sophisticated Web creation programs (such as FrontPage, Composer, or DreamWeaver). Teachers should choose the most appropriate tool for their students and ensure that their students are familiar with the tool before beginning the project (see Chapter 6 for more information on Web authoring tools).

The sample projects can be designed and developed by individual students or by groups of up to six students. In all cases, it is important to maintain a thorough review cycle before uploading the pages, particularly if they will be accessible through the Web.

My Personal Homepage

Lesson Description: This project challenges students to create a personal homepage that focuses on their interests. It is an appropriate introductory project for students because they can focus on the development process rather than having to research a new topic. A word of caution: if the projects will be accessible on the Internet (as opposed to the school network), you must warn the students about providing personal contact information. In most cases, it is not wise to include a student's picture, home address, phone number, or any other information that someone could use to contact them. Instead, recommend that students focus on their interests and their projects, such as artwork they have created, songs they have composed, or Web sites they like to visit (see Figure 9.1).

Figure 9.1. My Personal Homepage sample.

DECIDE. Begin the assignment by explaining to the students why some personal information should not be included in Web pages. Emphasize that Web pages are open to millions of people on the Internet and that it is important for students to protect their privacy. Explain that placing their pictures and home addresses on the Web would be similar to talking to strangers or handing out flyers with personal information at the shopping mall.

Continue the discussion by brainstorming the types of information that students might want to share on their personal pages. Ask each group to generate at least 20 possible ideas. Share these with the class and develop a list of potential topics for the pages. Items could include sports activities, stories or research papers the students have written, original artwork or music, information about their pets, links to favorite Web sites, class projects, community information, vacation stories, and so on.

DESIGN. Begin the design process by showing the students both good and bad examples of Web page design. Discuss general design issues (such as the use of contrasting colors) as well as design issues specific to the Web. Remind the students that bandwidth is still a major consideration for Web pages, so they must try to make their graphics as small (in file size) as possible and include audio or video only when it is essential. Following the discussion, provide students with a list of design guidelines for the Web (see the Web Design Guidelines blackline master included with this chapter).

During the next work period, students should develop their flowcharts and storyboards for the project. Flowcharts are particularly important because of the number of hyperlinks on most Web pages. Remind the students to provide an easy-to-use structure for their pages. They should also provide information about links so users will understand where they are branching and why. A storyboard template is provided at the end of Chapter 4 for Web projects. It can be modified as necessary to reflect the particular components involved in specific projects.

DEVELOP. After the students' storyboards have been approved, students can begin producing the HTML pages and the media elements for their projects. There are many ways to produce Web pages (see Chapter 6 for more information). Demonstrate or review the tools that are available for your students. If students are not working on the computers or on their storyboards, they can be:

- Conducting research about their ancestry

- Researching their hobbies or areas of interest

- Drawing pictures to scan into the computer

- Taking pictures of their school or classrooms (do not include names with photos)

- Creating storyboards and flowcharts

As students complete their pages, another team should review them for consistency, ease of use, and operational errors. The corrected pages, along with the project's rubrics, group and self-evaluations (see Chapter 7), and journal entries, are submitted to the teacher. All Web pages should be reviewed by the teacher or other adults prior to being uploaded to a Web server.

EVALUATE. In addition to the teacher and peer evaluations, students should be encouraged to solicit feedback from others via an e-mail address on the Web page. Student projects can be linked to a central class menu from which others can access the personal pages. Explain that upkeep and maintenance are important issues for Web pages. Plan to revisit the project a couple of weeks later and allow time for the students to check their external links to see if they are still active.

School Newsletter

Lesson Description: The School Newsletter project is an extension of the Personal homepages; however, it includes information about the entire student body rather than just individual students. This project is ideal for student groups. Each group can be assigned one particular aspect of student life, such as sports, clubs, drama, scheduling, faculty profiles, upcoming events, and so on.

The online school newsletter can supplement a print newsletter, or it can be developed separately. If the students are in a journalism course, or if the school newspaper is interested in establishing an online presence, the project can serve as an extension and integration of other school activities. If there is already an online newspaper at your school, this project can have a narrower focus, such as a newsletter for an individual class or club.

DECIDE. As a class, brainstorm potential topics that could be included in an online newsletter. Allow time for the students to investigate resources available at the school, such as statistics for sports, electronic files of school history, photographs, or other archival information.

Assign student teams that will focus on one particular aspect of student life. Allow plenty of time for the students to review other school Web sites and investigate the format of other online newspapers. Ask them to visit other school newsletters and Web sites (see Yahoo for a list of K–12 schools with a Web presence).

DESIGN. Discuss the overall flow of the lesson with the entire class. Emphasize the need for a consistent interface for the entire online newsletter, as well as the need for each section to be unique. Discuss navigation options and whether the project should incorporate frames or tables. Other ideas might include the following:

- Using the school mascot and colors as a theme

- Including audio clips with interviews

- Creating a visual tour of the school

- Linking to the district Web site

- Including information about the community

Remind the students that they must be careful not to include personal information (such as photos or home addresses) about individual students. Also, emphasize the need to involve the school's administrators in the review cycle.

DEVELOP. After the students' flowchart and storyboards have been approved, teams take turns at the computer stations (see Chapter 3). Other activities that the students can work on include the following:

- Reviewing hardcopy newsletters from the school

- Taking pictures of the school and community

- Reviewing films from sports events for possible inclusion in the project

- Recording greetings, speeches, and other narratives for the project

- Experimenting with alternative ways to display statistics and other data

EVALUATE. As students complete their portion of the online newsletter, another team reviews the pages for problems or errors. If possible, the pages should be tested on different computers (Macintosh and PC) as well as with different browsers. Be sure to include as many administrators, teachers, coaches, and students as possible in the review cycle. The club's president and faculty sponsor should authorize all content that relates to a particular club or organization before being uploaded to the Internet or intranet.

Our Town

Lesson Description: This project focuses on research, interactions with community members, and students' ability to organize and interpret collected information. Students are required to create a Web site for the community or nonprofit organization. If possible, they should collect or create photographs, video, and audio samples that reflect the flavor of the community and focus on its unique attributes.

DECIDE. As a class, discuss the community and possible topics for a Web site. Allow time for students to search for local organizations that already have Web sites. Brainstorm in small groups to generate as many ideas as possible for consideration. For example, they might create a Web site for the local park, or conduct research on the air or water quality and post the results on the Web. Other possibilities include creating a Web site for attract tourists or producing a site that presents a local historical event or person.

As the students conduct their field research, they should ask permission to record, videotape, or photograph anyone whom they want to include on the Web site. If existing graphics are used, they should seek permission to scan the images. Students can keep track of their sources using the Bibliography sheet in Chapter 3.

DESIGN. Allow time for the students to review Web sites that have similar content to what they are targeting. As they outline their intended content, remind them that they must keep the scope within the constraints allowed. In other words, if this is a short-term project, they may be limited to creating only a few pages. Ask them to consider the target audience for the Web site—it might include local people or a worldwide audience. They should also think about including words and phrases that would optimize the possibility of finding the Web site via a search engine.

DEVELOP. Teams can alternate between data collection, media production, and the creation of their Web pages. The focus should be on community involvement and focus. In addition to working on the computer, students can be doing the following:

- Creating a printable travel brochure for tourists

- Researching the town's history

- Interviewing senior community members about the community's evolution

- Photographing community groups and historical sites

- Recording unique sounds and videos

- Interviewing the mayor or other elected officials

EVALUATE. As students complete their Web pages, the teacher, other students, community members who were involved, and the administration should review the projects. It is important that each page be thoroughly reviewed before it is uploaded to the Internet. In addition, the copyright releases for all media elements should be documented and filed for future reference.

Sailing Through the Internet: A Research Project about Ferdinand Magellan

Lesson Description: This research project encourages students to use resources on the Internet as integral parts of the report. The project requires students to locate relevant information and integrate the resources into a report, with links at appropriate places throughout the report. Before assigning such a project, teachers should conduct Internet searches to verify that appropriate material exists for the topic areas assigned. Internet filters should be used to prevent students from accessing inappropriate information as they conduct their searches. The example focuses on a report on Ferdinand Magellan (see Figure 9.2). Because so many topics already have related Web sites, it is important to assign topics that are unique in some way and will require either a synthesis of existing Web sites or the creation of a unique approach/topic.

DECIDE. Provide an overview of the project's goals. Assign teams and allow the students to select a topic from a prepared list (in this case a list of explorers). As a class, brainstorm what students already know about their assigned explorer and what they need to know (see the KWL Knowledge Chart in Chapter 3). For example, they may know that these persons are famous explorers, but not the exact dates or routes of their explorations. Next, have the students speculate about the information they might find about the explorers on the Web. They can also speculate about how the information was added to the Internet and by whom. For example, if the research centers on contemporary artists, they may have developed their own personal homepages. If the research centers on a historical character (such as Magellan), someone else must have been responsible for creating the resource.

As students conduct their searches, emphasize that they need to ascertain the validity and accuracy of the content. Ask them to fill out a Fact or Fiction sheet (see the blackline master at the end of this chapter) when they are analyzing the reliability of the sources.

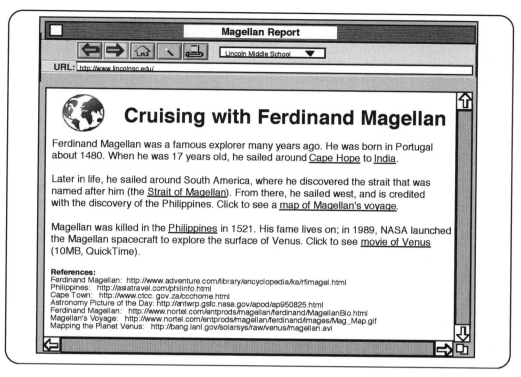

Figure 9.2. Ferdinand Magellan report.

DESIGN. Students may take two or three class periods researching their specific topic, depending on the number of Internet connections available for student use. If connections are limited, have the students print out potential sites (along with the URL) so they can read and evaluate the information offline.

As students complete their research, they should write the reports, linking to the Web at appropriate places. Flowcharts and storyboards are extremely important to help students map out their ideas and provide a structure for their reports.

Discuss using media elements in the projects. Point out that graphics that are not optimized for the Web (as far as size, resolution, etc.) may be slow to load. Encourage them to locate electronic maps that can be modified to depict trade routes and other information. Provide copies of the Web design guidelines and a storyboard template.

Remind students of copyright restrictions. Publishing on the Web is different from producing a multimedia project that will be used only within the classroom. All graphics, music, text, and video should be original or should be part of the public domain. If students locate a graphic or another media element on the Web, they should read the copyright statements to make sure that they can place that element on a Web page that will be accessible through the Internet.

DEVELOP. After the students' flowchart and storyboards have been approved, teams take turns at the computer stations (see Chapter 3 for a computer schedule). If teams are not working on the computers or on their storyboards, students can be doing the following:

- Conducting research about the topic in textbooks, videos, and encyclopedias to continue verifying the content found on the Web

- Building a model of Magellan's ship with paper or cardboard

- Reviewing maps that were available at Magellan's time

- Charting Magellan's journeys on a contemporary world map

- Writing a comparison of Magellan's journey to that of John Glenn (or another contemporary figure)

As students complete their Web-based reports, another group reviews them. If some of the links do not work, the reviewers should note them so they can be corrected. If possible, student review teams should also note any graphics or media elements that take too long to download, and they should test the site with different browsers and computers. The content of the report should be original and should access other resources as supporting documentation.

EVALUATE. Follow the general procedure for project evaluations (teacher evaluation, peer evaluation). If the projects are going to be uploaded to a Web server (and therefore accessible throughout the world), an additional review and revision cycle may be necessary. After the teacher has noted changes, students should revise the content as necessary before uploading the projects to the server. All class reports can be linked via a class page that explains the project and the parameters.

A Lesson in Life

Lesson Description: After your students master the basics of designing and developing a Web site with HTML and other tools, they can focus on more advanced interactions on the Web. There are various programs and techniques (such as JavaScript) that can produce interactions. Some tools, such as DreamWeaver, can automatically generate JavaScript interactions, such as feedback on questions. In addition, there are many Web sites that provide free access to game- and quiz-generating programs (see Table 9.1).

This project focuses on the students' ability to design a lesson that teaches about a concept they are currently studying. Interactions should be included whereby users can test their knowledge of the subject and receive meaningful feedback.

Table 9.1.

Game- and Quiz-Generating Programs on the Web

Web Site	Address
Quiz Center	http://school.discovery.com/quizcenter/quizcenter.html
QuizLab	http://www.quizlab.com/
QUIA	http://www.quia.com/
TestMaker	http://www.testmaker.com/
Easy Test Maker	http://www.easytestmaker.com/
Quiz Game Master	http://cybertrain.info/quizman/qmhome.html
APTE Puzzle Center	http://www.apte.com/puzzles/
Hot Potatoes	http://web.uvic.ca/hrd/halfbaked/

DECIDE. Before beginning the project, demonstrate several Web sites that are designed to deliver instruction and interactivity. Table 9.2 provides many examples of online courses. Prior to the demonstrations, review the sites and show the students examples based on student age, site content, and programming expertise required.

Table 9.2.

Instructional Sites on the Web

Web Site	Address
Explore E-learning (Math/Science)	http://www.explorelearning.com/
Physics Web	http://physicsweb.org/
Foreign Languages for Travelers (Learn over 35 languages)	http://www.travlang.com/languages/
InterActivate	http://www.shodor.org/interactivate/
Interactive Web sites	http://jc-schools.net/tutorials/interactive.htm
I Like 2 Learn	http://www.ilike2learn.com/ilike2learn/
Blue Web'n	http://www.kn.pacbell.com/wired/bluewebn/
Syvum	http://www.syvum.com/
Read Write Think	http://www.readwritethink.org/index.asp
MathMol	http://www.nyu.edu/pages/mathmol/
Florida Center for Instructional Technology	http://fcit.usf.edu/

Assign student teams as described in previous chapters. As a class, generate a list of possible topics about life that could be taught on the Internet. The topics could include subjects such as AIDS, life management skills, health, sex education, reproduction, air quality, and so on. Allow plenty of time for the students to generate possible topics and areas of investigation.

Demonstrate techniques for incorporating interaction on the Web. Discuss the advantages of delivering Web-based education, including access to a worldwide audience, ease of distribution, and ease of updates and maintenance. Allow the students to work through several sites on the Internet that deliver instruction.

DESIGN. After each group has selected or been assigned a topic, the groups can begin developing the flowcharts and storyboards. Most of this project should take place within a confined set of Web pages, without branches to external sites. Caution the students to carefully flowchart the lesson so the navigation is easy and intuitive. After the storyboards are complete, the teacher should review them carefully to make sure the content is chunked and presented in a logical manner. Questions and feedback should be checked for accuracy and relevance.

DEVELOP. After the students' flowchart and storyboards have been approved, teams can begin the production phase by creating the graphics, text, and interactions. The integration of interactive exercises (questions, puzzles, etc.) can create issues between different platforms (Mac vs. PC) and different browsers (Netscape, Internet Explorer, Safari, etc.). Extensive testing is required to ensure that the project will operate correctly on different delivery systems. If teams are not working at a computer, they can be involved in the following activities:

- Reviewing books and articles about the latest developments in Web authoring tools

- Taking pictures or drawing graphics that can be incorporated into their lesson

- Constructing questions or quizzes and pilot testing them with other students

EVALUATE. Following the reviews and evaluations by the teacher and peers, the students should be encouraged to pilot test their programs with other classes. The classes may be within the same school or located elsewhere in the world. After the program has been thoroughly tested, it can be uploaded to the Internet. Students should be encouraged to include e-mail feedback forms on the program to solicit responses from other students and teachers who implement the lesson.

SUMMARY

The possibilities for multimedia projects on the Web include informational pages, instructional sites, and worldwide research. This chapter presented sample Web projects focusing on students, schools, local communities, and instruction. As the Web continues to proliferate in our homes and schools, the development of Web-based programs will become an increasingly important tool for students.

BLACKLINE MASTERS

The Web is an invaluable resource for sharing and researching information. This chapter described several activities and two blackline masters for assisting students with their Web projects. Blackline masters in this chapter include the following:

Web Design Guidelines: a list of guidelines specific to Web projects

Fact or Fiction: a means to record and analyze information on the Web

Web Design Guidelines

The following guidelines can help make your Web pages more user-friendly for the visitors to your site.

General

Carefully plan your pages before you create them.
Place a descriptive title on the top of all pages.
Include the date of the last revision on the pages.
Limit the length of Web pages to three screens.
Test the pages with several different browsers and computers.
Check all pages for correct spelling and grammar.

Graphics

Make sure the graphics are relevant to the page.
Limit the file size of the graphics to less than 30K each.
Limit the number of graphics on each page.
Use GIF graphics for line drawings and simple graphics.
Use JPG graphics for photographs.
Limit the width of graphics to less than 470 pixels.

Text

Make sure there is high contrast between background and text.
Limit the length of text lines.
Include blank space between paragraphs.
Limit the use of blinking text.

Media: Audio and Video

Use audio and video only when necessary.
Include information about audio and video file sizes.
Include information about format (e.g., wav, avi, quicktime)

Fact or Fiction

Because anyone can create a Web page, it is important to try to determine if the information presented there is true or not. Fill out this form for Web sites that you are including in your project.

Web Site #1

Title of Site _____

Address (URL) _____

Author _____

Date last modified _____

Clues that help to determine if the information is Fact or Fiction

_____

Web Site #2

Title of Site _____

Address (URL) _____

Author _____

Date last modified _____

Clues that help to determine if the information is Fact or Fiction

_____

Web Site #3

Title of Site _____

Address (URL) _____

Author _____

Date last modified _____

Clues that help to determine if the information is Fact or Fiction

_____

Multimedia Projects: Presentation Tools

A SCENARIO

The students in Mrs. Calvin's class were about to give their class presentations on key individuals during the American Revolution. Mrs. Calvin had placed the students into groups of four and assigned each group a particular individual. In addition to specific content criteria outlined by Mrs. Calvin, students were to be graded on their group skills, their organization and presentation skills, and their ability to speak in front of an audience. Mrs. Calvin had provided student groups with the appropriate rubrics when the assignment was introduced and had explained the purpose of the groups' daily journal entries. The students spent two weeks researching and organizing information for their presentations. Now they were ready to present their research using PowerPoint, a presentation tool that was available on all of the school computers.

Joseph, David, Brian, and Michelle were the first presenters. Joseph and Brian had little experience speaking in front of a group, but David and Michelle assured them that they would do well. They had practiced together several times before today's big event. Both Joseph and Brian appreciated the opportunity to use a presentation program to assist them with their parts of the presentation. The bulleted text helped them to organize their thoughts, and the graphics, animation, and video segments seemed to make the presentation much more interesting than just standing up in front of the class and talking.

David started the group's presentation. Patriotic music captured the audience's attention and the title of the project dissolved in "George Washington: An American Hero." The group used several familiar icons associated with George Washington—the dollar bill, a quarter, a cherry tree—in their presentation as they discussed the contributions of George Washington. The group used the presentation screens to help them stay focused and explain George Washington's role in the American Revolution. The presentation screens included sounds, video segments, and photographs relative to their report. The students all appeared confident as they gave their part of the presentation. Their journals and group evaluation forms noted how much they appreciated the support of their teammates and the use of the presentation tool.

187

Michelle concluded the presentation, and the group took its well-deserved applause. Mrs. Calvin applauded the group as well, and she commended the students' teamwork, content presentation, and speaking skills. Joseph, David, Brian, and Michelle all beamed with contentment, even as they attributed their success to planning and practice. Joseph and Brian breathed deep sighs of relief, but they now felt easier about speaking in front of a group.

OVERVIEW

Designing and presenting multimedia projects provide students with invaluable real-world learning experiences; presentation and public-speaking skills are necessary in many occupations. In addition, presentation projects can be used to address a variety of standards, including those related to listening and speaking skills, writing, and so on. Students learn to work together, apply their research skills, plan and organize content, select appropriate media and layouts, and deliver professional-looking presentations.

Although professional-looking presentations can be created with authoring and Web tools, there are several tools on the market especially designed for creating large group presentations. Microsoft PowerPoint is probably the most common. Some integrated packages, such as the later versions of AppleWorks, also have slide show options for creating presentations. Scholastic Keys provides elementary students with a kid-friendly interface for Microsoft PowerPoint, as well as Word and Excel. Most presentation programs provide the option of using predesigned templates. Some programs also have "wizards" or other guides that prompt users through the design process.

This chapter presents several ideas for multimedia projects that can be created with presentation tools. A lesson description, the DDD-E process, and ideas for concurrent activities are provided for each project.

SAMPLE PROJECTS

The following projects can be created with most presentation tools. Teachers should choose the most appropriate tool for their students and ensure that they are familiar with the tool before beginning the project. Students should also be familiar with guidelines for presentations (see Guidelines for Presentations blackline master at the end of this chapter). The sample projects describe classrooms with four computers and 32 students; however, adjustments can be made to meet other conditions. Design teams consist of four students. See Chapter 3 for computer scheduling options.

Persuasive Automotive

Lesson Description: The goal of this lesson is to engage older students in persuasive speaking and writing strategies. Students structure ideas and arguments in a sustained, persuasive, and sophisticated way and support them with precise and relevant examples (California State Board of Education 2004). In this example, students research, compare, and analyze real-world considerations of purchasing an automobile. Each group of students is assigned a different automobile (e.g., a sports utility vehicle—SUV) from different manufacturers. As part of their research assignment, student groups must try to persuade classmates that their assigned SUV is the best. For example, students researching a Subaru Forester would create a presentation highlighting what they believe are its benefits— gas mileage, price, warranty, options, aesthetics, safety, buying options (current percentage rates and leasing options), and so on. Audience members would have the chance to ask questions and debate the presented issues. Other topics for persuasive speaking include school rules, laws, best places to eat or shop, the most influential person who ever lived, and so on. For younger students, teachers can have them try to persuade one another of Goldilocks' guilt or innocence in trespassing, what animal makes the best pet, and so forth. Students have the opportunity to state a clear position in support of a proposal, support a position with relevant evidence, follow a simple organizational pattern, and address reader concerns (California State Board of Education 2004).

DECIDE. As a class, determine what students know about buying an automobile (use the KWL Knowledge Chart in Chapter 3). Ask students what they know about their own or their parents' cars and why they purchased them. Complete the second column of the KWL Knowledge Chart by asking students what they would like to know about purchasing cars.

Introduce the project by assigning students to teams as described in previous chapters. Explain that groups will randomly choose an SUV to research and share with the class. As part of the assignment, explain that they will be required to present an overview and the benefits of the SUV via a presentation tool. Continue to explain that the purpose of the presentation is to persuade classmates that their SUV is the best. Groups must be prepared to answer questions and to debate the presented issues. As a group, design an evaluation form for the presentation. For an example, see the Persuasive Presentation Evaluation blackline master at the end of this chapter.

Provide student groups with the opportunity to brainstorm and research topics about their SUV. Check their progress and Bibliography sheets (see Chapter 3) before letting them move on to the DESIGN phase.

DESIGN. After the students' research has been approved, provide class time to create flowcharts and storyboards. To expedite the process, teachers may provide the students with a standardized template (see Figure 10.1). A limit of 15 screens could be imposed, if desired. Remind students of the purpose of bulleted text and the printout options available in the presentation tool.

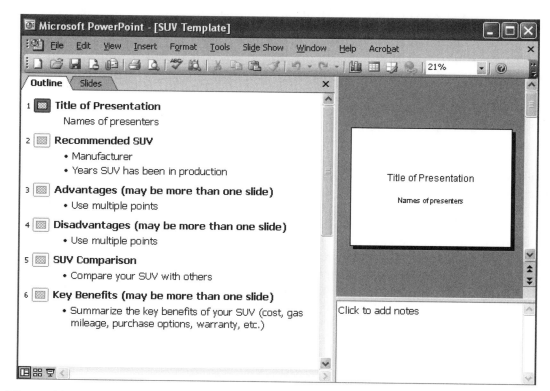

Figure 10.1. Sample template.

DEVELOP. After the students' flowchart and storyboards have been approved, teams take turns at the computer stations (see Chapter 3 for a computer schedule). If teams are not working on the computers or on their storyboards, students can be doing the following:

- Conducting additional research about their SUV

- Locating and charting where the majority of their SUV is sold

- Creating a brochure about their SUV

- Comparing and contrasting their SUV with other SUVs

- Creating a model, drawing, or collage of their SUV

Team members should review and practice their presentation before presenting it to the class.

EVALUATE. Teachers and students use the evaluation form created during the DECIDE phase of the project. Students may be evaluated on the effectiveness of their presentation, its organization and structure, its content and accuracy, their speaking skills, and so on. The evaluations are collected and averaged by the teacher. Students may also choose to conduct self- and intragroup evaluations (see Chapter 7).

Famous People in History

Lesson Description: The goal of this lesson is to engage students in an informative presentation about a famous person in history—a common requirement across grade levels, addressing social studies and language arts standards. Student groups have the opportunity to choose a famous person and to share their findings with the class. Media elements can be added to the presentations to highlight certain aspects of the famous person. For example, if students choose to do a presentation on Scott Joplin, music can be added to demonstrate his work. Or, if Neil Armstrong were chosen, students might opt to include an audio segment of his first words on the moon. In any case, the goal of the presentation should be to inform viewers about a particular person in history. Presentations should be clear, well organized, and interesting and should address the content criteria established by the teacher.

DECIDE. Assign student teams as described in previous chapters. Ask what makes a person famous. Students may discuss current celebrities. Ask them what makes these people different from others or debate whether they really are different. Discuss how celebrities or famous people of today compare with famous people of yesterday. Discuss what made people in history famous.

Following this discussion, have the groups decide on a famous historical person to research and present to the class. Ensure that each group chooses a different person. After their selection is approved, students conduct research on the person they have chosen. Evaluate their research before letting students continue the DESIGN phase.

DESIGN. Students need to examine their research findings and organize the information for their presentation. Make sure they understand the importance of flowcharts and storyboards. Provide groups with a list of design guidelines, a presentation storyboard template (see Chapter 4), and the journal entry form and project checklist. Explain each form. In addition, provide groups with the storyboard, design, content, and technical rubrics (see Chapter 7). Groups should keep these forms in a binder. Multiple copies of the journal entry form and the bibliography form should be available. Remind students of the purpose of bulleted text and the printout options available in the presentation tool (see Chapter 6). Teachers may choose to set a minimum and maximum number of screens in the presentation.

DEVELOP. After the students' flowchart and storyboards have been approved, teams take turns at the computer stations. If teams are not working on the computers or on their storyboards, students can be doing the following:

- Creating a Venn diagram that compares the life of their famous person to their own lives

- Designing a booklet about the career of their famous person

- Drawing a portrait of their famous person

- Creating a timeline of their famous person's life

EVALUATE. Peers and the teacher can evaluate group presentations by using the content, technical, and presentation rubrics in Chapter 7. The students receive a group grade based on combined scores. Students receive an individual grade based on their group, self-, and intragroup evaluations. The teacher may present a whole-class quiz to assess what was learned from each presentation.

Scientific Follow-Up

Lesson Description: The goal of this lesson is to engage students in reporting their scientific findings. This is one way to assess students' knowledge of what they have learned and can be applied to science projects across grade levels.

Following small-group science experiments, organize student groups into design teams to present their findings to the full class. Talk about how they think such presentations might relate to real life. Discuss the importance and purpose of presentations in the business world, in the scientific community, and in education.

DECIDE. In the DECIDE phase, student groups must decide how best to represent and discuss their findings by reexamining their data and methods. Students should organize their ideas with a planning sheet (see Chapter 4) before continuing to the DESIGN phase.

DESIGN. Depending on the experiment, students may want to incorporate a variety of media (e.g., charts, photos, animations) into their presentations to illustrate their methods and findings (see figure 10.2).

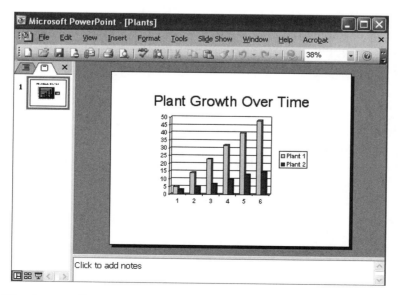

Figure 10.2. Chart example.

Make sure students understand the importance of flowcharts and storyboards. Provide groups with a list of design guidelines, a presentation storyboard template (see Chapter 4), and the journal entry form and project checklist available in Chapters 3 and 4. Explain each form. In addition, provide groups with the storyboard, presentation design, content, and technical rubrics available in Chapter 7. Remind students of the purpose of bulleted text and the printout options available in the presentation tool (see Chapter 6). Teachers may choose to set a minimum and maximum number of screens in the presentation.

DEVELOP. After the students' flowchart and storyboards have been approved, teams take turns at the computer stations (see Chapter 3 for a computer schedule). If teams are not working on the computers or on their storyboards, students can be doing the following:

- Conducting further research on their scientific investigation

- Conducting a similar experiment and comparing the results

- Creating a newsletter about the implications of their experiment

EVALUATE. Peers and the teacher can evaluate group presentations (see Chapter 7). The students receive a group grade based on the teacher and peer evaluations. Students receive an individual grade based on their self- and intragroup evaluations. The two grades can be averaged for a final score (see Final Grades in Chapter 7).

How To

Lesson Description: The goal of this lesson is to encourage students to teach each other how to do something and addresses standards related to listening and speaking skills. For example, students need to be able to give precise directions and instructions, restate and perform multiple-step instructions and directions, and so on. There are many advantages of using a presentation tool for instruction: step-by-step instructions can be bulleted; enlarged photographs can show procedures close up; video and animation can show a sequence of events; and learners can be provided with screen-by-screen handouts to assist them in the learning process.

DECIDE. Assign student teams as described in previous chapters. Introduce the project, explaining that the goal of the presentation is to teach their classmates how to do something. Discuss different strategies for communicating how to do something and the advantages of using different media elements. Following the discussion, let groups decide on something to teach. Next, students should brainstorm different ways to teach the procedure to the class.

DESIGN. When students are ready to move on to the DESIGN phase, make sure they understand the importance of flowcharts and storyboards. Discuss the design issues explained in Chapter 4 and, if possible, show the students samples of "how-to" presentations. Again, review the significance of certain media elements. Once the students' flowchart and storyboards are approved, they can begin developing their presentations.

DEVELOP. After the students' flowchart and storyboards have been approved, teams take turns at the computer stations. If teams are not working on the computers or on their storyboards, students can be doing the following:

- Conducting further research on their how-to activity

- Practicing their presentation through their storyboards

- Researching and evaluating how-to books

- Creating a how-to commercial

EVALUATE. How-to presentations may be evaluated by the rubrics in Chapter 7 or by a customized rubric designed by the class. For an example, see the How-to Evaluation blackline master at the end of this chapter.

SUMMARY

In addition to planning and organizational skills, presentation tools provide students with the opportunity to practice speaking in front of a group and conveying their ideas verbally. Presentation tools can help support a presenter's train of thought, as well as provide visual cues for learners. Creating and delivering presentations through presentation tools provides students with valuable real-world and authentic learning experiences.

BLACKLINE MASTERS

Presentation projects provide students with opportunities to practice their speaking and presentation skills. This chapter includes additional evaluation forms for assessing specific student projects. Blackline masters in this chapter include:

- Guidelines for Presentations

- Persuasive Presentation Evaluation: a rubric designed to rate the presenter's ability to persuade his or her audience

- How-to Evaluation: a rubric designed to rate the presenter's ability to teach members of the audience a procedure

REFERENCES

California State Board of Education. 2004. English-language arts content standards [Online]. Available at: http://www.cde.ca.gov/be/st/ss/engmain.asp. Retrieved on January 8, 2005.

Presentation Guidelines

These guidelines can help you make effective presentations.

Computer Display

Keep the presentation simple and easy to follow.
Make sure the text is readable to everyone (about 24 pt font).
Mix upper- and lowercase letters for the bullets.
Keep consistent headings (titles) and subheadings.
Provide plenty of space between bullets.
Use a maximum of five colors.
Include a maximum of six bullets.
Each bullet should only have about six words.
Include key phrases in bullets -- not the entire presentation.
Use high contrast between the text color and the background.
Do not place text on a highly textured/patterned background.
Make sure your graphics are large enough for everyone to see.
If you include charts, make large labels and legends.

Media: Audio and Video

Use audio and video only when necessary and appropriate.
Test the speakers and projection unit before the presentation.
Make sure everyone can hear and see the media.

Presentation Techniques

Rehearse the speech before presenting it.
Make notes to yourself on cards or on the computer.
Face the audience -- not the projection screen.
Start with a brief introduction and overview of the topic.
Don't read the bullets to the audience; expand on them.
Always plan a little extra in case you talk too fast.
Don't talk too fast -- pause and let the audience reflect.
Stand tall and speak directly to the audience (don't slouch)!
Don't fidget with keys, coins, pens, pencils, etc.
End the presentation with a summary and conclusion.
Smile!

Persuasive Presentation Evaluation

CRITERIA	0	1	2	3
Clarity	Presenter(s) did not speak clearly and did not speak loud enough.	Presenter(s) spoke loud enough, but did not speak clearly.	Presenter(s) spoke clearly but not in a loud enough voice.	Presenter(s) was articulate and spoke in a loud enough voice.
Supporting facts	Presenter(s) did not provide facts to support his or her opinion.	Presenter(s) provided one or two facts to support opinion.	Presenter(s) provided three or four facts to support opinion.	Presenter(s) provided five or more facts to support his or her opinion.
Viewpoints	Presenter(s) did not consider other opinions and didn't provide compelling reasons for own opinion.	Presenter(s) did not consider other opinions, but provided compelling reasons for own opinion.	Presenter(s) considered other opinions, but didn't provide compelling reasons for own opinion.	Presenter(s) considered other opinions and provided compelling reasons for own opinion.
Organization	Presenter(s) was very disorganized, distracting the presen-tation.	Presenter(s) was somewhat organized but needs to improve a lot.	Presenter(s) was well organized most of the time.	Presenter(s) was well organized throughout the presentation.
Appeal	Presenter(s) did not captivate or hold my attention.	Presenter(s) held my attention for a short period of time.	Presenter(s) held my attention for most of the time.	Presenter(s) captured and held my attention the whole time.
Persuasiveness	Presenter(s) did not change my opinion; he or she reinforced my other beliefs.	Presenter(s) did not change my opinion.	Presenter(s) changed my opinion, but I'm not completely convinced.	Presenter(s) changed my opinion; I'm completely convinced.
				Total _____

How-to Evaluation

CRITERIA	0	1	2	3
Clarity	Presenter(s) did not speak clearly and did not speak loud enough.	Presenter(s) spoke loud enough, but did not speak clearly.	Presenter(s) spoke clearly but not in a loud enough voice.	Presenter(s) was articulate and spoke in a loud enough voice.
Directions	Presenter(s) did not provide clear or step-by-step directions.	Presenter(s) provided step-by-step directions, but they were not clear.	Presenter(s) provided clear directions, but they were not step-by-step.	Presenter(s) provided clear, step-by-step directions.
Organization	Presenter(s) was very disorganized, distracting the presentation.	Presenter(s) was somewhat organized but needs to improve a lot.	Presenter(s) was well organized most of the time.	Presenter(s) was well organized throughout the presentation.
Instructional approach	Presenter(s) did not use a variety of instructional approaches.	Presenter(s) used two different instructional approaches.	Presenter(s) used three different instructional approaches.	Presenter(s) used four or more different instructional approaches.
Appeal	Presenter(s) did not captivate or hold my attention.	Presenter(s) held my attention for a short period of time.	Presenter(s) held my attention for most of the time.	Presenter(s) captured and held my attention the whole time.
Outcome (Fill in the blank based on the topic.)	I did not learn anything about how to ____.	I learned a little about how to ____.	I learned a lot about how to ____.	I successfully learned how to ____ and I could teach someone else.
				Total _____

Chapter 11

Multimedia Projects: Video

A SCENARIO

Betty, Bill, Bobby, and Danny never realized how outgoing and personable Thelma could be until they were videotaping her as she portrayed Betsy Ross. The class was divided into groups, and each group was assigned an historical event to reenact. Usually timid and not very outgoing, Thelma presented a whole new side to herself that most of her classmates had never seen. "Is that really Thelma?" Bobby asked. When Thelma was finished, she went back to being her quiet self. "Thelma," Betty motioned, "you were great!" Thelma blushed as her smile lifted her cheeks. "Really!" Betty said, "You're a natural! You make it look so easy!" Thelma noted, "I just pretend I am a famous actress—something I hope to be one day." The group was stunned. Who would have ever thought Thelma would want to be an actress—she seemed so shy. Bill, on the other hand, who was usually the class clown, was obviously nervous during his taping.

Mr. Booker was observing the students during their production and was happy to see that they were learning about history, themselves, and each other. This generally happened during group projects, especially when his students were engulfed in learning through multimedia. Not only did multimedia projects provide students with multiple opportunities and modalities of learning, they provided students with opportunities to express themselves in many ways. Creating digital videos with motion segments, graphics, titles, and music provided yet another dimension for students to express themselves and convey what they know.

OVERVIEW

Students live in a visual world, watching television, going to movies, and playing video games. Now, thanks to video editing programs that are inexpensive and easy-to-learn, video projects are feasible for students in all grades. As discussed in Chapters 5 and 6, video projects can be created from either analog or digital sources with popular, easily available programs such as iMovie on the Macintosh and Movie Maker on Windows computers.

Integrating video production into classroom activities has many benefits for students. Similar to other multimedia projects, video production encourages collaboration and requires students to be active and constructive (Jonassen, Peck, and Wilson 1999). It also has social benefits, such as improving students' self-confidence and providing public relations opportunities for school events (Valmont 1994). Written and oral communication skills have always been important in academics. Now, we have the tools to enhance students' understanding of and aptitude with visual communications (Hoffenberg and Handler 2001).

SAMPLE PROJECTS

Video projects can range from a simple, one-shot video of a demonstration, interview, or event to a complex, multiple-edit production. For example, students may take a camera on a field trip to record their experiences, create video yearbooks, or produce the school news programs. Some view video as "the ideal format for the culminating product of a project-based learning experience" (Hoffenberg and Handler 2001); others see it as another tool that can be used on a daily basis to document and supplement the curriculum.

The sample projects included in this chapter offer a variety of approaches for video. Video may be recorded or imported using analog or digital cameras, television, videotapes, or Web sites. After editing the video in a digital format, final products may be exported to videotape, recorded on a DVD, or displayed on a computer.

Before assigning a video product, carefully analyze the skills and experiences of your students. Obvious differences in requirements and outcomes should be expected based on students' understanding of the technical and design aspects of video production (video scripting guidelines are presented at the end of this chapter). Remember, however, that although the quality of the finished product may be higher with a high school media production class than an elementary class, the learning benefits can be the same or even greater!

As with other multimedia projects, you'll want to assess your resources. If you have three computers in your classroom, one of which is set up for video editing, the others may be used to design graphic logos or other elements that may be incorporated into the students' videos. Scheduling and rotation lists will depend on the number of computers and video cameras available in the classroom. As groups take turns shooting their video segments, other groups may be using the computers for research, graphics, or digital editing. Those who are not working with computers or cameras can be assigned other tasks that are related to the project. The following projects are designed to give you ideas of how to incorporate digital video into your own classroom.

Welcome to Our World

Lesson Description: A good introductory video project is one in which the students can concentrate on the process rather than new content. This project focuses on compiling a video overview of a familiar environment, such as the students' classroom, school, or community. Innovative approaches could include assuming the perspective of a dog, cat, or bug.

Depending on the amount of video recording and editing equipment available, the parameters of the project should be constrained to a reasonable limit. In other words, teachers may encourage compiling a limited number of video clips—one that establishes the setting of the "world," one that includes close-ups of the "inhabitants," and still frames or graphics of some of the objects in the "world." Audio can be limited to a single voiceover track that describes the world as the video plays.

DECIDE. As a class, discuss the possible topics for the "worlds," emphasizing that it can be as broad as the earth or as narrow as their classroom. In addition, students may choose to take a unique perspective, such as ants in an anthill, bees in a beehive, or a cell in the body. Brainstorm in small groups to generate as many ideas as possible for consideration.

After a list of topics is generated, help students filter the list by discussing issues that may facilitate or complicate the shooting. For example, would it be easier to create a "world" from a student's, dog's, or an ant's point of view? In which cases might props or special graphics be required? Does the project timeline allow sufficient time to improvise and create scenery?

Divide the class into groups of four or five students, based on their interest in various topics. Be sure that at least one student in each group is proficient with a digital camera and editing software. Discuss criteria for the project and conduct any research that may be relevant.

DESIGN. Assist students in the pre-production phase: outlining their project, creating a shot list, and writing the narration. Recommend that they include a title screen to set the stage and an initial still frame or video that establishes the setting and the perspective. Emphasize that they should use a variety of shots—some close-up and some wide angle—to add interest and variety.

DEVELOP. When it is time to shoot the video, team members should assume various roles, such as actors, lighting technicians, camera operator, and producer. After the video is imported into an editing program, ensure that all students have input into the appropriate cuts and transitions. If a team is waiting for a camera or computer, other members can be:

- Researching related information about their assumed perspective (e.g., ant)

- Practicing the narration

- Locating background music or sound effects

- Analyzing, comparing, and identifying the various perspectives of newspaper or magazine articles regarding a particular topic (e.g., movie reviews, policies, world events)

- Writing about why it is important to value and understand different perspectives

EVALUATE. When the projects are complete, display them for the entire class. Have students discuss the different interpretations and perspectives. Which of the videos are the most similar or the most different? Why?

If this is an initial video project, have students discuss lessons learned by answering the following questions:

- Which part or parts of the project were easier than originally thought?

- Which part or parts of the project were more difficult to complete?

- How did the video contribute to the effectiveness of this project? In other words, could a PowerPoint presentation have been as effective?

- What are two "lessons learned" that you would like to share with your classmates?

Creating a Convincing Commercial

Lesson Description: Students are very familiar with commercials on television. However, have they ever stopped to analyze commercials and consider the persuasive tactics that are employed? This project involves student groups in creating a short commercial that could be used to convince others to purchase a specific product.

DECIDE. Begin the assignment by showing examples of television commercials. You may have access to prerecorded commercials on DVD, videotape, or the Web. Web sites with commercials can be located at the following addresses:

- Classic TV Ads at http://www.roadode.com/classicindex.shtml

- Advertisement Ave at http://www.advertisementave.com/

- ClipLand at http://www.clipland.com/index_tvc.shtml

- TV Commercials at http://www.specialweb.com/tv/commercials.html

- SongTitle (music from commercials) at http://www.songtitle.info/

As the commercials are being viewed (either individually or as a group), have the students note the following:

- The length of time each ad runs

- How many edits (different scenes) are used in each commercial

- Where and how the commercials "imprint" the company—by logo, by jingle, or by words and actions

- The emotions that are evoked by the commercial

- The targeted audience—children or adults; males or females; local, national, or international audiences

Form groups of four to six students and have them continue the discussion by brainstorming possible products that they could target for the commercials. These products can be real or fictional; however, do not allow them to target a product that is already being advertised on television. Ask each group to generate at least 20 ideas of possible content items. Help them select a product that is feasible, based on their interests and the availability of props, images, and resources. Encourage innovation, creativity, and fun.

DESIGN. Discuss general design issues for commercials. Emphasize the need to convey a very persuasive position in a very short time frame. Encourage them to search the Web for information about producing commercials and possible lessons learned by marketing companies.

Students should create storyboards or video scripts, or both, that detail the types of video shots needed, along with the narration. Continually remind them of the short length of the final video; encourage them to brand the product with a logo, a jingle, or a phrase. Review the following design guidelines that apply to commercials:

- The most important portion of the commercial is the visual aspect. Even if the sound is turned off or down, a message should be conveyed.

- Commercials aim to motivate viewers and to touch their emotions. Concentrate on one or more emotions.

- Grab the viewer's attention quickly. Within a couple of seconds, the viewers may decide (consciously or unconsciously) to leave the room if they are not "hooked" by the commercial.

- Keep the message simple and visual. Include the name of the company and logo visually on the screen.

- Be repetitive. Repeat the product name several times in the commercial.

- Keep it short. Commercials are often designed for 30-second slots; however, many are only 10 or 20 seconds.

At this time, it may be a good idea for the class to design a rubric for evaluating their commercials. Criteria may include the appeal of the commercial (how well it motivates or touches the viewer's emotions), how well the message is conveyed and remembered, how well it grabs the viewer's attention, whether it convinced students to purchase the product, and so on.

DEVELOP. When it is time to shoot the video, team members should assume various roles, such as actors, lighting technicians, camera operator, and producer. After the video is imported into an editing program, ensure that all students have input into the appropriate cuts and transitions.

If a team is waiting for a camera or computer, members can be doing the following:

- Researching and comparing the cost of time slots for commercials (e.g., advertising during the Super Bowl versus advertising at 3:00 A.M.)

- Analyzing and comparing the commercials of different time periods (e.g., 1950s vs. 2006)

- Practicing the narration (if applicable), as well as rehearsing for the commercial

- Locating background music or sound effects, if appropriate

- Surveying other students about their favorite or least favorite commercials, including why they are their favorite or worst and what makes them remember the commercials

- Analyzing and comparing commercials aired during different shows and time slots throughout the day (these may be videotaped for use during class time)

EVALUATE. Record the projects to videotape for class evaluation. Students use the rubric designed in the DESIGN phase to evaluate and discuss each group's commercial. A sample rubric appears at the end of this chapter.

Digital Storytelling

Lesson Description: The term *digital storytelling* can be used to refer to many approaches and content areas. For example, in the literal sense, students write a story and "act it out" via video. This is one method for integrating video projects into the language arts curriculum and meeting standards addressing speaking, reading, writing, and other skills. Video storytelling can also refer to producing documentaries. Whether the video story is fiction or nonfiction, it provides students with a means to act out or convey what they know through an interactive environment.

Depending on the grade level and topic to be addressed, select or have your students create a story to act out on video. For example, students may act out a play about the famous ride of Paul Revere or write the script themselves based on research. Students may reenact the Boston Tea Party or other historical event; act out fairy tales, nursery rhymes, or chapters of books they are reading; or create and act out a story of their own. They may document the day of a teacher, a student, or school custodian; document the growth of a plant over time, the life cycle of a butterfly; and so on.

DECIDE. Make sure the selected topic is relevant and is aligned with your state or district standards. For example, if you are a fourth-grade teacher in California, you may want to design a timeline of the events that led up to the California Gold Rush and group your students to research and act out one of the events. The videotaped events can be imported, edited, combined, and sequenced inside the computer and exported onto a "final" videotape about the California Gold Rush.

Students can work in teams toward one topic, as described earlier, or perhaps work on different documentaries or stories that will be made accessible through a CD-ROM or DVD. For example, younger students could act out and record short nursery rhymes, and the teacher can link these within PowerPoint. Older students could be assigned to document specific concerns relative to their community and produce a community-based DVD to share with city council members. Whichever approach you decide to take, make sure your students understand what will be required of them (define the criteria) and assign them to appropriate teams.

DESIGN. Assist students in the pre-production phase: outlining their project, creating a shot list, and writing the narration. Emphasize that they should use a variety of shots—some close up and some wide angle—to add interest and variety. Define the evaluation criteria for the design of their project.

DEVELOP. When it is time to shoot the video, team members should assume various roles, such as actors, lighting technicians, camera operator, and producer. After the video is imported into an editing program, ensure that all students have input into the appropriate cuts and transitions.

If a team is waiting for a camera or computer, members can be doing the following:

- Constructing a picture, diorama, or brochure related to their topic

- Practicing the narration (if applicable), as well as rehearsing for their video

- Locating background music or sound effects, if appropriate

- Reading books related to their topic

EVALUATE. The evaluation of the selected project will be based on the criteria defined during the DECIDE and DESIGN stages. Projects can be presented during Open House or shared with other classes studying the same topics.

Historical Movie

Lesson Description: Digital storytelling can also be used to illustrate historical documents or recreate historical events. For example, a fifth-grade project that is showcased at depicts students creating a class movie by using period Civil War pictures to create help visualize the Gettysburg Address.

DECIDE. Introduce the topic and provide background information for the students. Use a KWL chart to list what students know and want to learn about the document and the related historical events. Have students brainstorm ideas of where to locate information about the Gettysburg Address and the history of the Civil War. Create a rubric for the project, based on desired content or facts and the project design. Give students time to conduct the necessary research.

DESIGN. Divide the class into pair groups and assign a section of the Gettysburg Address to each group to memorize and recite. Have students choose pictures from a Civil War Web site that can be used to illustrate the document. Students should have enough pictures to cover their narration, with each picture displayed no more than eight seconds. Such criteria should be added to the rubric for evaluation.

DEVELOP. Have each group read and record their assigned section of the document into iMovie. Team members can take turns reciting, or they can recite their part together. Import and combine all of the audio clips into a master file. Distribute the master file to all groups. Each group will then add the photographs to the sound track to create their final movie. Encourage students to add transitions and titles where appropriate.

If a team is waiting for a computer, members can be doing the following:

- Rehearsing for narrative for the video

- Searching the Web for relevant photographs to include in the video

- Locating background music to serve as an introduction to the movie

- Creating maps or diagrams that could be incorporated into the movie

EVALUATE. Record the projects to videotape or DVD for class evaluation. Evaluate the projects based on the rubric created in the DECIDE and DESIGN stage. Optimize the videos for the Web and post them on the school Web site (using first names of students only).

Show and Tell

Lesson Description: Students videotape segments that demonstrate how to do a particular task. For example, students could create video shots that demonstrate different tennis serves and shots. The digital video segments are made accessible through a program like iDVD so viewers can pick and choose which serves or shots they would like to see demonstrated, the order in which they would like to see them, and how often they want to see each segment.

DECIDE. Have students explain what is meant by "a picture is worth a thousand words." Discuss the advantages and disadvantages of text, pictures, and video. Have students share experiences of how they learned something by watching someone else or give examples of how they could learn something by watching someone else. Discuss what makes it easy or difficult to learn by watching someone.

Place students in groups and have them brainstorm ideas of what could be learned by watching someone do something. For example, how to swing a bat, dribble a basketball, tie a knot, make a balloon animal, overhand shuffle a deck of cards, and so on. Remind students that learning is the first step before doing—just because someone *knows* how to ride a bike (get on the seat, balance oneself, and pedal) does not mean he or she can do it without practice! Some learning tasks are more difficult than others.

Have student groups select a multistep task (like making a balloon animal) or variations of a single task (e.g., multiple ways to shuffle a deck of cards, different tennis swings, and so on). Have students share what would make a "how-to" video useful—types of shots (e.g., close-up, angles), pace, clarity, and so on. Create a rubric based on the criteria defined by the class.

Discuss how text and pictures may be used to enhance or support the video clips. Create a rubric with the students that includes the important elements of the assignment. See the "How-to Evaluation" blackline master in Chapter 10 for more ideas.

DESIGN. Assist students in the pre-production phase: outlining their project, creating a shot list, and writing the script (if applicable) for the video. If the videos will be incorporated into a PowerPoint presentation, Web site, or other program, students will also need to develop a flowchart and storyboards. These should indicate the placement of the video clips. Flowcharts, storyboards, and the video outline and shot list are reviewed before teams are allowed to go to the next stage.

DEVELOP. When it is time to shoot the video, team members should assume various roles, such as actors, lighting technicians, camera operator, and producer. After the video is imported into an editing program, ensure that all students have input into the appropriate cuts and transitions.

If a team is waiting for a camera or computer, members can be doing the following:

- Practicing the narration (if applicable), as well as rehearsing for their video
- Locating background music or sound effects, if appropriate
- Researching interesting facts or the history of their particular topic
- Researching and identifying experts related to their particular topic
- Listing what they want to learn how to do and why

EVALUATE. Use the class-created rubric(s) to evaluate the projects. Superior class projects may be stored in the school's media center for student checkout.

SUMMARY

Today's technologies make it easy and relatively inexpensive to create, edit, and produce video. Video projects may be recorded to videotape or DVD for viewing, or they be incorporated into other multimedia projects (e.g., PowerPoint presentations or Web pages). Creating videos is a powerful addition to a student's arsenal of learning tools, creating opportunities for high-level thinking, organization, planning, and management skills that can be applied in the real world. Developing digital videos encourages creative thinking, multiple perspectives, and teamwork. They can be implemented across the curriculum for meaningful learning and provide a real-world way to actively engage students in the learning process.

BLACKLINE MASTERS

Blackline masters in this chapter include the following:

- Video Guidelines: a list of guidelines specific to writing video scripts
- Commercial Evaluation: a sample rubric for evaluating student commercials

REFERENCES

Hoffenberg, H., and M. Handler. 2001. Digital video goes to school. *Learning & Leading with Technology*. 29(9): 10–15.

Jonassen, D. H., K. L. Peck, and B. G. Wilson. 1999. Learning with technology: A constructivist perspective. Upper Saddle River, NJ: Merrill.

Valmont, W. J. 1994. Making videos with reluctant learnings. *Reading and Writing Quarterly: Overcoming Learning Difficulties*, 10(4): 369–78.

Video Guidelines

The following guidelines can improve your digital videos.

Pre-Production

Make sure you have charged batteries or an electrical connection.
Obtain talent and copyright releases.
Label all tapes and log all shots.
Record with the best possible camera -- digital, if possible.
Use external microphones instead of built-in camera microphones.
Target the scripts at the intended audience.
Carefully plan your shots to tell a story.
Keep the script simple -- include only one or two main points.
Create a shot list and use it to sequence the recording.
Consider impact of distribution media (videotape or DVD vs. Web).

Production

White-balance the camera before shooting.
Shoot with your back to the light.
Use natural lighting; avoid fluorescent lighting.
Beware of cluttered backgrounds and excess movement.
"Set the stage" for the video with a wide shot of the area.
Shoot people interacting with each other, not the camera.
Use a tripod (or stand still and keep the camera very still).
Minimize panning, tilting, tracking, and other movements.
Shoot excess footage at both ends of a shot (to be edited out later).
Continue recording until the audio portion ends.
Carefully frame your shots and "lead" the eye of the viewer.
Use over-the-shoulder shots to draw the audience into the action.
Minimize harsh, close-up shots of people.
Maintain a continuous time code.

Post-Production

Minimize special effects and transitions.
If in doubt, leave it out.
Smooth sound is more important than smooth video.
Keep an archival copy of the source video.

Commercial Evaluation

CRITERIA	0	1	2	3
The commercial's length was appropriate.	Commercial's length was way too short.	Commercial's length was way too long.	Commercial's length was almost appropriate.	Commercial's length was appropriate.
The commercial struck a variety of my emotions.	Commercial did not strike my emotions.	Commercial struck one of my emotions.	Commercial somewhat struck a variety of my emotions.	Commercial struck a variety of my emotions.
The commercial's message was clearly conveyed and is rememberable.	Commercial's message was not conveyed.	Commercial's message was somewhat conveyed, but it is not something I will remember.	Commercial's message was clearly conveyed, but it is not something I will remember.	Commercial's message was clearly conveyed and is something I will remember.
The commercial motivated me to purchase or support its product.	It made me not want to purchase or support this product.	It did not motivated me to purchase or support its product.	I'm unsure whether or not I will purchase or support this product.	It motivated me to purchase or support this product.
The commercial captured and held my attention.	Commercial did not captivate or hold my attention.	Commercial held my attention for a short period of time.	Commercial held my attention for most of the time.	Commercial captured and held my attention the whole time.
The commercial included the company logo and repeated the product names several times.	Commercial excluded logo and didn't repeat product name.	Commercial included logo but didn't repeat product name.	Commercial excluded logo but did repeat product name several times.	Commercial included logo and repeated product name several times.
				Total _____

Glossary

alternative assessment. A form of assessment other than the true or false, multiple-choice, matching, and fill-in-the-blank responses that are often associated with standardized tests. Performance-based assessment, authentic assessment, and portfolio assessment are forms of alternative assessment.

analog video. Video that is stored as an electrical signal with a continuous scale. Videotape and video disc generally store analog video.

authentic assessment. A method of evaluating a student's performance based on observations, performance tests, interviews, exhibitions, or portfolios. The context, purpose, audience, and constraints of the task must connect to real-world situations and problems.

authoring system. A computer program designed specifically to create computer-based instruction.

AVI. A Microsoft video file format that stands for Audio Video Interleave. This format is used extensively on the Windows platform—especially to download and play files.

bandwidth. The transmission capacity of a telecommunications system. The greater the bandwidth, the greater the amount of digital information that can be transmitted per second.

bitmapped image. A computer image that consists of individual dots or picture elements (pixels).

bits per second (bps). A common method of measuring the speed of a modem. Most telephone modems transfer information at 56,600 bps (also referred to as 56K). DSLs (digital subscriber lines) and cable modems are faster.

branch. To move from one location of a program to another. For example, if a button initiates a video file, it is said to *branch* to video.

bug. An error in a program.

button. An object or area of the screen used to initiate an action, such as a branch to another card.

byte. Eight bits working together. A single byte can have any value from 0 to 255.

capture. The process of collecting and saving text or image data.

card. The basic unit of HyperCard and HyperStudio, equivalent to one screen of information.

CD-audio (compact disc-audio). High-quality audio stored on a compact disc in a linear format. Each compact disc can store 74 minutes of sound with no degradation of quality during playback.

CD-R. A recordable compact disc, allowing users to write to the disc one time (see CD-RW).

CD-ROM (compact disc–read only memory). A prerecorded, nonerasable optical storage disc that stores approximately 650–700 MB of digital data.

CD-RW. A recordable compact disc that allows users to write to the disc many times.

clip. A short video or audio segment.

clip art. Graphics that are commercially distributed for use in product development.

compression. Reduction of data for more efficient storage and transmission; saves disk space but may also reduce the quality of the playback.

constructivism. The belief that learning takes place through the construction of knowledge.

cooperative learning. A way of structuring student-to-student interaction so that students are successful only if their group is successful. Students are held accountable for their individual learning, they receive specific instruction in the social skills necessary for the group to succeed, and they have the opportunity to discuss how well their group is working.

DDD-E. A model for the systematic design of multimedia projects, consisting of four phases: DECIDE, DESIGN, DEVELOP, and EVALUATE.

debug. The process of correcting problems (e.g., code, grammar, and spelling) in a program.

dialog box. A window that asks a question or allows users to input information.

digital camera. A camera that records images in true digital form. The images are usually downloaded directly into a computer through a USB or FireWire connection.

digital video. Video that is stored in bits and bytes on a computer. It can be manipulated and displayed on a computer screen.

digitizing. The process of converting an analog signal into a digital signal.

disc. Usually refers to a videodisc or compact disc. Computer diskettes are generally referred to as *disks* (with a *k*), and compact discs are referred to as *discs* (with a *c*).

disk. *See* disc.

dpi (dots per inch). Refers to printing resolution of an image. Most printers can print 300–1200 dpi.

DV. Digtital video. Often used to refer to the format of the used by a digital camcorder with "DV" tapes. Also used to refer to the compression type used by DV systems.

DVD (digital video disc). A second generation of the original CD-ROM format. It provides up to two layers of digital information on a single-sided compact disc. It stores up to 4.7 gigabytes for one layer; 8.5 gigabytes for two layers. Advanced digital video and audio features are specified.

e-portfolio. A meaningful collection of student work in an electronic format.

eZediaMX. Multimedia authoring and editing software for Windows and Macintosh, by eZedia.

FireWire. The Apple Computer trace name for the IEEE 1394 standard that enables direct transfer of digital video between devices, such as a camcorder and computer.

flash memory. Flash memory is used to record photographs in a digital camera. The flash memory space (usually on a memory card or stick) can be erased and used again.

flowchart. A visual depiction of the sequence and structure of a program.

fps. Frames per second. Describes the frame rate—the number of frames displayed each second.

frame. One complete video picture.

frame rate. The number of video frames displayed each second.

frequency. The number of times per second that a sound source vibrates. Frequency is expressed in hertz (Hz) or kilohertz (kHz).

full-motion video. Video frames displayed at 30 frames per second.

GIF (Graphic Interchange Format). A file format for Web graphics that allows for 256 colors. It uses a lossless compression and is best used for line art and graphics with solid areas of colors. GIFs also support interlacing, transparency, and animation. GIF89a is another name for transparent or animated GIFs.

Group Investigation. A cooperative group technique similar to the Jigsaw method except that students do not form "expert groups." Student teams give class presentations of findings.

hertz (Hz). Unit of frequency measurement; numerically equal to cycles per second.

HTML (HyperText Markup Language). Coding language used to create hypertext documents to be posted on the Web. HTML code consists of embedded tags that specify how a block of text should appear or that specify how a word is linked to another file on the Internet.

HTTP (HyperText Transfer Protocol). The protocol for moving hypertext files across the World Wide Web.

HyperCard. A hypermedia development program developed by Apple Computer.

HyperStudio. A hypermedia development program for Windows and Macintosh computers, developed by Roger Wagner Publishing.

icon. A symbol that provides a visual representation of an action or other information. An icon or an arrow is often used to denote directional movement in hypermedia.

image. A graphic, a picture, or one frame of video.

iMovie. A free desktop video editing program developed and distributed by Apple Computer.

Internet. A group of networks connecting governmental institutions, military branches, educational institutions, and commercial companies.

Internet service providers (ISPs). Organizations that provide connections to the Internet. They may be universities or private companies.

Jigsaw. A method of cooperative group learning that assigns each of its members a particular learning task. Team members meet with members of other groups to form "expert groups" to discuss and research their topic. Following research and discussion, the students return to their own teams and take turns teaching their teammates about their topic.

JPEG (Joint Photographic Experts Group). A common format for storing images (especially photographs) on the Web.

kilohertz (kHz). Unit of frequency measurement; equal to 1,000 hertz.

Learning Together. A method of cooperative group learning that incorporates heterogeneous student groups that work on a single assignment and receive rewards based on their group product.

link. A connection from one place or medium to another. For example, buttons contain the linking information between cards.

liquid crystal display (LCD) panel. A panel that connects to a computer to display the computer screen when the LCD panel is placed on top of an overhead projector.

MIDI (Musical Instrument Digital Interface). A standard for communicating musical information among computers and musical devices.

movie file. The file that is created by combining audio, video, and images.

Movie Maker. A free video editor available on Windows Millennium and XP systems.

MPEG (Moving Picture Experts Group). A common format for storing digital video files.

MP3. An audio-only compression format that can decrease the size of an audio file but maintain high-quality sound.

multimedia. A type of program that combines more than one media type for disseminating information. For example, a multimedia program may include text, audio, graphics, animation, and video.

object-oriented drawings. Graphics that are composed of separate geometric objects that can be layered one atop the other to create images. Also known as vector drawings or, simply, drawings.

objects. In hypermedia, generally refers to elements that are placed on the screen, such as buttons, fields, and graphics. Objects are components that can be manipulated and can contain links to other objects.

performance-based assessment. An assessment method whereby teachers evaluate a student's skill by asking the student to create an answer or product that demonstrates his or her knowledge or skills.

pixel. A single dot or point of an image on a computer screen. *Pixel* is a contraction of the words *picture el*ement.

plug-and-play. A device that is automatically recognized and assessable when plugged into a computer.

PNG (Portable Network Graphics). PNG is a lossless format that supports interlacing and transparency.

portfolio assessment. An estimation of a student's abilities based on a systematic collection of the student's best work, records of observation, test results, and so on.

post-production. The phase of a video project that includes editing the video.

PowerPoint. A presentation program developed by Microsoft.

PPI (pixels per inch). Refers to image resolution. Most monitors can display 60–120 ppi.

pre-production. The planning phase of a video project—includes setting a goal, writing scripts, and so on.

production. The phase of a video project that consists of shooting the video and compiling the media.

QuickTime. A file format that allows computers to compress and play digitized video movies.

RealAudio. A compression and transfer technique that allows audio files to play over the Internet as they are transferring.

resolution. The number of dots or pixels that can be displayed on a computer screen. Higher resolutions create sharper images. Also refers to the sharpness or clarity of a computer screen. Displays with more lines and pixels of information have better resolution.

sampling rate. The number of intervals per second used to capture a sound when it is digitized. Sampling rate affects sound quality; the higher the sampling rate, the better the sound quality.

scanner. A hardware peripheral that takes a picture of an item and transfers the image to a computer.

scripting language. A set of commands that is included in some icon- and menu-based development systems. The scripting language allows complex computer instructions to be created.

scripts. A series of commands written in a language embedded in a hypermedia program.

sequencer. A device that records MIDI events and data.

slide show (electronic). Computer screens designed in a sequence for projection purposes.

sound module. A peripheral for MIDI that uses an electronic synthesizer to generate the sounds of musical instruments.

stack. A group of cards in the same HyperStudio file, usually based on the same theme.

storyboard. A visual representation of what will be placed on a computer screen. In addition, storyboards contain information that helps the programmer and the production specialists develop media components.

streaming. Files that can be played as they are sent over the Web.

Student Teams Achievement Divisions (STAD). A cooperative group technique: Students learn something as a team, contribute to their team by improving their own past performance, and earn team rewards based on their improvements.

synthesizer. A musical instrument or device that generates sound electronically.

Team Assisted Individualization (TAI). A cooperative group technique that combines cooperative learning with individualized instruction. Students are placed into groups but work at their own pace and level.

Teams Games Tournament (TGT). A cooperative group technique similar to STAD except that weekly tournaments replace weekly quizzes. Homogeneous, three-member teams formed from the existing heterogeneous groups compete against similar ability groups to earn points for their regular, heterogeneous group.

text-to-speech synthesis. Sounds created by applying computer algorithms to text to produce spoken words.

Theory of Multiple Intelligences. A theory proposing that there are multiple ways of knowing, suggesting that people possess several different intelligences.

timeline. A method for organizing video clips in sequential order.

transitions. Visual effects, such as dissolves or wipes, that take place as a program moves from one image or screen of information to the next.

Uniform Resource Locator (URL). The exact location (address) of an Internet resource, such as a Web page.

upload. The process of sending a complete file to a host computer.

vector image. A computer image constructed from graphic formulae. Images that are made up of lines, boxes, and circles (such as charts) usually are vector images.

.WAV. The extension (last three letters) for sound files saved in Microsoft wave format.

WebQuest. A Web-based project designed to guide learners as they research a specific issue and to incorporate the results of the research into an authentic product or project.

Web browser. A software program that can display Web pages.

window. An area on a computer screen that displays text, graphics, messages, or documents.

Windows Movie Maker. A software editing program that can be used to create digital movies that is included with Windows Millennium Edition and XP.

World Wide Web (WWW). Hypermedia-based Internet information system. Graphical user interfaces allow users to click a mouse on desired menu items, accessing text, sound, pictures, or even motion video from all over the world.

Index

About the Authors

KAREN S. IVERS is Professor of Elementary and Bilingual Education at California State University, Fullerton. She has received honors for teaching and technology innovations, outstanding teaching and scholarship, and service. She is currently Chair of the department and has taught graduate level technology courses for teachers, as well as having worked with preservice teachers in the field of educational technology. She is a former elementary school teacher and received her doctorate at the University of South Florida.

ANN E. BARRON is Professor of Instructional Technology at the University of South Florida. She is the recipient of numerous teaching awards and has published books and articles related to the integration of technology in education.